The Joan Palevsky  Imprint in Classical Literature

In honor of beloved Virgil—

"O degli altri poeti onore e lume . . ."

—Dante, *Inferno*

The publisher gratefully acknowledges
the generous contribution to this book
provided by the Classical Literature Endowment
Fund of the University of California Press Associates,
which is supported by a major gift from Joan Palevsky.

Encomium of Ptolemy Philadelphus

CONTENTS

PREFACE

Theocritus's *Encomium of Ptolemy* is not one of his best-known or most-admired poems, but these are exciting times for the study of Ptolemaic culture, and the need for a new study of this poem seemed, at least to me, self-evident. How far this book goes toward filling that need is a matter for others.

The preparation of this book has taken me into scholarly areas where I am, at best, a novice, and the advice of friends has been more than ever important. Kathryn Gutzwiller, John Ma, Katja Mueller, Susan Stephens, and Dorothy Thompson all read earlier versions of some or all of the typescript, and their observations, corrections, and encouragement have been invaluable. I would also like to thank Kate Toll of the University of California Press for her enthusiastic support.

CONVENTIONS
AND ABBREVIATIONS

T. = Theocritus throughout. Except where it is relevant to the argument, poems of the Theocritean corpus are all cited as though "genuine"; thus 1.7, 23.7, not 1.7, [23].7. Translations are my own, unless the translator is identified. In the spelling of Greek names, ease of recognition has been the principal aim. The names of authors are usually "latinized," whereas other names may be transliterated. References of the form "cf. 100n." are to notes in this commentary; thus "cf. 100n." refers to the note on v. 100.

The following editions of Theocritus are cited by author only:

A. S. F. Gow, *Theocritus*, 2d ed., 2 vols. (Cambridge 1952)

C. Gallavotti, *Theocritus quique feruntur Bucolici Graeci*, 3d ed. (Rome 1993)

R. Hunter, *Theocritus: A Selection* (Cambridge 1999)

The epics of Homer *(Il., Od.)* and Apollonius *(Arg.)* are cited b title only. Unless otherwise specified, references to Callimach are to the edition of R. Pfeiffer (Oxford 1949–53). *EA* = Bion *Epitaphios Adonidos; EB* = [Moschus] *Epitaphios Bionis.*

The list of references provides full references for modern works cited by author and date in the footnotes and commentary. Abbreviations for periodicals usually follow the system of *L'Année Philologique.* Collections of texts and works of reference are abbreviated as follows:

ANET	J. B. Pritchard, ed., *Ancient Near Eastern texts relating to the Old Testament,* 2d ed. (Princeton 1969).
CA	J. U. Powell, ed., *Collectanea Alexandrina* (Oxford 1925).
CEG	P. A. Hansen, ed., *Carmina epigraphica Graeca* (Berlin 1983, 1989).
Denniston	J. D. Denniston, *The Greek particles,* 2d ed. (Oxford 1954).
FGrHist	F. Jacoby, ed., *Die Fragmente der griechischen Historiker* (Berlin 1923–30; Leiden 1940–58).
GGM	C. Muller, ed., *Geographi Graeci minores* (Paris 1855–61).
GLP	D. L. Page, ed., *Greek Literary Papyri* (Cambridge, Mass. 1942).
GP	A. S. F. Gow and D. L. Page, eds., *The Garland of Philip and some contemporary epigrams* (Cambridge 1968).
GV	W. Peek, ed., *Griechische Vers-Inschriften,* vol. 1 (Berlin 1955).
HE	A. S. F. Gow and D. L. Page, eds., *The Greek Anthology: Hellenistic epigrams* (Cambridge 1965).

K-B   R. Kühner and F. Blass, *Ausführliche Grammatik der griechischen Sprache, Erster Teil: Elementar- und Formenlehre*, 3d ed., 2 vols. (Hanover 1890–92).

K-G   R. Kühner and B. Gerth, *Ausführliche Grammatik der griechischen Sprache, Zweiter Teil: Satzlehre*, 3d ed., 2 vols. (Hanover 1898–1904).

LdÄ   *Lexikon der Ägyptologie*, ed. W. Helck, E. Otto, and W. Westendorf (Wiesbaden 1972–92).

LfgrE   *Lexikon des frühgriechischen Epos*, ed. B. Snell et al. (Göttingen 1979–).

LIMC   *Lexicon iconographicum mythologiae classicae* (Zurich 1981–97).

LSJ   *A Greek-English Lexicon*, ed. H. G. Liddell, R. Scott, H. Stuart Jones, and R. Mackenzie, 9th ed. (Oxford 1968).

OGIS   W. Dittenberger, ed., *Orientis Graecae inscriptiones selectae* (Leipzig 1903–5).

PMG   D. L. Page, ed., *Poetae melici Graeci* (Oxford 1962).

RE   *Paulys Real-Encyclopädie der classischen Altertums-wissenschaft* (Stuttgart 1893–1980).

SEG   *Supplementum epigraphicum Graecum* (Leiden 1923–).

SGO   R. Merkelbach and J. Stauber, *Steinepigramme aus dem griechischen Osten*, vol. 1 (Stuttgart 1998).

SH   H. Lloyd-Jones and P. Parsons, eds., *Supplementum hellenisticum* (Berlin 1983).

SIG   W. Dittenberger, ed., *Sylloge inscriptionum Graecarum*, 3d ed., vol. 1 (Leipzig 1915).

SVF　　　　J. von Arnim, ed., *Stoicorum veterum fragmenta* (Stuttgart 1905–24).

Welles, *RC*　　C. B. Welles, *Royal correspondence in the Hellenistic period: A study in Greek epigraphy* (New Haven 1934).

Introduction

BEGINNING FROM ZEUS

Theocritus's *Idyll* 17 *(EP)*[1] celebrates Ptolemy II "Philadelphus,"[2] who became co-regent of Egypt and the Ptolemaic empire with his father, Ptolemy I "Soter," in 285[3] and then assumed the throne in his own right on Soter's death in 283/2; he died in 246, to be succeeded by his son Ptolemy III "Euergetes." Much of the surviving high poetry of Alexandria dates from his long reign, which also saw the full flourishing of literary and scientific schol-

---

1. The conventional modern numbering of all of the *Idylls* derives from H. Stephanus, *Poetae Graeci principes heroici carminis & alii nonnulli* (Basel 1566), and for *Idylls* 1–18 follows that of the "Vatican family" of manuscripts, as already in the *editio princeps* (Milan 1480) and the Aldine of 1495; cf. pp. 361–62 of Gallavotti's edition.

2. Throughout this book I shall, for clarity's sake, refer to Ptolemy II as "Philadelphus," though this name was not used for him alone until many years after the period from which *EP* dates; cf. below, p. 192.

3. All dates are B.C.E., unless specified.

arship in the famous Museum and its associated Library,[4] as well as a period of active foreign expansion and exploration; from a modern perspective this combination of political and cultural power gives Philadelphus's reign something of the flavor of a "Golden Age." The period is richly documented: beyond the great poetry of the third century and the narratives of the later historiographical and anecdotal traditions, thousands of papyri illustrate the nature of life outside the metropolis, and in particular the complexity and detail with which the lives of ordinary Egyptians and the Greek settlers were ordered. Of particular interest and importance is an extract from the historian Callixenus of Rhodes (second century B.C.E.), preserved in the fifth book of Athenaeus's *Deipnosophistai* (late second to early third century C.E.), describing the "Dionysiac section" of an extraordinary procession (πομπή) and lavish display staged by Philadelphus in Alexandria.[5] Both the date and occasion (the Ptolemaia of 279/8?) of this festival are matters of fierce critical debate,[6] but with due caution this description can be used to illustrate many of the same themes of Ptolemaic ideology as are reflected in *EP*; it is likely enough, in fact, that the procession and *EP* are not too far from each other in time.

4. Cf. below, p. 33.

5. Cf. Dunand 1981; Rice 1983; Walbank 1996; Thompson 2000; Coarelli 1990. This description will usually be referred to in this book as the "Grand Procession."

6. In addition to the bibliography in n.5 see Foertmeyer 1988 (the Ptolemaia of 275/4); Hazzard and Fitzgerald 1991; and Hazzard 2000, 4, 30–32 (Ptolemaia of 263/2). Walbank, Thompson, and Coarelli (see previous note) date the procession to the founding Ptolemaia of 279/8.

Both Philadelphus and his sister-wife Arsinoe II have also a very
rich Greek and Egyptian epigraphical and iconographical tradi-
tion.[7] Major hieroglyphic documents such as the "Pithom Stele,"
a record of Philadelphus's activities in the east of the country and
his donations to the temple of Atum at Pithom,[8] allow us to fill
out the copious Greek record with some knowledge of how
Philadelphus presented himself to and was seen by at least the
priestly class among his Egyptian subjects. This picture of royal
ideology may also be filled out (with caution) from later docu-
ments, such as the surviving decrees, in Greek, hieroglyphic, and
demotic, issued by synods of the Egyptian priesthood in honor of
Philadelphus's successors (the most famous of which is the Rosetta
Stone, of 196).[9]

The standard criteria[10] used to establish the date of *EP* are the
fact that Arsinoe is still alive and married to her royal brother;
that nothing is said of the cult of the Theoi Adelphoi ("Brother
and Sister Gods"), which we know to have been established in
Alexandria in 271 (*PHibeh* II 199);[11] and the historical circum-
stances suggested by vv. 86–90. Arguments have also been con-
structed on the basis of the relation between *EP* and the *Hymns*

7. Cf. Quaegebeur 1971a; 1998, with further bibliography.

8. Naville 1902–3; Roeder 1959, 108–28; cf. Grzybek 1990, 69–112; there is,
to my knowledge, no recent English translation (cf. Naville 1885, 16–19). A new
edition is in preparation by C. Thiers (cf. *Göttinger Miszellen* 157 [1997] 95–101).

9. Most accessible in Simpson 1996; on the nature of these decrees cf.
Clarysse 2000, 41–65.

10. Cf. Griffiths 1977–78; Mineur 1984, 16–18; Weber 1993, 213 n. 2, with
bibliography.

11. Cf. Koenen 1993, 51–52.

of Callimachus to Zeus and Delos and between *EP* and *Idyll* 16 for Hieron of Syracuse. Of these various considerations, the first is perhaps the strongest.

The exact date of Arsinoe's marriage to her brother, between 279 and 274, is unknown;[12] it is tempting to place *EP* close in time to the marriage, because of the wedding imagery and language of vv. 129–34, but on any reckoning the poem must fall within ten, and probably six, years of the wedding, and the language of weddings has in fact a significance within the portrayal of the royal couple that can be explained without recourse to the chronological argument (cf. 129, 133–34nn.). Arsinoe's death is standardly dated, on the basis of Egyptian documents, to July 270; E. Grzybek has argued for July 268, but the revised dating has not found wide favor.[13]

As for the other arguments that have been adduced, silence about the Theoi Adelphoi would be unsurprising if the poem was to be performed to Greek audiences outside Alexandria, although the praise of Philadelphus for having established the cult of his parents (vv. 121–34) might indeed seem strange if he and his sister-wife were already themselves the object of cult. The catalogue of conquests and possessions in vv. 86–90 offers in fact no narrowly precise date and would seem to suit any time in the second part of the decade (see 86–92n.); it may well be, of course, that if we knew the date of the poem, those verses would appear more historically nuanced than they do now. As for arguments based on

12. Cf. Fraser 1972, 2: 367.

13. Grzybek 1990, 103–12; cf. Koenen 1993, 51–52. For the earlier date cf. Minas 1994; Cadell 1998.

the (undeniable) intertextual relation with Callimachus, these are always likely to be no more than suggestive. The *Hymn to Zeus* is standardly (and attractively) dated early in Philadelphus's reign, on the basis of the apparent allusion in vv. 57–67 to Philadelphus's elevation to the co-regency in 285 and subsequent accession in 283 ahead of his older brothers;[14] if Callimachus's poem does indeed predate *EP*, then Theocritus has used a (famous?) "Hymn to Zeus" in the construction of analogies and differences between Zeus and Philadelphus that run right through the poem (cf. 1n.). Callimachus's *Hymn to Delos*, on the other hand, must postdate Philadelphus's quelling in 275/4 of the rebellion of the Celtic mercenaries hired to assist him in his struggle with Magas of Cyrene (cf. vv. 171–87);[15] that the fetal Apollo prophesies that Cos is reserved for "another god" (θεὸς ἄλλος) is usually taken as a sign that Callimachus's hymn is later than 271 (cf. above), though that is hardly a necessary conclusion, given that the speaker is Apollo and his mode is the allusive style of prophecy.[16] It is right to ask

14. Cf., for example, Clauss 1986; Cameron 1995, 10.

15. Cf. Meincke 1965, 116–24; Weber 1993, 213 n. 3, with bibliography. Little weight can be attached to Perrotta's argument (1978, 83–84) that T. could not have failed to mention the incident of the mercenaries if it had already happened. Why not? Many reasons for such a silence, ranging from the original performance context to the whole nature of the poem, can be imagined: the incident seems important to us, but that is because of Callimachus. Similarly, Gelzer (1982, 21) argues that Callimachus's *Hymn* must predate the First Syrian War, for this would have provided the poet with much more heroic material than the defeat of the mercenaries; this incident owes its place in the poem, however, to the parallel that it allows the poet to draw between Apollo and Ptolemy, and not to the fact that Callimachus could think of nothing else to say.

16. Cf. rightly Griffiths 1977–78, 96.

whether the idea of the birth of Ptolemy on Cos as parallel to that of Apollo on Delos is more likely to have been borrowed by Theocritus from Callimachus, or vice versa, but it is unlikely that any answer will command universal assent; it is, moreover, not improbable that the conceit had a wider contemporary currency than just these two poets.[17] Cos appears in the catalogue of islands and cities visited by Leto in the *Homeric Hymn to Apollo* (v. 42), and this—together with the knowledge that Philadelphus was born on Cos—would surely have been enough of a hint for Callimachus, without Theocritus showing him the way (v. 160);[18] his description of the island, ὠγυγίην . . . Κόων Μεροπηΐδα νῆσον, looks in fact directly to the *Homeric Hymn* (Κόως . . . πόλις Μερόπων ἀνθρώπων, v. 42), whereas Theocritus's introduction of the personified island ignores her legendary history entirely.

Finally, the many similarities between *Idylls* 16 and 17 have led to a modern biographical construction in which Theocritus seeks Hieron's patronage and, when disappointed, moves to Alexandria in what was to prove a successful search for Ptolemaic patronage; as *Idyll* 16 is most likely to have been composed c. 275,[19] *EP* will

17. Unlike Schlatter (1941, 30–34), however, I do not doubt that there is an intertextual relation between the poems. Perrotta (1978, 166) and Reinsch-Werner (1976, 376–79) hold that the motif of "likeness to the father" (17.63; Callim. *H.* 4.170) comes as a surprise in Callimachus and is therefore likely to have been borrowed from T. Note, however, Σαωτήρων ὕπατον γένος in v. 166; it is also relevant that Zeus's pride in his son has an important role in the *Homeric Hymn to Apollo*; cf. vv. 10–11, 204–6.

18. Griffiths (1977–78, 98) sees T. as the imitator in all these motifs and (99) calls attention to the fact that the very comparison of Philadelphus to Apollo may be considered digressive in a poem that has at its heart the comparison of Philadelphus to Zeus. The point carries some weight.

19. Cf., for example, Hunter 1996, 82–87.

follow shortly after that.[20] The suggested dating may in fact be correct, but the reasoning is flawed, and not merely because it takes too literal a view of the narrative of *Idyll* 16 as a "search" for patronage: purely on the basis of the poems themselves, there is no good reason to assume that *Idyll* 16 preceded *EP*. What evidence there is for the date of *EP* tends, therefore, to converge on the second half of the 270s, but greater precision than that hardly seems possible.

Two other poems of Theocritus must be mentioned in this context. *Idyll* 15 portrays a festival of Adonis staged by Arsinoe, after her marriage to Ptolemy, in honor of her now divinized mother (vv. 106–11). These facts suggest a *terminus post quem* of the middle years of the decade (cf. above and 50n.), in other words, a date not too far from the most likely date for *EP*. It is noteworthy, though perhaps unsurprising, that the two poems share certain encomiastic motifs.[21] The second poem, the lost *Berenice* (fr. 3 Gow), which was perhaps transmitted in antiquity separately from the bulk of Theocritus's poems that have survived for us,[22] presumably celebrated this same Queen Mother and may have concerned, at least in part, her deification in association with Aphrodite.[23] Unfortunately, the single fragment allows us to go no farther, but there is at least nothing here that tells against the

20. For this narrative cf. Gow 2: 326, who himself enjoins caution.

21. Cf., for example, 38–39n. on Ptolemy-Arsinoe as the Homeric Alcinous-Arete.

22. Cf. below, pp. 70–71.

23. Cf. Gow ad loc. on the associations of Aphrodite with fish. An interesting (if unanswerable) question is the identity of the speaker of this fragment: someone seems to be explaining a current, or perhaps future, ritual in honor of "this goddess." Are we present at the foundation of the cult?

hypothesis of a set of poems for the Ptolemaic royal house, all written at roughly the same period.

GENRE

EP announces itself emphatically as a ὕμνος (cf. 8n.) and concludes with an *envoi* of a type familiar from the Homeric and Callimachean *Hymns* (cf. 135–37n.); at its center, moreover, lies a reworking of the birth of Apollo from the *Homeric Hymn to (Delian) Apollo*, a scene that Callimachus too refashioned for his *Hymn to Apollo*, and throughout the poem there seems to be an intertextual dialogue with Callimachus's *Hymn to Zeus*, another poem in praise (very probably) of Ptolemy II. The generic placement of *EP* as a hymn would thus seem to be straightforward. On the other hand, this poem is clearly not a version of a *Homeric Hymn* in quite the way that, say, *Idyll* 22 for the Dioscuri is:[24] the opening verse announces not the name of Ptolemy, who is to be the principal object of praise, but rather Zeus (though in retrospect this comes to be seen as the first move in a poetic game about the relation of the Olympian Zeus to Ptolemy), and there is no central narrative section, such as is normal in the extended *Homeric Hymns;* in its structure and thematic concerns too, as we shall see, *EP* is quite different from the tradition of hexameter hymns. At the heart of this difference lies the fact that the subject of the poem is a man, not (yet) a god, and that just as both he and his forebears move smoothly between levels of existence, so the poem in his honor slips between genres. *EP* is, in fact, in many ways an isolated example of poetic form among

---

24. Cf. Hunter 1996, 46–47; Sens 1997, 13.

what survives of Hellenistic poetry, though there is good reason to believe that it was not so isolated in antiquity.[25]

The manuscripts entitle the poem either Ἐγκώμιον εἰς Πτολεμαῖον or Ἔπαινος Πτολεμαίου,[26] though only εἰς Πτολεμαῖον survives in the Antinoopolis papyrus, and this short form has some claims to authenticity.[27] The *Suda* ascribes to Aratus poems entitled εἰς Ἀντίγονον (*SH* 99), εἰς Παυσανίαν τὸν Μακεδόνα (*SH* 112), and εἰς Φίλαν (*SH* 116), and this prepositional form seems to have been the regular one for poems in praise of (living or past) individuals, such as the postclassical "paians," including a Rhodian "paian" for Ptolemy Soter, of which Athenaeus provides a list.[28] What noun was felt to be understood with such titles may be debated (ὕμνος or ἔπαινος is as likely as any), but the history of such poems can in fact be sketched in reasonable detail. One thread of this history leads back through the hymnic tradition, both the hexameter *Homeric Hymns* and also the lyric ὕμνοι of Pindar, all of which are hymns "for" (εἰς) a particular god, or in certain cases (e.g., Heracles, the Dioscuri), heroes who became gods. The εἰς form is also found in the fifth century, together with the noun τὸ ἐγκώμιον, to designate a song in praise of a particular individual's victory: consider, for example, Aristophanes fr. 505 K-A, Ἰσθμιακὰ λαβόντες ὥσπερ οἱ χόροι | ᾄδωμεν εἰς τὸν δεσπότην ἐγκώμιον;

---

25. A formal public contest in ἐγκώμιον ἐπικόν does not, however, seem to be attested before the first century B.C.E. (Oropos, *IG* VII 416, 418–20, where it appears alongside a contest in "prose encomium"); cf. Hardie 1983, 89; Pernot 1993, 1: 49.

26. On the distinction between the two modes of praise cf. below, p. 17.

27. Cf. Cameron 1995, 269 n. 41.

28. Cf. Ath. 15.696d–97a; Käppel 1992, 346–49; Cameron 1995, 269.

and Plato *Lysis* 205d–e, πρὶν νενικηκέναι ποιεῖς τε καὶ ᾄδεις εἰς σαυτὸν ἐγκώμιον . . . ἐγκώμια ὥσπερ νενικηκότι;[29] among the surviving titles of Ion of Chios is an "Encomium for (εἰς) Skuthiades" (*PMG* 743). Pindar used the adjective ἐγκώμιος to describe songs that "accompanied the *komos*" in honor of the victor,[30] and it is easy to see how such a use soon brought ἐγκώμιον close in sense to the more explicit ἐπινίκιον.[31] Other, nonepinician songs of Pindar in praise of patrons were indeed labeled ἐγκώμια by Alexandrian scholars (frr. 118–28 Maehler), and such praise poems clearly abounded in the archaic age.[32] To this extent, *EP* is a hexameter version of an earlier lyric form, and such a realignment finds many parallels in the poetry of the Hellenistic age. One Pindaric fragment offers a tantalizingly broken glimpse of how close the themes of such lyric poems might be to those of *EP*:

> . . . πρέπει δ᾽ ἐσλοῖσιν ὑμνεῖσθαι . . .
> . . . καλλίσταις ἀοιδαῖς.
> τοῦτο γὰρ ἀθανάτοις τιμαῖς ποτιψαύει μόνον
> θνᾴσκει δὲ σιγαθὲν καλὸν ἔργον . . . (fr. 121 Maehler)

> . . . it is proper for good men to be hymned . . . with the most noble songs, for that alone touches upon immortal honours, but a noble deed dies when left in silence.
> (trans. W. H. Race)

---

29. Cf. Harvey 1955, 163.

30. Cf. *Ol.* 2.47, *Nem.* 1.7, etc.; Fraustadt 1909, 17–18.

31. Thus Plutarch (*Dem.* 1.1) refers to Euripides' epinician for Alcibiades (*PMG* 755) as "an encomium for Alcibiades (εἰς Ἀλκιβιάδην ἐγκώμιον) on the occasion of his Olympian chariot victory."

32. Cf. Pl. *Ion* 534c2, *Rep.* 10.607a4 ("hymns for the gods and *enkomia* for great men [τοῖς ἀγαθοῖς]"), etc.; cf. below, p. 25. For the Alexandrian classification cf. Harvey 1955, 164–65; Rutherford 2001, 92, 157.

A passage of Aristophanes also shows how the language of victory encomium might easily be extended. At *Clouds* 1204–11 Strepsiades celebrates his good fortune in having a son who will be able to defeat his creditors in court:

> ὥστ᾽ εἰς ἐμαυτὸν καὶ τὸν υἱὸν τουτονὶ
> ἐπ᾽ εὐτυχίαισιν ἀιστέον μοὐγκώμιον.
> "μάκαρ ὦ Στρεψίαδες
> αὐτός τ᾽ ἔφυς, ὡς σοφός,
> χοῖον τὸν υἱὸν τρέφεις",
> φήσουσι δή μ᾽ οἱ φίλοι χοὶ δημόται
> ζηλοῦντες ἡνίκ᾽ ἂν σὺ νι-
>   κᾶις λέγων τὰς δίκας.

> Now I ought to sing a song of praise to myself and my
> son here over this good fortune. "O blest Strepsiades, how
> clever you are yourself and what a son you're bringing up!"—
> so my friends and my fellow-demesmen will say of me in
> envy, when you win my lawsuits with your speeches. (trans.
> Sommerstein)

In celebrating this comic victory, Strepsiades imagines himself praised for his *sophia* and for his offspring, both standard topoi of later rhetorical encomia.

The same passage of the *Lysis* cited above offers a striking illustration of what compositions, in both verse and prose (ποιή-ματα . . . καὶ συγγράμματα, 204d4–5; cf. 205a5), in praise of (εἰς) an individual (in this case an *eromenos*) might look like. Here Ctesippus describes with disgust the praises of Hippothales for the lovely Lysis:

> He fills his poems and speeches (ποιεῖ τε καὶ λέγει) with things
> the whole city could sing about Democrates [Lysis's father] and

the boy's grandfather Lysis and the whole tribe of his ancestors—the wealth, the stables, the chariot and horse victories at the Pythian, Isthmian, and Nemean Games, and even older stuff than this. The other day he treated us to a poem about entertaining Heracles, how his ancestor, who was himself a descendant of Zeus and the daughter of the deme's founder, received Heracles in his house because of his family tie . . . (205c–d)

Heracles was indeed the favorite ancestor for elite families to claim (cf. 26–27n.), and in this the Ptolemies, like the Macedonian kings before them, were no exception; one wonders in fact if Hippothales' alleged poem included a description of Heracles at a symposium (cf. vv. 20–33).[33] Be that as it may, Hippothales is teased with the composition of "poems and lyric songs" ($\mu\acute{\epsilon}\tau\rho\alpha$ . . . $\mu\acute{\epsilon}\lambda\eta$), as well as prose encomia, of his beloved (205b1), and the poems are presumably imagined as in hexameters or elegiacs. Critias certainly composed an elegiac poem "in honor of " ($\epsilon\emph{i}s$)[34] Alcibiades (like Lysis, another "marvelous boy"), and such a tradition continues in Hellenistic elegiac poems for rulers and patrons;[35] Callimachus's major elegiac poems for Berenice II and the Ptolemaic courtier Sosibios are, in part, representatives of this encomiastic line. Another passage of Plato also shows how traditional are some of the themes of *EP*:

When [the philosopher] hears an encomium for a tyrant or king, he thinks that he is listening to the praises of some herdsman . . . and when he hears that someone is extraordinarily rich, that he

33. I hope it goes without saying that for my argument nothing depends on the "historicity" of Plato's dialogue.

34. Cf. Heph. *Ench.* 2.3, citing Critias fr. 4 West.

35. Cf. Cameron 1995, 289–91; Barbantani 1998, 2001.

owns ten thousand *plethra* of land or more, he thinks that this is very little because he is accustomed to consider the whole earth. And when people sing the praises of families, how someone is noble because he has seven wealthy grandfathers, he thinks that such praise is dull and short-sighted. . . . And when people take pride in twenty-five generations of ancestors and trace themselves back to Heracles, son of Amphitryon, their pettiness seems to him absurd . . . (*Tht.* 174d–75b)

Hippothales' alleged prose works about his beloved Lysis may be set beside prose encomia of mythical subjects, a kind of composition that flourished in the fourth century to such an extent that mock encomia of humble objects (bees, salt, etc.) became a recognizable sophistic exercise.[36] Gorgias concludes his *Encomium of Helen*, which is a probably untypical example of the genre, with the famous words "I wanted to write this speech *(logos)* as Helen's encomium, but my little sport *(paignion)*," which seems to signal not merely a title, but also a generic placement of the work. Taking itself far more seriously than such *paignia* is Isocrates' *Evagoras* (c. 370), which shows an extensive debt to the encomiastic lyric tradition, above all that of Pindar;[37] in this essay Isocrates appears to claim an absolute novelty for his undertaking to write the praises of a recently deceased king:

I am aware of the difficulty of what I am about to do, namely, to eulogize a man's virtue in prose (ἀνδρὸς ἀρετὴν διὰ λόγων

36. Cf. Pl. *Symp.* 177a–b; Arist. *Rh.* 1.1366a28–32; Pease 1926. On rhetorical encomium generally see Fraustadt 1909; Buchheit 1960; Russell and Wilson 1981, xviii–xxxiv; Nightingale 1995, 93–106; Schiappa 1999, 187–90.

37. Cf. Race 1987, 131–55. For Isocrates' recognition of Pindar as a forerunner in encomium cf. *Antidosis* 166.

ἐγκωμιάζειν).[38] The best proof of this is the fact that although those who concern themselves with philosophy undertake to speak on many other subjects of the most varied kind, none of them has ever attempted to write a composition on such a subject as this. (*Euag.* 8)

There are various possible approaches to this claim: Isocrates may (broadly) be speaking the truth (i.e., previous prose encomia by serious "philosophers" and rhetoricians were on the whole devoted to mythic subjects—Heracles, Isocrates' own *Helen*, and the encomia of Eros in Plato's *Symposium*—or were "jokes" [*paignia*] such as the praise of salt); alternatively, we may give a strict interpretation to the range of possible authors to whom Isocrates refers ("those who concern themselves with philosophy"), thus leaving open the possibility that others had written such speeches.[39] However we interpret Isocrates' self-advertisement, however, it is clear already in his *Busiris* (early fourth century) that the methods and tropes proper to encomium were a subject for discussion among professional rhetoricians from a relatively early date. Moreover, this discussion did not have to start from scratch, for there existed already a well-developed tradition of epideictic praise, from which the new encomiastic oratory could borrow significantly. The principal manifestation of this tradi-

38. Pindar had used the simple κωμάζειν for "celebrate in a *komos*" (*Nem.* 2.24, 10.35; Slater 1969 s.v. *b*), but ἐγκωμιάζειν subsequently becomes normal for celebration divorced from a formal *komos*.

39. Cf. Nightingale 1995, 99 n. 16. As she notes, "In order to resolve this scholarly dispute, agreement as to what constitutes an encomium would have to be reached." Buchheit (1960) accepts Isocrates' claim at face value. The fullest study of ancient encomiastic rhetoric is Pernot 1993.

tion was the "funeral oration" *(epitaphios logos)*, which itself was indebted to the praise poetry, both of the living and the dead, of the archaic age.[40] That *encomia* and *epitaphioi logoi* shared many themes and commonplaces was well known to the subsequent tradition of technical rhetorical teaching.[41] Thus, for example, the *Evagoras* concerns not a living individual, but a recently deceased king, and the praise of Alcibiades that is included in a speech that Isocrates wrote for the famous Athenian's son *(On the Chariot* 25–41) is an excellent illustration of the links between encomium, funeral oration, and epinician. It is a great pity that we know nothing of the speech composed by a Xenocrates in praise of the deceased Arsinoe.[42]

There is, in fact, little evidence for prose encomia of Hellenistic rulers,[43] but the two principal surviving fourth-century rhetorical texts discuss the nature and arrangement of encomiastic speeches in some detail, and we are clearly already dealing with a flourishing epideictic mode. The so-called Rhetoric to Alexander (mid-fourth century?) sets out the pattern of τὸ ἐγκωμιαστικόν in chapter 35. The author first notes that the proper subject of encomium, as of vituperation *(kakologia* or *psogos)*, is the deeds that the *laudandus* has performed (1440b12); this apparently simple point is to assume significance in a consideration of the relation between *EP* and the rhetorical tradition.[44] As for the subjects to be handled, the author lays down the following division:

40. Cf. Buchheit 1960, 75; Loraux 1986.

41. Cf., for example, [Dion. Hal.] *Rhet.* 278.16–18 U-R, which lists these shared topoi as "country, family, nature, upbringing, achievements (πράξεις)."

42. Cf. Fraser 1972, 2: 939 n. 420.

43. Cf. Pernot 1993, 1: 45.

44. Cf. below, pp. 21–24.

After the introduction one should make a distinction between
the goods external to virtue and those actually inherent in virtue,
putting it thus: goods external to virtue fall under high birth,
strength, beauty, and wealth; virtue is divided into wisdom,
justice, courage, and creditable habits (ἐπιτηδεύματα ἔνδοξα).[45]
Those belonging to virtue are justly eulogised, but those ex-
ternal to it are kept in the background (κλέπτεται), since it is ap-
propriate for the strong and handsome and well-born and rich
to receive not praise (ἐπαινεῖν) but congratulation (μακαρίζειν).
Having then made this distinction, we shall place first after the
introduction the genealogy of the person we are speaking of,
as that is the fundamental ground of reputation or discredit
for human beings, and also for animals; so in eulogising a hu-
man being or a domestic animal we shall state their pedigree,
although when praising an emotion or action or speech or pos-
session we shall base our approval directly on the creditable
qualities that actually belong to it. (*Rhet. Alex.* 1440b16–28,
trans. H. Rackham)

After describing the method of praising the family of the *laudan-*
dus, the author then advises a roughly chronological progression
through the subject's life that highlights and magnifies (αὐξάνειν)
the accomplishments (ἔργα, πράξεις) of each stage of life. The ac-
complishments of adult life are to be divided according to the parts
of virtue—justice, wisdom (if appropriate!), courage (if appro-
priate!), and so on (1441b3–13). There are certain obvious points
of contact here with *EP*, notably in the amplified treatment of
Ptolemy's parents (cf. 13n.), but the much stronger impression is
of difference between poem and rhetorical paradigm: what is most

45. The fourth "cardinal virtue" is usually σωφροσύνη; cf., for example, Pl. *Rep.*
4.427e–28a; North 1966; below, p. 17.

strikingly lacking from *EP*, when it is viewed from the perspective of the "Rhetoric to Alexander," is the standard division of praise by "the parts of virtue" and any cataloguing of Ptolemy's "deeds." In particular, the absence of any treatment of Philadelphus's observance of justice may be particularly noted, as this might have been expected both from the perspective of rhetorical tradition and because of the importance of the idea of the king as the embodiment of the law (νόμος ἔμψυχος) in Hellenistic kingship theory. To the reasons for this I shall return.

Of particular interest for *EP* is Aristotle's discussion of rhetorical praise in the ninth chapter of book 1 of the *Rhetoric;* elsewhere, Aristotle distinguishes between ἔπαινος, or general praise of an individual, and ἐγκώμιον, or praise of a particular deed or action, but it is doubtful whether that distinction is relevant to this major discussion of the subject.[46] As we have already seen in Isocrates and the "Rhetoric to Alexander," praise in encomiastic rhetoric is praise of *arete* (cf. already 1362a12–13); for Aristotle, *arete* in this context "is an ability that is productive and preservative of goods, and an ability for doing good in many and great ways (δύναμις εὐεργετικὴ πολλῶν καὶ μεγάλων), actually in all ways in all things," 1366a36–39.[47] *Euergesia* is indeed fundamental to the portrait of Philadelphus that Theocritus paints (vv. 95–120), but when Aristotle comes to the "parts of *arete*," here listed as "justice, courage, moderation (σωφροσύνη), magnificence, magnanimity, liberality, gentleness, practical wisdom (φρόνησις), and intelligence (σοφία)"

---

46. Cf. Kassel's apparatus on p. 45 of his edition (Berlin 1976). The relevant passages are *Eth. Eud.* 2.1219b8–16 and *Eth. Nic.* 1.1101b31–34.

47. This and subsequent translations of the *Rhetoric* are taken from Kennedy 1991.

(1366b1–3), it is again clear that whereas there is, unsurprisingly, some overlap with Theocritus's praise of Ptolemy, the differences between the two texts stand out even more sharply. As with the "Rhetoric to Alexander," at the heart of praise stand "actions" (πράξεις, 1367b28); noble birth, education, and so on can serve to add persuasiveness to one's encomium, "for good parents are likely to have good children" (1367b30), but are not the heart of the encomiast's business. Naturally, this distinction between inherited and earned praise is not to be exaggerated: poets of the archaic age wrote epinicia and encomia for young boys that concentrated very largely on the achievements of their family, and the occasional necessity to make the best of a bad job must have been one of the reasons for the interest of professional encomiasts in genealogy. Nevertheless, Theocritus is, as we have seen, remarkably silent about Ptolemy's "great deeds" (πράξεις in the stricter meaning of the term), and an obvious affinity between *EP* and the rhetorical prescriptions of the fourth century should not blind us to these striking differences.

One further point worth noting from this chapter of the *Rhetoric* is Aristotle's insistence on the close link between praise and deliberation or advice (συμβουλαί):

> Praise and deliberations are part of a common species in that what one might propose in deliberation becomes encomia when the form of the expression is changed. When, therefore, we know what should be done and what sort of person someone should be, we should change the form of expression and convert these points into propositions: for example, that one ought not to think highly of things gained by chance but of things through one's efforts. When so spoken, it becomes a proposition; but as praise it takes the following form: "He did not think highly of

what came by chance but of what he gained by his own efforts."
Thus, when you want to praise, see what would be the underly-
ing proposition; and when you want to set out proposals in de-
liberation, see what you would praise. (1367b36–38a8)

Praise and advice use the same material but frame it differently;
an important aspect of the relation (and difference) between *Idyll*
16 in praise of Hieron of Syracuse and *EP* is here theorized:
Ptolemy is praised for doing precisely what Theocritus urges
prospective patrons in *Idyll* 16 to do. Pindaric epinicia, to say noth-
ing of the epic tradition, show how closely praise and advice could
be joined in a single poem (as indeed they conspicuously are in
Idyll 16), and Isocrates presents his *Evagoras* to Nicocles as a spur
to urge Nicocles and his generation toward emulation of Evago-
ras (*Euag.* 75–81), while at the same time carefully negotiating
around the possible implication that Nicocles is not in fact already
developing in the right direction (*Euag.* 78–81). So too, the lav-
ish praise bestowed by an encomiastic poet comes with the seri-
ousness and moral weight of a Hesiod (cf. below).

EP falls easily into sections divided by topic:

1–12	Proem
13–33	Philadelphus's father
34–57	Philadelphus's mother[48]
58–76	Philadelphus's birth
77–94	Philadelphus's territory: Egypt (77–85) and beyond (86–94)

48. Meincke (1965, 88) places vv. 53–57 with the birth narrative; they obvi-
ously form a "gliding transition," but cf. 56–57n.

These sections, and their arrangement, clearly correspond to some extent with the fourth-century prescriptions for the arrangement of encomia, although the topics themselves—family, wealth, territorial rule—are those already familiar from Pindaric praise poetry. Led partly by these similarities and partly by the apparently very clear sectioning of *EP*, modern scholars have long constructed a very close relationship between Theocritus's *Encomium* and the rhetorical tradition of prose encomia; it is in fact now virtually an article of faith that *EP* is "rhetorically" constructed along lines laid down by rhetorical theorists, which are seen (by different scholars) as being adhered to more or less closely.[49] There are different questions that may be asked here: Given that *EP* clearly does share certain themes and structural elements with what we know of the rhetorical prose encomium, has Theocritus molded his poem to reflect the patterns of such works? If so, are we intended to notice this molding? And, if so, what is its effect? In attempting to answer these questions, the fact that we have no other comparable Hellenistic poem enjoins caution. Moreover, as we have seen, the common features may be, in part at least, accounted for by the debt that the rhetorical tradition itself owes to the poetic traditions of both hymn and encomium. Nevertheless, it would seem both difficult and pointless to deny all influence from epideictic rhetoric, and in one particular at least Theocritus clearly wants us to

49. Cf., for example, Buecheler 1875, 57–58; Fraustadt 1909, 92; O. Crusius, *RE* 5.2582; Meincke 1965, 88; Hardie 1983, 87; Schwinge 1986, 60, etc.

notice the relationship between *EP* and model rhetorical schemata. The very deliberate, formal structuring of the poem gestures toward the teaching of rhetorical theory, as one way of marking the relation between encomiast and object of praise through siting that relationship within a familiar tradition. The poem thus emphasizes that Ptolemy is indeed a fit subject for such an *epideixis*. The structure of the poem is itself an encomiastic move.

The most elaborate and influential analysis of *EP* as a "rhetorical" poem is that of Francis Cairns, who sees Theocritus's poem as a *basilikos logos*, "speech for a king/emperor," patterns for which are prescribed in the surviving treatises ascribed to Menander "the rhetorician" (c. 300 C.E.).[50] There are a number of topoi, of course, that are shared between *EP* and Menander's prescriptions,[51] and there is an obvious temptation to see in Theocritus's poem a forerunner of the "poems on the emperor" of festival competitions under the Roman Empire.[52] Moreover, the huge chronological gap between Theocritus and Menander can, if necessary, be narrowed both by noting that competitions in ἐγκώμια for living men can be traced epigraphically from as early as the first century B.C.E. and by an appeal to the general conservatism of the language of praise throughout antiquity; there is in fact no doubt that some of the material in Menander's treatise goes back a very long way. Nevertheless, it is dangerously circular to interpret *EP* in the light of a subsequent tradition that itself, all but certainly, draws upon po-

50. Cf. Cairns 1972, 100–20; Russell and Wilson 1981, 76–95.

51. Russell and Wilson (1981, xxxii–iii) rather overstate the similarities between *Idyll* 17 and Menander's prescriptions.

52. Cf. Jamot 1895, 364 (Thespiae); Hardie 1983, 17. For rhetorical encomia of the later period in general cf. also Robert 1938, 17–31.

ems such as *EP.* Menander's debt to poetic, especially hymnic, traditions of praise is very well established:[53] poems such as *EP,* which draw many of their themes and conventions from the hymnic tradition, themselves fed into the rhetorical practice that Menander standardized and systematized. The *basilikoi logoi* that are really relevant to the understanding of *EP* are in fact, first, Hesiod's celebration of "reverend kings" (*Theog.* 80–97) and the blessings enjoyed by the "just city" (*WD* 225–37),[54] and, second, prose treatises "on kingship," such as the one Aristotle wrote for Alexander;[55] by evoking the flavor of such works Theocritus suggests an affinity between himself and the wise adviser of great men. On the other hand, Cairns's long list (p. 110) of the Menandrean topics allegedly omitted by Theocritus—country, race, physical appearance, and upbringing; military prowess; mildness to subjects, choice of deputies, taxes and laws; luck; children; loyalty of the bodyguard; "cardinal" virtues—itself suggests how self-defeating is the wholesale application of Menander's template to this poem. Comparison with Menander can, of course, serve as a useful heuristic technique for focusing on what is prominent in Theocritus; such things are prominent, however, not because Theocritus chose to omit the other possible topics suggested by Menander, but because of the kind of poem this is and the particular position of the honorand. We must place the poem within the traditions of praise appropriate to it, not assume that it lies in one particular tradition, and then seek to explain its many divergences from that selected mode.

53. For the influence of Hellenistic on later poetic encomia cf., for example, Giangrande 1971, 214–15.

54. Cf. below, p. 156.

55. Cf. Arist. fr. 646–47 Rose; 104–5n. below.

As noted above, the most obvious difference between *EP* and the prescriptions of the rhetorical tradition[56] lies in the absence of any detail about Philadelphus's achievements, military or otherwise.[57] For most critics there is an easy explanation: "There weren't any achievements (πράξεις)," was Gennaro Perrotta's pithy summing up; "one could not, without producing laughter, celebrate military deeds which did not exist."[58] For Francis Cairns, "[Theocritus] could not . . . insert a section on Ptolemy's personal military prowess since Ptolemy was, in fact, a weak and somewhat effete man personally, and any attempt to fly in the face of this fact would have produced a credibility gap."[59] It may be wondered how vv. 85–94 and 102–3 avoid this "credibility gap," if that indeed is the way the strategy of the poem is to be interpreted. We must again be wary of assuming what was expected in such a poem, but an understandable concern with the relation between *EP* and the rhetorical tradition has stopped critics asking why the poem is, in many ways, as surprising as it is: not just "Why so little about Ptolemy's 'deeds'?" but also, for example, "Why so little about the 'cardinal virtues,' which both the rhetorical tradition and Greek kingship theory would have led us to expect?"[60]

---

56. The "actions" of a single *basileus* were also a standard structural form for Hellenistic historiography; cf. the writers gathered in *FGrHist* 154–99.

57. For the emphasis upon "deeds" in the later tradition of rhetorical didaxis cf., for example, Aelius Theon II 109.20 Spengel; Cic. *De or.* 2.345–48.

58. Perrotta 1978, 83.

59. Cairns 1972, 111.

60. Cairns (1972, 112) at least recognizes the problem. For the cardinal virtues in Hellenistic encomium in general cf. Fraustadt 1909, 100; Doblhofer 1966, 27–33; Wallace-Hadrill 1981, 298–323; and for the earlier period cf. Isoc. *Euag.* 23.

The answer to at least some of these problems will lie, inevitably, with the special nature of Ptolemy's position, as both Graeco-Macedonian *basileus* and Egyptian pharaoh.[61]

POETS AND PATRONS

Plutarch preserves an account, partly from the historian Douris of Samos (late fourth–early third century), of the honors bestowed upon the Spartan admiral Lysander in the period immediately after the Peloponnesian War:

> Lysander was the first Greek to whom the cities erected altars as to a god and made sacrifices, and he was the first to whom paians were sung. The opening of one of these [*PMG* 867] is recorded:

> τὸν ῾Ελλάδος ἀγαθέας
> στραταγὸν ἀπ᾽ εὐρυχόρου Σπάρτας
> ὑμνήσομεν ὤ ἰὲ Παιάν.

> It is the general of holy Greece, coming from wide-dancing Sparta, whom we shall hymn, O! Io Paian!

The Samians voted to rename their festival of Hera the Lysandreia. As for the poets, Lysander kept Choirilos with him to celebrate his achievements in verse (κοσμήσοντα τὰς πράξεις διὰ ποιητικῆς), and when Antilochos composed some middling verses in his honor (εἰς αὐτόν), Lysander showed his pleasure by filling his cap with silver and giving it to the poet. Antimachus of Colophon and a certain Nikeratos of Heracleia competed with their poems at the Lysandreia before Lysander, and when he awarded the garland to Nikeratos, Antimachus destroyed his poem in his distress. (Plut. *Lys.* 18 = Douris, *FGrHist* 76 F 71, 696 F 33c)

---

61. Cf. below, pp. 46–53 and, for example, 86–92n.

Much here seems to foreshadow the Hellenistic age: divine cult for a successful military commander;[62] poets attached to his retinue (we think, above all, of Alexander and his cultural entourage) who might hope for substantial monetary reward (cf. *Idylls* 16.24, 29; 17.114), alongside the traditional garlands of victory;[63] public festivals named for him (cf. the Ptolemaia) at which poets compete, all but certainly with poems of praise for the "patron." Choirilos's poems for Lysander were very probably in hexameters; that of Antimachus may have been.[64] This festival pattern is clearly related to that of archaic and classical royal "courts" where poets might live or visit, whether of their own accord or in response to a "commission":[65] Polycrates of Samos, Hieron of Syracuse, and Archelaos of Macedon are among the best-known of such rulers who gathered poets and intellectuals around them, and whose praises were sung by their "guests." Ibycus's famous poem for Polycrates (*PMG* 282) is only the most visible tip of a very large iceberg.

In the Hellenistic period, the patronage offered directly by great men, such as Philadelphus, worked both alongside and often through the support that individual cities offered both to their own poets and to those from outside, through a complex network of honorific awards and prizes. This civic patronage continued the institutional recognition and support of poetry and its

62. Cf. Habicht 1970, 3–6. Whether the *paian* was composed during Lysander's lifetime is disputed; cf. Rutherford 2001, 57–58.

63. Cf. below, pp. 182–84.

64. Cf. Cameron 1995, 270.

65. On the distinction between the "bidden" and the "unbidden" poet cf. Hardie 1983, 30–36; the idea is particularly important for *Idyll* 16; cf. below, pp. 38–39.

performance that had always been a regular feature of great aristocratic gatherings and religious festivals; thus Hesiod tells how he won a tripod at the funeral games of Amphidamas at Chalcis (*WD* 650–59). A principal textual model for *EP*, the *Homeric Hymn to Apollo*, records the performance at Delos of a wandering Chian poet whose poem tells the most important Delian "myth" of all, the birth of Apollo, and who claims that "all [his] songs are hereafter supreme (ἀριστεύουσιν)"; this does not necessarily mean that the poet has won a poetic competition at the festival, but such a conclusion would be very easy for later interpreters to draw.[66] In this poem, the familiar reciprocity of later poems of praise—*kleos* in return for "gifts"—that Theocritus holds out to both Hieron and Philadelphus is replaced by a striking exchange of reciprocal *kleos:* the singer carries the fame of the Delian performances around the world, and the performers themselves are charged with responsibility for the singer's own renown (vv. 166–76). Structurally, however, this reciprocity functions just like the claimed mutual dependence of "host" and "guest," which is a prominent element of the rhetoric of later praise poetry, and here again the *Hymn to Apollo*, a poem that we find constantly reworked in Alexandrian poetry, is seen as a very important pointer to later traditions.

The primary evidence for civic patronage of poetry in the Hellenistic and imperial ages is the epigraphic record of rewards and privileges, such as *proxenia*, freedom from tax, grants of land, and so on, bestowed upon poets, both lyric and hexameter, by the grateful citizens of towns honored in their verses.[67] Thus, for ex-

---

66. Cf. *Idyll* 15.98: the singer "who last year did best in (ἀρίστευσε) the dirge."

67. The principal study is Guarducci 1926; cf. also Cameron 1995, 47–49; Bouvier 1985.

ample, we see the Delians in the first half of the third century honoring Demoteles of Andros for poetry "on [Delian] local myths" and Amphiklos of Chios for poems that "brought luster (κεκόσμηκεν) to the temple and to the Delians" (Guarducci 1926, 650); the pattern of the *Homeric Hymn to (Delian) Apollo*—a visiting bard sings of the mythic glories of his host city—is here again played out in the realities of Greek cultural life. The Aristophanic picture of the lyric poet "on the make," who arrives unannounced at the new foundation of Cloudcuckooland with celebratory verses making clear his hopes for a reward (*Birds* 903 ff.), looks to such a pattern, as much as to the satirical view of a Simonides or a Pindar as poets with their eye firmly on the (monetary) main chance; distinctions between such patterns tend, of course, to have more significance in historical analysis than in practice and are, in any case, of little moment for a comic poet. In *EP* Theocritus too makes plain his hopes (or perhaps gratitude) for recompense from the *laudandus* (vv. 112–20); it was traditional so to do.

We know a little, but not nearly enough, about the workings of Ptolemaic patronage.[68] The catchall term "patronage" can in fact easily mislead, suggesting as it does "a [personal] relationship . . . of some duration,"[69] particularly in the field of literature and the arts, where the well-documented subject of artistic patronage in the Renaissance and subsequent centuries seems to offer dangerously tempting analogies. There is in fact no evidence,

68. Cf. esp. Pfeiffer 1968, 87–104; Fraser 1972, 1: chap. 6; Weber 1993, 87–95; Burton 1995, chap. 4. The extent of our ignorance is rightly stressed by Goldhill (1991, 272–74).

69. Saller 1982, 1.

even circumstantial, for direct contact between Theocritus and
Philadelphus, and no evidence that Theocritus ever lived and
worked under royal protection, as did, say, Callimachus, Apollo-
nius, and Eratosthenes.[70] On the face of it, *Idylls* 14 and 15 might
be thought clearly to suggest that Theocritus hoped to, or actu-
ally did, enjoy Ptolemaic favor and support, but we in fact know
nothing about the conditions under which those poems were com-
posed and circulated;[71] possible indications of a Ptolemaic con-
text in the bucolic poems are at best merely suggestive.[72] It is per-
haps hardly bold to conclude that *EP* seeks patronage (in a very
loose sense of the term) through victory at one of the rich net-
work of poetic festivals behind which lay, and which in turn rein-
forced, Ptolemaic political power and wealth, but that is unillu-
minating as long as no relationship between poet and ruler can
be established; the mere fact that Theocritus seems to have com-
posed a group of "Ptolemaic" poems (*Idyll* 15, *EP*, *Berenice*, and
perhaps others),[73] probably all close in time to each other, remains
without an explanatory context in the absence of evidence from
beyond the poems themselves. If it is correct, as is now widely be-
lieved, that there is a detailed "Ptolemaic" subtext to the narra-

---

70. Whether or not Strabo 17.3.22 (Κυρηναῖος δ᾽ ἐστὶ καὶ Καλλίμαχος καὶ Ἐρ-
ατοσθένης, ἀμφότεροι τετιμημένοι παρὰ τοῖς Αἰγυπτίων βασιλεῦσιν) and Aul. Gell.
17.21.41 (*Callimachus, poeta Cyrenensis, Alexandriae apud Ptolomaeum regem celebra-
tus est*) (264 B.C.E.) refer to actual "court titles" or honors is disputed. Gelzer (1982)
would see a reflection of the differences in position between Callimachus and The-
ocritus in the respective manners in which they write of the royal family; it is cer-
tainly true that Callimachus's "laureate" poems convey a very particular tone of
intimacy. Cf. further below on *Idyll* 15.

71. Cf. further below, p. 45.

72. Cf. my notes on 3.50b–51 and 4.31.

73. Cf. above, pp. 7–8.

tive of Heracles and the snakes in *Idyll* 24,[74] with the infant hero evoking various aspects of the young Philadelphus, then it may be thought that Theocritus must have had at least a more than passing familiarity with important elements of Ptolemaic self-projection, as indeed *EP* would seem to confirm; moreover, the witty near burlesque of the description of Amphitryon and Alcmena in *Idyll* 24 is close in tone to the work of poets (Callimachus, Apollonius) who are known to have enjoyed Ptolemaic patronage in a fuller sense of that term.[75] What, however, we cannot say is what degree of intimacy between court and poet is necessary for that knowledge.

How Theocritus "supported himself" we do not know. *Idylls* 11 and 13 are addressed to the doctor and poet Nicias of Miletus, and *Idyll* 28 and *Epigram* 8 honor Nicias and his wife. These poems do indeed suggest one model of private patronage, but when we are told that "Nicias was wealthy enough to commission *Idylls* 11, 13 and 28 as well as *Epigram* 8,"[76] we will want to ask just what is involved in this practice of "commissioning," and how it differed—if it did—from, say, the relations between Pindar and those for whom he wrote. Ideas of *philia, xenia,* and *charis* are central to the construction of the relationship between Theocritus and Nicias and his wife in *Idyll* 28, and these are of course also crucial in the archaic language of patronage;[77] their prominence in *Idyll* 28 may in fact, like the Aeolic dialect, be part of a

74. Cf. Koenen 1977, 79–86; Griffiths 1979, 91–98; Weber 1993, 241–42; Cameron 1995, 54–55; Stephens 2003, 123–46.

75. I have discussed *Idyll* 24 in greater detail in Fantuzzi and Hunter 2002, 275–86.

76. Cairns 1976, 304.

77. Cf., for example, Kurke 1991, 135–59.

literary reconstruction of the past, which is of course not to say that such terms may not also have been entirely appropriate for the "real" relationship between Theocritus and Nicias. So too, it would be dangerous to draw conclusions from the graceful, half-amused praise of Nicias in *Idyll* 11 (vv. 5–6; cf. 81) and the generalizing and inclusive opening of *Idyll* 13 ("not for us alone, as we thought . . . we who are mortal and do not see tomorrow") about the relationship between the two men, though the fact that Nicias and Theocritus use each other's names in the vocative in their respective poems on the Cyclops[78] suggests at least a rhetoric of "equality," perhaps again in imitation of modes of archaic sympotic poetry. The conclusion of *Idyll* 11 does, however, play with the respective value of song and money, and *Epigram* 8 celebrates the skill ($\tau\acute{\epsilon}\chi\nu\eta$) of the sculptor of a wooden sculpture of Asclepius, for which Nicias paid "the peak of wages" ($\mathring{\alpha}\kappa\rho o\nu \ldots \mu\iota\sigma\theta\acute{o}\nu$). One wonders if Eetion was the only $\tau\epsilon\chi\nu\acute{\iota}\tau\eta\varsigma$ (cf. 17.112–14) to benefit from Nicias' "patronage."

If relations with Nicias figure large in the Theocritean corpus, it is also an easy guess that *Idyll* 7 (the *Thalysia*) was written for the Coan family of Lykopeus, whose ancestors' deeds are praised in the opening verses (cf. vv. 3–7), though what the realities of such "writing for" involved we can again hardly say. If, however, the initial position of honor in this poem is given to Lykopeus and his sons, another potential patron arises near its center. The young poet Simichidas introduces the best poem from his repertoire of songs, "which perhaps report has carried even to the throne of Zeus" ($\tau\acute{\alpha} \pi o\nu \kappa\alpha\grave{\iota} Z\eta\nu\grave{o}\varsigma \mathring{\epsilon}\pi\grave{\iota} \theta\rho\acute{o}\nu o\nu \mathring{\alpha}\gamma\alpha\gamma\epsilon \phi\acute{\alpha}\mu\alpha$, v. 93). The temptation to see here a reference to Ptolemy Philadelphus is hard to

---

78. Cf. Hunter 1999, 221.

resist: Simichidas is a "professional poet" on Cos, the island where Philadelphus was born and which remained under his close protection; of the two great poets he claims to aspire to surpass (vv. 39–41), one (Philitas) certainly had very close connections to the Ptolemaic court, and the other (Asclepiades) may have had such ties.[79] Whether we are to understand that Simichidas's ambition—royal patronage!—ludicrously outstrips his talent or that, with self-satisfied understatement, he is claiming already to enjoy Philadelphus's approval (much depends on the nuance placed upon που), the "narrative of patronage" that the verses evoke was in fact to become a familiar one: the potential patron "hears of" the work of a poet and then takes the initiative in offering financial and other support. It is, for example, this narrative that Horace, in a catalogue of the tactless follies of poets, describes as a deluded fantasy:

> cum speramus eo rem uenturam ut, simul atque
> carmina rescieris nos fingere, commodus ultro
> arcessas et egere uetes et scribere cogas. (*Epist.* 2.1.226–28)

> [It is bad] when we hope that things have come to such a
> state that as soon as you [Augustus] learn that we are writing
> poetry, you will generously summon us of your own accord,
> banish our poverty, and compel us to go on writing.

If in Horace's satirical vision poets are silly enough to think that writing poems, regardless of their quality, is enough to gain a patron, it is nevertheless this same pattern that Cicero invokes when he claims that the young Archias's reputation as a wonderful

---

79. Cf. Fraser 1972, 1: 559.

(Greek) poet preceded him to Rome, and it was through this reputation that he was taken up by the two consuls who happened to have literary interests (*Arch.* 5); Archias in fact clearly tailored some of his poetry to the business of catching the eye or ear of the great, as later did Varro of Atax, whose epic *Bellum Sequanicum* "was a piece of propaganda not only on Caesar's behalf but on his own."[80] Like Archias, Simichidas is already making his way in the world, and the game that is played out between Simichidas's voice and that of the poet behind that voice means that Simichidas's hopes for, or claims of, Ptolemaic approval are, at some level, also those of Theocritus. It is, however, crucial to the strategy of *Idyll* 7 that the claim to royal approval is presented as part of Simichidas's naively self-satisfied *epideixis* to Lycidas; the claim to patronage is itself part of Simichidas's role-playing as the "professional poet" ($Mo\iota\sigma\hat{a}\nu$ $\kappa a\pi\nu\rho\grave{o}\nu$ $\sigma\tau\acute{o}\mu a$ ... $\dot{a}o\iota\delta\acute{o}s$, vv. 37–38). This ironic distance with which Simichidas is depicted finds a counterpart in Theocritus's most elaborate representation of the business of patronage, namely, *Idyll* 15.[81]

The anecdotal tradition, above all Athenaeus, represents the early Ptolemies, like Philip and Alexander who preceded them, as able to joke, with varying degrees of self-consciousness, with the scholars and hangers-on who surrounded them. The social relations of a Ptolemy with parasites and *hetairai* appear in three anecdotes of Machon (frr. 1, 5, 18 Gow), who worked at Alexandria almost certainly under Philadelphus,[82] and it is entirely plausible that the later anecdotal tradition has its roots in the Ptole-

---

80. J. Zetzel in Gold 1982, 91.
81. Cf. below, p. 45.
82. Cf. Gow 1965, 3–11.

maic period itself. Thus the famous description by Timon of Phlius of the inhabitants of the Museum seems, whatever view of its imagery we take,[83] satirically to twist the idea of Ptolemy and his scholars as "table-companions," by laying bare true power relations within the context of the provision and consumption of food:

πολλοὶ μὲν βόσκονται ἐν Αἰγύπτωι πολυφύλωι
βιβλιακοὶ χαρακῖται ἀπείριτα δηριόωντες
Μουσέων ἐν ταλάρωι (SH 786)

In teeming Egypt are fed many creatures of the book,
fenced-in, constantly squabbling in the Muses' basket

σιτεῖσθαι, the verb with which Athenaeus glosses Timon's βόσκεσθαι, was, at least in Roman times, part of the "title" of the Alexandrian scholars or "those being fed in the Museum without payment" (οἱ ἐν τῶι Μουσείωι σιτούμενοι ἀτελεῖς);[84] how far back in time such language goes we cannot say, but σίτησις is the standard classical and Hellenistic word for "dining privileges" granted by a city to its benefactors, and under Augustus, Strabo saw attached to the Museum "a large building in which is the common dining-hall of the scholars who share the Museum" (τὸ συσσίτιον τῶν μετ-εχόντων τοῦ Μουσείου φιλολόγων ἀνδρῶν, Strabo 17.1.8). Even if "being fed" refers merely to monetary payments received by certain resident scholars,[85] the strategy of Timon's attack seems clear. The fundamental tension between treating the dinner table and

---

83. Cf. Fraser 1972, 2: 471; Cameron 1995, 31–32.
84. Cf. Fraser 1972, 1: 316–17, 2: 470–71; Weber 1993, 89 n. 2.
85. On the σύνταξις βασιλική cf. Fraser 1972, 1: 310–11.

symposium as sites for the meeting of equals, whether it be Alcaeus's aristocratic *hetaireia* or a gathering of free citizens of democratic Athens, and as sites for the display of difference between host and guest (as in the *Cena Trimalchionis*), or, put more harshly, between patron and parasite, underlies both anecdotal and satirical traditions;[86] the particular flavor of those traditions arises in fact from the awareness, which is shared and exploited by both host and guest, of that tension. It is this awareness that, in the anecdotal tradition, shapes the rules by which the game of patronage is played out. Within this pattern of knowing role-playing (on both sides), the king's avoidance of σεμνότης, that insistence upon distance that derives from the certainty of intellectual, social, or political superiority, was clearly important in projecting the new settlement of power as a "natural" outgrowth of traditional Greek and Macedonian values. No doubt this aspect of the anecdotal and literary traditions reflects, to some extent, a genuine feature of the early Ptolemaic court in its imitation of Macedonian traditions—it is only in the second and first centuries that a very elaborate set of court hierarchies developed—and poets too caught the mood.

This paraded approachability[87] is very clearly on show in the description of Ptolemy placed in the mouth of Thyonichus in *Idyll* 14:

[*AI.*] τἆλλα δ' ἀνὴρ ποῖός τις; [*ΘΥ.*] . . . τοισιν ἄριστος ·[88]
εὐγνώμων, φιλόμουσος, ἐρωτικός, εἰς ἄκρον ἀδύς,

---

86. Cf. Herman 1980–81 for related slippage in the treatment of the king's "friends." Note how Trimalchio's temporary withdrawal from the room brings both *libertas* and *sermones* (Petron. *Sat.* 41.9).

87. For the importance of this quality for Hellenistic kingship and beyond cf. Wallace-Hadrill 1982, 33–35.

88. The text is here damaged beyond repair.

εἰδὼς τὸν φιλέοντα, τὸν οὐ φιλέοντ' ἔτι μᾶλλον,
πολλοῖς πολλὰ διδούς, αἰτεύμενος οὐκ ἀνανεύων,
οἷα χρὴ βασιλῆ'· αἰτεῖν δὲ δεῖ οὐκ ἐπὶ παντί,
Αἰσχίνα. (14.60–65)

[Aisch.] What sort of man is he in other ways? [Thyon.]
The very best—humane, a friend of the arts, knows all
about love, charming in every way; he knows his friends,
and his enemies even better; he's generous to many, doesn't
refuse when asked, just as you would expect from a king—
but you shouldn't ask on any pretext, Aischinas.

The king's virtues as described here are those traditionally claimed
by the privileged elite, together with the precious addition of real
power, but it is a power that allows a man to keep his "freedom"
(v. 59).[89] At one level, we may see these verses as a translation to
a less formal level of language of the ideals of Pindar's description
of Hieron:

πραΰς ἀστοῖς, οὐ φθονέων ἀγαθοῖς, ξεί-
νοις δὲ θαυμαστὸς πατήρ. (*Pyth.* 3.71)

Gentle to the citizens, without malice to the good,
a marvelous father to strangers.

If, however, the substance of these Theocritean verses is broadly
traditional, we also recognize in them the congenial Ptolemy of
the anecdotal tradition—the cultured *bon viveur* who is "one of
us," but for the fact that he holds the purse strings. Even Thy-
onichus's warning about the need for moderation in requests finds

89. On this passage see esp. Burton 1992, 240–43; Weber 1993, 207–8.

a close echo in a story that Athenaeus tells about Philip and a parasite called Kleisophos, "when Philip reproved him for always making requests" (διότι ἀεὶ αἰτεῖ, Ath. 6.248d). Thyonichus is in fact repeating "popular gossip"—this is what the people, and particularly the Greek troops, say—and it is precisely δόξα, popular reputation, upon which the new power settlement rests and, most important of all, that poetry claims to be able to confer. If Ptolemy needs mercenaries, he needs poets to spread his *kleos* as much, if not more (cf. 17.116–20); Thyonichus, both recruiting-sergeant and encomiast, represents one way of positioning the poet in the new dispensation.

Thyonichus finds a close, and perhaps surprising, ally in the bawd Gyllis of Herodas 1, who seeks to persuade a younger friend that her man has forgotten all about her in the midst of the delights of Alexandria:

> κεῖ δ' ἐστὶν οἶκος τῆς θεοῦ· τὰ γὰρ πάντα,
> ὅσσ' ἔστι κου καὶ γίνετ', ἔστ' ἐν Αἰγύπτωι·
> πλοῦτος, παλαίστρη, δύναμις, εὐδίη, δόξα,
> θέαι, φιλόσοφοι, χρυσίον, νεηνίσκοι,
> θεῶν ἀδελφῶν τέμενος, ὁ βασιλεὺς χρηστός,
> Μουσῆιον, οἶνος, ἀγαθὰ πάντ' ὅσ' ἂν χρήιζηι,
> γυναῖκες, ὁκόσους οὐ μὰ τὴν Ἅιδεω Κούρην
> ἀστέρας ἐνεγκεῖν οὐρανὸς κεκαύχηται . . . (Herodas 1.26–33)

The home of the goddess is there. For everything in
the world that exists and is produced is in Egypt: wealth,
wrestling schools, power, tranquillity, fame, spectacles,
philosophers, gold, youths, the sanctuary of the sibling
gods, the King is an excellent chap, the Museum, wine,
every good thing he could desire, women, as many as by
Hades' Maid the stars that heaven boasts of bearing . . .
(trans. Cunningham, adapted)

This heterogeneous list[90] reflects not merely the rather chaotic mind of the speaker but also points to how Ptolemaic ideology overlays the traditional values and activities of the elite (wrestling schools, philosophers, τὰ ἐρωτικά, the symposium, here indicated by "wine") with a new, and necessarily hierarchizing, valuation for wealth and its display ("spectacles")[91] and a new political and religious settlement. Alexandria, with its "house of the goddess" (though no longer a Parthenon)[92] and its philosophers, is the new Athens, the center of the cultural and mercantile world. So too, in *Idyll* 15 a Ptolemaic "spectacle" is combined with the representation of Alexandria as a *cosmopolis* to which all the people and goods of the world flow; the Syracusan women and the Syracusan poet are moving with the tide.

For the most part, of course, *EP* operates at a quite different level than does the mime tradition: Ptolemy is treated with the seriousness appropriate to the object of hymnic praise. Nevertheless, the gentle humor of the Olympian symposium (vv. 16–33) comes recognizably from the same milieu that I have been sketching, and the "narrative of patronage" that is hinted at in vv. 115–16 ("the spokesmen of the Muses sing of Ptolemy in return for his benefactions") exploits our familiarity with standard models that

90. Interpolation has often been suspected, probably unnecessarily; cf. Cunningham 1965, 7–9; Simon 1991, 52–55. The heterogeneity is underplayed in Too's account (1998, 118).

91. Cf. above, p. 2, on the "Grand Procession." The classical world, most notably Athens, was of course also full of "spectacles," but these gain a new political significance in the relations between the Hellenistic monarchs and their subjects; cf. Dunand 1981.

92. The identity of the goddess is disputed: most commentators incline to Aphrodite, though Simon (1991, 52) argues for Tyche.

confirm Ptolemy in a traditional role as generous patron, no less than do the explicit words of *Idyll* 14.

For the Hellenistic period, we can in fact say more about the literary representation, both positive and negative, of poetic patronage than about its actual workings. One possibly important source for this representation requires particular care but should not be neglected. This is the abundant material concerning poetic patronage at Rome. Although it is the case that no major Hellenistic poet expresses himself like "Vergil, Horace, Tibullus, Propertius, and Ovid [who] each boast attachments to one or two important persons who occupy more of their attention than their other acquaintances among the . . . elite,"[93] the possibility that Roman representations of patronage evoked, and in extreme cases were modeled upon, aspects of Greek practice offers a potentially fruitful resource for the study of the Hellenistic situation.[94] In the final part of this section I shall try to tease out some relevant strands of Greek and Roman patronage narratives that may shed light on Theocritus's poetry of praise.

Broadly speaking, two partly overlapping models dominate ancient narratives of poetic patronage. The first, which was considered above, represents the initiative for the patronage relationship as coming from the poet himself (as with the lyric poet in Aristophanes' *Birds*); it is this model of "the begging poet" that lies at the heart of *Idylls* 15 and 16 (cf. below). Alternatively, the would-be patron asks a famous artist, poet, philosopher, or scientist to visit him or, particularly from the late fifth century on,

93. White 1993, 3.

94. The Alexandrian pattern is still too often neglected in discussions of Roman poetic patronage and the poetry of praise, but cf. Griffin 1984; Barchiesi 1996.

to come to stay at his court; the most common verb for such invitations is μεταπέμπεσθαι, "to send for."[95] Biographical sources record such invitations for a host of leading Greeks under the first Ptolemies. Most famously, perhaps, two letters of Alciphron (4.18–19 Benner-Fobes) dramatize the invitation of Ptolemy Soter to the Athenian comic poet Menander, an invitation that the dramatist, along with certain philosophers, refused.[96] Sometimes the role of an intermediary, who may recommend an individual to the patron, is stressed; this pattern is probably most familiar from Horace's later account of his introduction to Maecenas in *Satires* 1.6:

> nulla etenim mihi te fors obtulit: optimus olim
> Vergilius, post hunc Varius, dixere quid essem.
> ut ueni coram, singultim pauca locutus
> (infans namque pudor prohibebat plura profari)
> non ego me claro natum patre, non ego circum
> me Satureiano uectari rura caballo,
> sed quod eram narro. respondes, ut tuus est mos,
> pauca: abeo, et reuocas nono post mense iubesque
> esse in amicorum numero. (*Sat.* 1.6.54–62)

It was no chance that put you in my way: at one time Virgil, best of men, and then Varius, told you about me. When I came into your presence, I stammered a few words through my gulps, because shyness gripped my tongue and prevented me from saying any more: I told you not that I am the son of a distinguished father, not that I ride around my country estate on a Tarentine pony, but I told you what I am. In reply

---

95. This is the standard verb throughout Plato's *Seventh Letter* of his relations with Dionysius of Syracuse.

96. Cf. Weber 1993, 74 n. 5.

you said little, as is your custom; I went away, and nine
months later you called me back and bid (*iubesque*) me be
counted among your friends.

Similar patterns perhaps lie behind the account in the *Suda* Life
of Callimachus ("before being introduced [συσταθῆναι] to the
king . . . , he taught at Eleusis"),[97] and the *Lives* of Aratus[98] sug-
gest an intermediary role between the poet and Antigonos Go-
natas for the Stoic philosopher Persaios.

Many aspects of poetic patronage may in fact be illustrated
equally from Greek and Roman sources; thus, for example, the
Greek συμβιοῦν, "to live with" (Strabo 14.1.16: Anacreon and Poly-
crates; Alciphron 4.18.13: Menander and Ptolemy), or συνοικεῖν,
"to dwell with" (*Suda* α3745: Aratus and Antigonos Gonatas), or
συνεῖναι, "to be with" (e.g., *Vit. Arat.* 4 Martin), correspond to the
Latin *conuiuere* (cf. Cic. *Arch.* 6; Hor. *Sat.* 1.6.47).[99] On the other
hand, the differences between the two cultures are not to be min-
imized. One such difference seems to lie in the language of re-
quest. Whereas Roman poetry and the ancient biographies of Ro-
man poets are replete with allusions to the processes by which a
patron may "ask for" a particular kind of poetry, and display a rich
vocabulary of request,[100] there is apparently little to set against
this from Greek sources. This may be partly a result of the
wretched survival of third-century Greek poetry, but we should

97. Cf. below, p. 45; LSJ s.v. συνίστημι IV. For an attempt to reconstruct Cal-
limachus's "real" biography cf. Cameron 1995, 1–7.

98. Cf. below, pp. 41–42.

99. Cf. T. P. Wiseman in Gold 1982, 32–33.

100. Cf. White 1993, 64–91.

also recognize a distinctively Roman mode of discourse with deep roots in the customs of the Roman elite. Even here, however, the extant *Lives* of Aratus offer a partial parallel, and it will be worth dwelling on them briefly.[101]

In these *Lives* the initiative for the writing of the *Phainomena* came from King Antigonos, as that for Aratus's "edition" of the *Iliad* from King Antiochus (*Vita* I, p. 8 Martin). According to *Vita* 1, on the authority of letters ascribed to Aratus, but all but certainly the typical product of a later age of such fictional writing, once Antigonos had formed a high opinion of Aratus, he gave the poet a copy of a prose work of Eudoxus and urged (προτρέπειν, ἀξιοῦν) him to versify it, adding the famous quip "You will add to Eudoxus's *doxa*" (εὐδοξότερον ποιεῖς τὸν Εὔδοξον); in *Vita* 3 the verbs are *iubere* and κελεύειν. These *Lives* are, of course, epitomes of attempts to make sense of various traditions, as well as of whatever indications Aratus's poetry itself provided, and their common basis is not to be read as the best approximation to "what really happened." Rather, their accounts of the patron-poet relationship give us, admittedly later, versions of how such a relationship could be represented, with varying degrees of irony, and the multilayered texture of their transmitted form is itself instructive for how contextualized such anecdotes are. Thus when the author of *Vita* 1 reports a rival chronology to his own, one that in his view reveals deep ignorance, Antigonos's "charge" to Aratus and Nicander becomes precisely that, an instruction (ἐπιτάττειν); the shift of vocabulary, which would well suit "a joke made up to explain why

---

101. On these *Lives* cf. esp. Martin 1956 and Cameron 1995, 194–214, though Cameron's concerns are rather different from mine. The *Lives* are translated into French by Martin on pp. xii–xxi of his Budé edition (Paris 1998).

both poets wrote on subjects they knew nothing about,"[102] both obscures the more nuanced language of the main narrative of the *Vita* and shows us precisely what is at stake in the linguistic choices that different narratives make. The narrative allegedly derived from the "letters of Aratus" in fact offers a suggestive parallel to the substantial Roman material: however the poet in fact came to write the *Phainomena*, the patron, in an act of graceful homage, is given some role in its conception. What, if anything, in the poetry of Aratus lies behind these *Lives* we can only guess; that Virgil's famous *tua, Maecenas, haud mollia iussa* (*Georg.* 3.41) picks up a reference to Antigonos in Aratus (cf. *SH* 85) is an attractive, if unprovable, suggestion.[103] More important, however, for our present purposes is the fundamental fact that such narratives have no essential and unchanging meaning; like smaller-scale anecdotes, it is how and for what purpose they are told that matters. Thus Antigonos's "request" to Aratus could, for example, be treated as an intellectual challenge complimenting Aratus's skill (as apparently the author of *Vita* 1 takes it) or as a malicious jest at the helpless dependency of the poet, and it is in this openness to interpretation where the true value of such narratives lie, for the patronage relationship itself was, as abundant testimony demonstrates and

102. Cameron 1995, 195. I do not, of course, intend to suggest that there is always a clear distinction between the various verbs I have cited; Fraser (1972, 1: 312) cites the case of Apollonius of Citium's statement in the proem to his commentary on the Hippocratic *Dislocations* that he undertook the work on the instructions (τὰ προσταχθέντα) of Ptolemy Auletes. A parody of this kind of discourse may be represented by the work on dining by Chaerephon, addressed to his fellow parasite Kurebion ("Pod"), which began ἐπειδή μοι πολλάκις ἐπέστειλας, "since you have often bidden me" (Ath. 6.244a).

103. Cf. Kidd 1997, 5.

Horace most memorably dramatizes through the misunderstandings of "the pest" in *Satires* 1.9, fundamentally always negotiable and interpretable, both by those on the inside and those observing from without. In *Idyll* 7 Lycidas teases Simichidas as a parasite on his way to a free meal, a forerunner (quite literally) of Petronius's Eumolpus (vv. 24–25); it was an easy "mistake" to make.

If *EP* is a particular kind of poem for a real or prospective patron, *Idylls* 15 and 16 dramatize the search for poetic support and the fragile relations between poet and patron.[104] In both poems (as probably also in *Idyll* 7)[105] the journey to the patron's house is a central conceit, but the use made of it is very different.[106] In *Idyll* 16, the idea of the begging/wandering poet is rewritten as the "trick-or-treating" round of a band of children, but a band of children who will accept only the hospitality of a house that really welcomes them and invites them in. The patron must be morally worthy of the poetry, and in *EP* Ptolemy is indeed the very embodiment of such a patron. Hospitality had been also of course very important for Pindar:

> ἔσταν δ' ἐπ' αὐλείαις θύραις
> ἀνδρὸς φιλοξείνου καλὰ μελπόμενος,
> ἔνθα μοι ἁρμόδιον
> δεῖπνον κεκόσμηται, θαμὰ δ' ἀλλοδαπῶν
> οὐκ ἀπείρατοι δόμοι
> ἐντί. (*Nem.* 1.19–23)[107]

104. This remains true, whether we wish to see these poems as actually written under royal "patronage," or just looking for it.

105. Cf. above, p. 30.

106. I have discussed both of these poems at length elsewhere (cf. Hunter 1996, 77–138), and here restrict myself to a brief account.

107. Cf., for example, *Nem.* 9.1–2.

And I have taken my stand at the courtyard gates of a generous host as I sing of noble deeds, where a fitting feast has been arranged for me, for this home is not unfamiliar with frequent visitors from abroad. (trans. Race)

The relation between the poet and his patron's οἶκος or *domus* is in fact one of the most persistent motifs of ancient "patronage" poetry: physical presence in (or outside) the house may refer both to the real practices of social life and to the more intangible structures governing a relationship. Thus Martial is forced to tell a patron:

> sed non solus amat qui nocte dieque frequentat
>   limina nec uatem talia damna decent. (10.58.11–12)

> The person who hangs around your door day and night
> is not your only friend, nor does such a waste befit the poet.

Pliny (*Epist.* 3.21) proudly quotes to a correspondent Martial's verses (10.19.12–21) in his honor (verses for which the poet had been well rewarded): "[Martial] addresses the Muse and tells her to seek out my house on the Esquiline, but to approach respectfully:

> sed ne tempore non tuo disertam
> pulses ebria ianuam, uideto.

> Make sure that, drunk as you are, you do not knock upon
> that eloquent door at an inappropriate time.

Another version of this anxiety is staged in Horace's poem to Vinnius Asina (*Epist.* 1.13), who is supposedly carrying books of poems to Augustus and who is harried on his way by the poet's instructions and fears. It is this fragile network of links that tie the patron (and his house) to the poet that is explored in *Idyll* 16. What is most important, however, is that it is a network constructed, if not merely fantasized, by the poet: however much poets and poetry could contribute to the status and (self-) image of the patron, the relationship between the two is anything but dynamically equal. What gives *Idyll* 16 its special flavor is the remarkable historical perspective of its ironic acknowledgment that the language of patronage has been preserved, but its meaning irretrievably altered in the march of time and circumstance: the attempt to recreate the archaic relationship of Pindar and Hieron I must always remain an imaginative, literary *mimesis*.

Idyll 15, however, is loudly contemporary. The coming of the Syracusan Theocritus and the traditions of Syracusan mime to Alexandria are figured as the difficult and comical approach of Gorgo and Praxinoa to the royal palace.[108] Royal sponsorship of the arts is again located at a center that acts as a magnet for both artists and audiences. We may wonder indeed whether behind the story in the *Suda* Life that, before finding royal patronage,[109] Callimachus worked as a schoolmaster in Eleusis, a marginal suburb of Alexandria, there lies a similar construction of patronage to that of the dramatized movement of the women from Syracuse to the margins of Alexandria and then (briefly) to the center. The end of Callimachus's "story" is his adoption into the intellectual life of the court, whereas Gorgo and Praxinoa return from the splendors of the Ptolemaic palace to the routine of their daily lives. Which ending more nearly approximates Theocritus's fate, we do not know.

108. Cf. Hunter 1996, 118.
109. Cf. above, p. 40.

AN EGYPTIAN DIMENSION?

The nature of Ptolemaic society, socio-legal interaction, questions of ethnicity, and cultural exchange are currently the focus of sustained scholarly activity; these broad historical issues are not the concern of this book. In seeking, however, to set *EP* within its historical context, the question of to what extent, if any, Egyptian and pharaonic themes resonate in the poem, and in Ptolemaic ideology more generally, is obviously of the greatest importance. Given that we do not know the circumstances of the poem's composition and original performance, it would be rash merely to assume a positive or negative answer to this question; a more fruitful procedure would seem to be to set out possible ways in which the pharaonic ideology that the Ptolemies inherited might have been important for Ptolemaic poetry, and to seek to build a cumulative case (for or against). This is what the present commentary sets out to do. Nevertheless, as this subject has dominated much recent discussion of Alexandrian poetry, a brief general consideration may be helpful.

The impulse for work in this area comes from two directions, from readings of the poems themselves,[110] and from broader historical considerations. The cultural complexity of Ptolemaic kingship and society is now generally recognized, and the recent recovery from the harbor at Alexandria of the art and monuments of the Ptolemaic palace has given the whole question a new urgency.[111] It is now clear that the Egyptian interior, most notably

110. Among the most important "'Egyptianizing'" contributions are Merkelbach 1981; Gelzer 1982; Koenen 1977, 1983, 1993; Bing 1988; Selden 1998; and Stephens 2003.

111. Cf. Empereur 1998.

the sacred site of Heliopolis, was ransacked for monuments with which to adorn the new capital as symbols of Ptolemaic control over the ancient land; both city and palace "must in parts have had an Egyptian feel, with sphinxes lining the streets and with obelisks towering in front of the temples and in public open spaces."[112] Monumental images of a Ptolemy as pharaoh and a Ptolemaic queen as Isis[113] now reveal this expression of cultural power in its full force. There are, however, at least two major problems with using this suggestive situation in the interpretation of the Alexandrian poetry of the first half of the third century. The collection (and composition) of imposing artworks is one thing; any serious grasp of pharaonic ideology by Greeks might be thought to be quite another, even without any consideration of how this would severely limit the comprehending audience of a Greek poem. Second, there is chronology. Most of the material recovered from the Alexandrian harbor was probably brought to the city or manufactured after Philadelphus, but in any case it might be very dangerous to see later developments foreshadowed as early as the 270s. It is indeed very clear that there were important changes over time in the way that the Ptolemies presented themselves before their two populations. In the course of a helpfully skeptical account (written before the discoveries at Alexandria),[114] Graham Zanker argues that the search for "Egyptian influence" in Alexandrian poetry has not only been cavalier in its treatment of this change over time but is also based on a view of Alexandrian society that is fundamentally flawed. At least under

112. Empereur 1998, 75.
113. Ibid., 76–77.
114. Zanker 1989, 91–99.

Soter and Philadelphus, he argues, the Alexandrian elite was fiercely chauvinistic in its Greekness, so that reference to Egyptian ideas and practices is inherently unlikely; under these Ptolemies, there is no reason to suppose that poetry was any different from art and cult, in which the two traditions remained strictly separated.[115] Moreover, there is no good evidence that the leading scholar-poets were much interested in Egyptian antiquities, whereas, for example, it is clear that the *Aitia* reflect many of the same interests that we can trace in Callimachus's prose researches. This view of Alexandrian society as purely "Greek" has come under increasing challenge in recent years, but there are also more general considerations of poetic interpretation in play here.

To accept the possibility that Alexandrian "court poetry" might allude to or allow Egyptian ideas or iconography to resonate is of course, pace Zanker, neither the same thing as believing that "the regents . . . encouraged their court-poets to subject to a wholescale *interpretatio Graeca* the Egyptian mythology and ideology introduced into the Ptolemaic ruler-cult,"[116] nor is it to assume that "the audience of the Ptolemies' Egyptian cult-practices and images was the same as that of their Greek cult and court-poetry."[117] As for *EP*, it is, as the commentary throughout will demonstrate, the Greek poetic tradition that is the fundamental basis for Alexandrian encomiastic poetry. Nevertheless, it is hardly perverse to bear in mind the possibility that poets like Callimachus, Theocritus, and Apollonius were familiar with

115. For the separateness of the two artistic traditions—itself (unsurprisingly) a very disputed matter—cf. also Bianchi 1988.

116. Zanker 1989, 91.

117. Ibid., 95.

some central motifs of, say, Egyptian royal cult and of the Egyptian vocabulary for and iconography of the "Ptolemy-pharaohs" and, moreover, selected and shaped the Greek material of their poems in such a way as to allow Egyptian patterns, as well as Greek, to resonate; there were certainly enough Greek-speaking Egyptian men of learning available to offer instruction, should someone seek them out. With such a scenario, we would then not be faced with a simple choice between "Greek" and "Egyptian" readings.

An excellent and very skeptical recent survey by Gregor Weber[118] reveals in fact how few are the cases where the determinative presence of Egyptian ideas in Greek poetry—that is, where knowledge of such ideas is necessary for understanding—has so far won any kind of general acceptance; a passage in Callimachus's *Hymn to Delos* remains the most discussed instance,[119] but in general most scholars still hold that the Greek poetry of this period looked solely to Greek ideas and earlier Greek poetry. It must always be acknowledged that the fact that many Greek and Egyptian ideas are similar enough to make the presence of Egyptian resonances difficult to establish clouds our appreciation, but even with every allowance, the absence of overt Egyptian material remains palpable. Nevertheless, the question of material that accommodates both Greek and Egyptian interpretations remains open. What is at stake may perhaps be seen most clearly in a specific example.

118. Weber 1993, 371–88.

119. Cf. below, p. 168. After the discussions of Koenen (1993) and Selden (1998) one should perhaps add the "Lock of Berenice" to this; see also the interpretation of *Idyll* 15 in Reed 2000.

Callimachus's poem on the death of Philadelphus's sister-wife, the *Ektheosis of Arsinoe* (fr. 228), is in many ways a very typical product of his art: the conception and meter (an archaic lyric length, the "archebulean,"[120] used stichically) are strikingly novel, but much of the power of the poem depends upon the reworking of famous archaic models. Callimachus uses Andromache's learning of the death of Hector in *Iliad* 22 and the narrative structure of the *Homeric Hymn to Demeter* to tell how Arsinoe's already deceased and deified sister, Philotera, learned of the queen's death. As she traverses Lemnos, Philotera is disturbed by signs of a funeral pyre in far-off Africa:

> ἄρτι γάρ οἱ Σικελὰ μὲν Ἔννα
> κατελείπετο, Λαμνιακοὶ δ' ἐπατεῦ[ν]το
> Δηοῦς ἄπο νεισομέναι· σέο δ' ἦν ἄπ[υ]στος
> ὦ δαίμοσιν ἁρπαγίμα (Callim. fr. 228.43–46)

She had recently left Sicilian Enna behind, and was walking on the Lemnian . . . after her return from Demeter. Of you she was unaware, Lady Snatched by the Gods . . .

Philotera here plays the role of Demeter, whom she has just been visiting in Sicily, with Arsinoe as Persephone, the maiden snatched away by a god;[121] so too Charis, Hephaestus's wife, whom Philo-

---

120. This may be thought of as an anapaestic pentameter.

121. Cf. Fraser 1972, 1: 669; Griffiths 1979, 59–60. Arsinoe was celebrated at Alexandria as "Eleusinia" and "Karpophoros." There was a Thesmophorion in the city (Fraser 1972, 1: 199), and although the evidence for the celebration of the traditional rites in the city is very slender (cf. Hopkinson 1984, 32–43), it would seem excessively skeptical to doubt their existence; cf. in general Thompson 1998. For echoes of *Iliad* 22 in this poem (Philotera as Andromache, etc.) cf. Di Benedetto 1994; D'Alessio 1997 ad loc.

tera dispatches to discover what is wrong, fulfills the roles of Hecate and Helios in informing Philotera of the death of her sister. It is tempting to speculate that the evocation of the *Homeric Hymn* was not limited to this passage, but that the poem as a whole moved, like the archaic hymn, from mourning to the celebration of a new god; the surviving summary of the poem, the *Diegesis*, informs us that the *Ektheosis* included the establishment of an altar and precinct of Arsinoe at Alexandria, just as the people of Eleusis (the name also of a suburb to the east of Alexandria) build a temple and altar of Demeter in the *Homeric Hymn* (vv. 270–72, 296–98). Here then is a thoroughly sophisticated and thoroughly Greek poem. Before Philotera learns of her sister's death, the poet seems to address the dead queen:

> νύμφα, σὺ μὲν ἀστερίαν ὑπ' ἄμαξαν ἤδη
> κλεπτομέν]α παρέθει σελάναι (Callim. fr. 228.5–6 Pf.)

Bride,[122] already you beneath the starry wagon . . . <your soul> which had been snatched away was racing beside the moon . . .

Despite the serious problems of text and interpretation,[123] we can see here an imaginative reuse of traditional Greek ideas of the ψυχή joining the stars in the upper air after death[124] and of

122. On this form of address cf. Gelzer 1982, 24.

123. The best discussion remains Pfeiffer 1922, 4–12, and I follow Pfeiffer in my translation; cf. further D'Alessio ad loc., citing the quite different interpretation of Grzybek (1990, 110–12). Wilamowitz's παρέθει <ς> may well be right, but Pfeiffer notes the possibility of a parenthesis.

124. Cf. Ar. *Peace* 832–41; Eur. *Supp.* 532, *Hel.* 1013–16; Alexis fr. 163 K-A; Rohde 1898, 2: 384 n. 2, 387 n. 1; Lattimore 1962, 31–34.

heroes "snatched away" to join the immortals (cf. the stories of Ganymede, Pelops, etc.); just so in *EP* does Theocritus represent Aphrodite "snatching away" (ἁρπάξασα) Arsinoe's mother, Berenice (v. 48). Ascent to the stars and the sun is, however, also "the central dogma of Egyptian belief about the pharaonic afterlife";[125] certainly, as far as Egyptian documents attest, Arsinoe "departed to the sky" in the classic manner.[126] It is certainly not necessary to believe that Callimachus's text alludes to Egyptian ideas (however imperfectly understood) as well as Greek ones, but to deny the possibility closes off one potential avenue for appreciating both Callimachus as a poet and the particular nature of Ptolemaic kingship. Did he (and his audience) have no inkling at all of what the Egyptian tradition was saying about the late queen? Not dissimilar perhaps is the case of Theocritus's description of the apotheosis of Berenice at 15.106–8, where we may sense an evocation of pharaonic burial practice behind the rewriting of Homer.[127] Neither instance relies upon the niceties of pharaonic ideology or sacred narratives,[128] nor does the possi-

125. *LdÄ* s.v. *Himmelsaufsteig*; cf. also s.v. *Jenseitsvorstellungen*; and Kees 1956, 67–97.

126. On the "Mendes stele" Arsinoe "ascended to the heaven"; cf. Bevan 1927, 65; Roeder 1959, 181; Sauneron 1960.

127. Cf. Hunter 1996, 132–34.

128. As such, they are importantly different from the poems treated by Selden (1998) and Stephens (2003). It is also worth stressing here that Egyptian religious ideas and kingship ideology changed over time; I am aware that the citation of Egyptian material in the commentary may suggest a far more "monolithic" ideology over centuries than was really the case, but for the purposes of this book this procedure can perhaps be justified. Within this shifting ideology there is also an accretive tendency through which newer ideas are added to, rather than displace, older ones; older texts, therefore, remain suggestive for the Ptolemaic context.

bility of an Egyptian "audience" arise in either case; the Egyptian color is painted with the very broadest brush and in ways that it is hardly unreasonable to think could have been appreciated by many cultured Greeks.

The choice of certain encomiastic themes, and the omission of others, in *EP* may indeed be determined by the poet's desire to reflect the particular position of Philadelphus as both Greek king and Egyptian pharaoh,[129] though it should be repeated that this is a thoroughly Greek poem;[130] some, however, of what has seemed to modern critics awkward, even embarrassing, in this poem can perhaps be better understood against the background of the coexistence of two traditions of praise and power, which are straddled by, if not united in, the figure of Ptolemy.

THE LANGUAGE OF THE ENCOMIUM

The language of later Greek hexameter poetry is based upon the inherited poetic language of Homer and early epic; within this heritage poets innovated and added, by means of analogy (i.e., the creation of forms that "could have appeared" in Homer), by the inclusion of material from other "high" poetic registers, such as lyric and tragedy, and under the influence of regionally specific morphological and lexical items and the requirements of partic-

129. This is, of course, quite independent of the contested question of whether or not Philadelphus went through a pharaonic coronation ceremony; cf. (for) Koenen 1977, 58–63; (against) Burstein 1991.

130. Throughout the commentary I have deemed it better, where appropriate, to adduce Egyptian "parallels," even if their significance for the interpretation of *EP* is doubtful, as others may judge differently from me, and this is, above all, a matter of critical judgment.

ular genres. Theocritus[131] is no exception to this rule. His position is, however, made more complex by the fact that most of his poems show a Doric linguistic texture, of greater or less thickness, in contrast to the Ionic language of the epic tradition. It is extremely important to establish as accurately as possible the dialectal character of each poem, as nearness to and divergence from the inherited language of epic carries significant generic force. Doric forms do not merely offer linguistic variation but have ramifications for poetic self-consciousness and, ultimately, for the meaning of a poem. Whether in v. 1 the Muses were addressed in the traditional epic-Ionic language as Μοῦσαι *(Pap. Ant.)* or as Μοῖσαι *(codd.)*, in the Doricizing language of lyric,[132] will have been an important marker for how the poem was to be sited with respect to literary tradition.

Although it is clear that, broadly speaking, Theocritus's "bucolics" are much more thoroughly Doricized than the "epic" poems (i.e., *Idylls* 13, 16, 17 *[EP]*, 22, and 24), the detailed situation is confused and uncertain. In the majority of cases, most notably in the principal Doric diagnostic feature, namely, retention of long alpha where epic-Ionic has eta, alternative dialectal forms are metrically equivalent and thus equally possible as readings (at least as far as meter is concerned). Together with later assumptions about Theocritus as *the* "Doric" poet par excellence, this may in fact be one of the reasons for the great dialectal confusion, the result of both accidental corruption and deliberate alteration, throughout

131. Cf. Hunter 1996, 28–45, a discussion that will be assumed here.

132. Μοῖσα is (probably) an Aeolic form that is also used in high "Doric" lyric (Pindar, etc.); the common Doric form was in fact Μῶσα. For discussion and bibliography cf. Dover 1971, xl–xli; Hunter on 1.9.

the surviving manuscripts; papyri show that this confusion was already widespread in antiquity. Thus, for example, our earliest witness to the text of *EP, POxy.* 3551, of the third century c.e., has ἔκαλοι in v. 97 with ἔκηλοι as a superscript correction; in v. 62 the Antinoopolis papyrus (fifth–sixth century c.e.) offers ἃ δέ against the unanimous ἦ δέ of the MSS, but in vv. 50 and 68 it has the Ionic forms against the Doric of the MSS, and so on. Moreover, metrical criteria can never do more than establish a partial picture, as there is no reason, except the despair of a modern editor faced with having to decide what text to print, to believe that the only "inconsistencies" of dialect that Theocritus allowed in any given poem were those forced upon him by meter.[133] The text printed here must be read in this light.

EP shows in fact very few of the standard Doric features of the bucolics,[134] and the most striking of such features (e.g., present infinitives in -εν, short vowel accusative plurals in -ος and -ας, Doric κα) do not occur. The following transmitted "Doricisms" may, however, be noted:

1. τῆνος, vv. 16, 46, 118. *(ἐ)κεῖνος* is in fact extremely rare throughout the corpus (cf. Gow on 7.104).

2. Feminine participles in -οισα are unanimously transmitted in vv. 36 and 130; -ουσα is unanimously transmitted in vv. 42 and 45, and the transmission is divided, though not to a consistent pattern, in vv. 62, 64, and 132.[135] Nowhere, of course, is either form metrically guaranteed.

---

133. Good remarks in Darms 1981, 170–71.

134. For a summary of these features cf. Dover 1971, xxvii–xlv; Hunter 1999, 22–26.

135. For a bibliography on this problem cf. Hunter 1999, 26; to which add Verdier 1972, 37–52.

3. ποτεοικότα, v. 44. Such forms are already familiar in the language of epic and high lyric.[136]

4. Third-person present indicatives in -οντι are unanimously transmitted at vv. 73, 91, 108, and 115 but are nowhere guaranteed, as they may always be replaced by -ουσι; -ουσι(ν) is, however, protected by ephelkystic nu at vv. 78 and 97 (where, however, περιστέλλονται may be correct) and universally transmitted at v. 33.

5. καλεῦνται, v. 25; ἀριθμεῦνται, v. 27; and αἰτεῦ, v. 137 (cf., for example, 10.20: μυθεῦ) show "Doric" contractions familiar from the bucolic poems, though Theocritus would also have found such forms in his texts of Homer (cf. *Od.* 10.229, καλεῦντες, etc.), where they seem to be due to fourth-century developments in Ionic.[137] (Cf. further below on uncontracted forms.)

6. ὅκα is universally transmitted in v. 14, as is ὅτε in vv. 59 and 80.

Against this very meager haul may be set features[138] that point to the inherited epic-Ionic language of high hexameter poetry. Most of these features also occur sporadically in the bucolics, but it is the distribution and quantity that are significant here. Moreover, epic forms, which also occur regularly as part of the mixed poetic language of the bucolics, may be "(re)marked" as distinctively epic by the principal component of the linguistic context in which they occur.

---

136. Cf. Hunter 1996, 42.

137. Cf. Chantraine 1973, 1: 58–62; West 1998–2000, 1: xxii–xxiii.

138. The following survey makes no claims to exhaustiveness.

Verb Forms

1. ἀρχώμεσθα, v. 1. The epic and poetic -μεσθα occurs also at 4.39, in a passage of mock high-style;[139] at 7.36 in βουκολιασδώμεσθα, where the epic ending sits in pointed contrast to the "popular" implications of the verb; at 13.4 and 14.68 (both with the high-style verb πέλεσθαι). -μεθα occurs throughout the corpus (1.21, 10.33, 12.11, 14.51, 15.51, 18.56, 22.166, etc.).

2. ἔην, v. 13. This epic form occurs elsewhere only at 24.133 and 25.218.

3. Unaugmented past tenses occur at vv. 54, 58, 59, 64, 65, 119, and 132.

4. ἔειπεν, v. 71. Such epic forms occur elsewhere only at 22.153; 25.77, 179; and 26.18 and 19.

5. στόρνυσιν, v. 133. This, rather than στόρνυτι, is protected by ephelkystic nu; such a form occurs nowhere else in the corpus.

Noun/Adjective Case Endings

1. Dative plurals in -οισι and -αισι occur throughout the poem and are not rare in the bucolics; they are also familiar in high Doric lyric (Pindar, etc.). Nevertheless, Theocritus seems to avoid them in much the same poems in which he also does not use certain strongly marked epic forms, such as genitive -οιο, and this perhaps suggests something of the flavor that could be attached to them.[140]

---

139. Cf. Hunter on 4.38–39.

140. Cf. Darms 1981, 168; for the evidence cf. Di Benedetto 1956, 52–55. Particularly striking is the case of *Idyll* 7, in which both these dative plurals and genitives in ⁻οιο are numerous.

The relative οἷσι in v. 12 is, however, paralleled only at 25.33. The form in -ῃσι, which can never be guaranteed against -αισι, is universally transmitted in vv. 22 and 65; in v. 101 it is in the MSS, whereas *Pap.Ant.* has -αισιν. Elsewhere it occurs occasionally in the transmission even of the "Doric" bucolics, where its status is extremely doubtful, although it is transmitted unanimously in the very probably non-Theocritean and highly epicizing *Idyll* 25 (vv. 163, 242, 262, and 268) and is also accepted by modern texts at 12.18 and 22.18, 96, and (by emendation) 80.[141] In 17.35 Gow prints the shorter form in -ῃς, which also occurs in part of the tradition at 12.18; Gallavotti prefers -ῃσ' at 17.35.

2. Dative plurals in -εσσι (vv. 16, 61, 65, 69, 83, 88, 90, 102, 109, 111, and 125) occur throughout the corpus and are not necessarily an "epic" form, as they are attested from Doric areas of both the mainland and the west;[142] nevertheless, their frequency in *EP*, alongside so many other epic features, might be thought to enhance the epic resonance of the language.

3. Genitive singular in -οιο occurs in vv. 20, 21, 29 (twice), 109, and 119.

Pronouns

1. σφέων, v. 24; σφιν, v. 26; σφισιν, v. 84, and σφέτερος, 41–42n., all occur in *EP*; of these only σφισι occurs in the genuine "bucolics" (7.33), but all occur in other "epicizing" poems.[143]

2. σύ etc., rather than Doric τύ etc., occurs in vv. 53, 56, and

---

141. Cf. Darms 1981, 177–83; Molinos Tejada 1990, 212–19.

142. Cf. Hunter 1996, 33–34.

143. Cf. Hunter 1996, 41–42.

58. σέθεν (vv. 46, 135) occurs once in the genuine bucolics (4.38, where see my note and Hunter 1996, 42), but otherwise only at 25.162; 29.32, 37 (Aeolic); and in the spurious *Idyll* 27 (vv. 43, 45).

3. The third-person pronominal adjective ἑός (vv. 25, 39) occurs elsewhere only at 12.33, 22.147, 24.59, and in the spurious poems. Theocritus also uses it as a second-person adjective in v. 50.[144]

4. The Ionic-epic μιν is universally transmitted in v. 93.

Miscellaneous

There is a clear distinction between bucolic and epicizing poems in the freedom with which the definite article is omitted; broadly speaking, omission is a mark of "high" poetic style. *EP* is very clearly with the "epic" poems, in omitting the article far more freely than do the bucolics (cf. Leutner 1907, 19).

The following forms occur in *EP* but never in the genuine "bucolics":

1. ἐνί, vv. 3, 106. Cf. 2.26; 14.49; 18.33; 22.94, 190; 25.163.

2. ἐπήν, v. 2, which Theocritus very likely found in his texts of Homer (cf. K-B I 223), is also found at 16.12, 28; 25.28; 27.40; and *Epigr.* 17.2. For the distribution of ἄν, which is not found in the genuine bucolics, see Molinos Tejada 1990, 360–66; Hunter 1996, 42.

3. πτόλις, v. 111. Cf. 2.35 (ἀνὰ πτόλιν, a Homeric phrase, *Il.* 8.55) and 22.157 (πτολίεθρα); note also the Homeric φιλοπτολέμοισι (v. 89).

---

144. Cf. Rengakos 1993, 117. Disputed cases are 22.173 and 24.36.

4. The epic participle γεγαῶτες (v. 25) is paralleled only at 22.176.

5. The form Κόως (v. 58, where see 64n.) shows epic diectasis and is found already in Homer.

6. ἠδέ, v. 124.[145]

7. The Ionic μοῦνος (v. 121) is universally transmitted, as it is at 18.18, where, however, modern editors adopt Wilamowitz's μῶνος. At 2.64 the transmission is divided between the Ionic and Doric forms.[146]

The clear picture that emerges from this analysis of a markedly epicizing poem is reinforced by the sheer number of close Homeric echoes and of words and phrases borrowed almost verbatim from early epic.[147] These are signaled throughout the commentary, and here a brief sample must suffice: ἐπιστάμενος καλὰ εἰπεῖν (v. 7), μελέων ἐξείλετο (v. 24), δαίτηθεν ἴοι (v. 28), βαθύκολπος (v. 55), αἰχμητής (vv. 56–57), χείρεσσι φίλῃσι (v. 65), ἔθνεα μυρία (v. 77), ποταμοὶ κελάδοντες (v. 92), and πατρώϊα πάντα (v. 104). This very strong Homeric linguistic flavor goes together with the presentation of Philadelphus as a latter-day Agamemnon or Achilles, and thus as the true heir of Alexander; the Macedonian monarchy saw itself as a continuation of the Homeric situation, and this is here reflected in linguistic form. This epic language is also, of course, traditionally appropriate to a hexameter hymn, as *EP* proclaims itself to be (cf. 8n. and above, p. 8). Such generic considerations must not, however, determine editorial linguistic choice in the face

---

145. Cf. Hunter 1996, 41.

146. μώνα also occurs at 20.45.

147. Cf. briefly Legrand 1898, 359; Meincke 1965, 160–61.

of other evidence, as there is no reason *a priori* to expect conservatism rather than innovation in the matching of genre and poetic dialect from a third-century poet.[148] Instincts about what kind of poem this is can never (and rightly so) be eliminated from editorial decisions among alternative forms, but these instincts must also bear in mind the new directions traveled by third-century poetry.

It may also be worth asking why, if the linguistic form of *EP* seems so predominantly epic-Ionic, there is also Doric color. More than one answer suggests itself. Theocritus's own native Syracusan was a Doric dialect, and such forms, which are not of course specifically Syracusan, may act as markers of his own tradition, a kind of linguistic *sphragis* asserting authorship. If so, however, we must distinguish clearly between the dialect of this poem and the language of local poets such as Isyllos of Epidauros (late fourth century) with whose hexameters Wilamowitz compared the language of *Idylls* 13, 16, and 17.[149] Isyllos's hexameters (*CA* 132–35) in fact show a mixture of (probably both local and "common") Doric[150] and epic/*koine* forms, some of them of course direct reminiscences of Homer, which is quite unlike the much more uniform *EP*.[151] It may be that, for his contemporaries, these poems of Theocritus had something of the flavor of stylized versions of the kind of unsophisticated Doricization of the traditional epic language that Isyllos represents, but the linguistic difference be-

---

148. Cf. Hunter 1996, 38–39, citing the discussions of Latte and Halperin.

149. Wilamowitz 1886, 25–28.

150. For the Doric "koines" of the Hellenistic period cf. Bubeník 1989, 193–213; Horrocks 1997, 40–41.

151. Note ποί (v. 20), πολιάταις (v. 21), ῥέπεν (v. 24; if this is the correct reading), the recurrent mixture of σύ and τύ and σός and τεός forms, etc.

tween the two is clear and was for Theocritus probably of the greatest importance. Less likely, perhaps, is the hypothesis that Theocritus is deliberately perpetuating a known feature of archaic epic, namely, the presence of a scatter of "Doric" features within epic language itself;[152] neither the items chosen nor their distribution suggests such a scholastic motive. More attractive is the idea that the mild Doric flavor may be a kind of linguistic homage to the tradition of choral "encomia" (above, pp. 9–11) that has clearly played an important role in the formation of generic consciousness within this poem.

Finally, we should consider whether the Doric touches are aimed in part at the poem's honorand. Dorian traditions were extremely important to the Ptolemaic house, which traced its ancestry to Heracles and the Temenid dynasty of Argos.[153] Whatever the historical nature of the Macedonian language,[154] the language of the Ptolemaic court may have been a Doric *koine*,[155] though the evidence is scattered and difficult to interpret. A recently published epigram by Poseidippos in which Philadelphus himself is made to celebrate the Olympian victories of the Ptolemaic house in a poetic dialect of strongly Doric flavor (*P.Mil.Vogl.* VIII 309, col. XIII 35–39)[156] is at least suggestive in this context, and the prominence given to Doric Cos in the course of the poem (cf. 68–70n.) may be thought to strengthen the possibility that the Doric elements of the language of *EP* carry an unusually

152. Cf. Giangrande 1970.

153. Cf. 68–70n. below.

154. I hope to discuss this issue in greater detail elsewhere.

155. Cf. Clarysse 1998. For Ruijgh's view of the importance of Cyrenean cf. Hunter 1996, 37.

156. Bastianini and Gallazzi 2001, 99.

charged political color. Just, then, as hymnic form has been accommodated to the changed conditions of the Ptolemaic court, so has traditional hymnic language.

The one fragment of the *Berenice* (fr. 3 Gow),[157] however, suggests that poems in honor of the royal house were not linguistically uniform in this, any more than in any other, particular. The fragment concerns the sacrifice of a fish by a fisherman to a goddess, perhaps the deified Berenice:

κεἴ τις ἀνὴρ αἰτεῖται ἐπαγροσύνην τε καὶ ὄλβον
ἐξ ἁλὸς ὧι ζωή, τὰ δὲ δίκτυα κείνωι ἄροτρα,
σφάζων ἀκρόνυχος ταύτηι θεῶι ἱερὸν ἰχθύν
ὃν λεῦκον καλέουσιν, ὃ γάρ θ᾽ ἱερώτατος ἄλλων,
καί κε λίνα στήσαιτο καὶ ἐξερύσαιτο θαλάσσης
ἔμπλεα

And if a man whose livelihood is from the sea, whose nets are
his ploughs, sacrifice to this goddess at nightfall the holy fish
which men call Leukos, for it is holy beyond all other fish, and
pray for luck in his fishing and for wealth, then might he set
out his nets and draw them from the water filled. (trans. Gow)

Gow (on v. 1) notes: "There is no sign of Doric in [the fragment] and κείνωι . . . ought to mark it as epic or Ionic." To Gow's observation we may add καλέουσιν, which shows an ending guaranteed also in *EP* (above, p. 56), and ὃ γάρ θ᾽ ἱερώτατος ἄλλων, which, together with 25.93, provides the only example of this epic use of γάρ τε in the Theocritean corpus.[158]

---

157. Cf. above, p. 7.

158. For this use cf. Denniston 529; Ruijgh 1971, 720–22. In the *Berenice* fragment Gallavotti adopts Schweighäuser's ὃ γὰρ φιερώτατος κτλ.

THE METER OF THE ENCOMIUM

The meter and prosody of *EP*, no less than the language, are strongly Homeric in flavor, when seen within the developments of the third century; this too will mark the traditions within which Philadelphus is being placed.

Dactyls and Spondees

1. Of the verses in *EP*, 19.1% are wholly dactylic, and a further 48.5% contain only one spondee in the first five feet; the corresponding figures for Homer are 18.9% and 41.7%. Although the vastly differing numbers of verses involved make comparisons all but worthless, this apparent increase in the predominance of dactylic rhythm over the archaic situation is in line with other third-century elite poetry (with the important exception of Theocritus's bucolic and mimic poems):[159] the corresponding figures for the *Argonautica* are 21.9% and 45.5% and for Callimachus 22.3% and 50.8%.[160] *EP* is in fact very close to *Idyll* 22, another hymn, where the figures are 18.4% and 47.1%,[161] and *Idyll* 18 (18.7%, 50%), though less dactylic than *Idyll* 24 (25.3%, 45.6%), which is notably high on this count.[162]

159. Cf. Hunter 1999, 18–19. The corresponding figures for *Idylls* 1, 3–7, and 10–11, taken together, are 14.5% and 38.5%, and for *Idylls* 2 and 14–15, taken together, 16.2% and 41.8%. Two other poems that buck the dominant trend are *Idyll* 26 (13.1%, 34.2%) and *Idyll* 16 (10%, 36.7%).

160. Hollis (1990, 16) rightly notes that such overall statistics tend to conceal differences between poems.

161. Cf. Sens 1997, 43–44.

162. Cf. Legrand 1898, 340.

2. The three verse forms *ddddd, dsddd,* and *sdddd* account for well over half of *EP* (74 of 136 whole verses), as they do also for *Idylls* 22 and 24; in Homer, these forms, though more common than any others, account for less than half the verses. These facts accord with a general third-century tendency to reduce the number of verse forms that occur with any regularity; the figures for these three verse patterns in Callimachus (59%) and the *Argonautica* (53%) are not significantly out of line with the Theocritean hymns.[163]

3. Theocritus's "epicizing" poems differ from the bucolics and mimes most markedly in the treatment of the third and fourth feet.

a. *EP* has a notably low number of third-foot spondees, 4.4%, although *Idyll* 24 (5.7%) is not significantly different, and Callimachus's *Hymn to Delos* (4.3%) is even slightly lower; *Idyll* 22 (7.6%) is somewhat higher, as is the overall picture in Callimachus (8.7%), and *Idyll* 16 (10%) is notably so. The figure for *Idylls* 1–7, 9–11, and 15.1–83 taken together is 22.6%,[164] which itself is far higher than for Homer (c. 15%).

b. In *EP,* 27.9% of fourth feet are spondaic against 30% for Homer, 29.1% for *Idyll* 22, 23.1% for *Idyll* 24, and roughly 19% for both Apollonius and Callimachus; in *Idylls* 1–7 taken together, however, only some 15% of verses have a spondaic fourth foot (cf. further below).[165]

---

163. In addition to the sources already cited, I am indebted to a computer-assisted count conducted by Dr. D. Fusi of the University of Rome (La Sapienza). There are again differences between poems: thus Mineur (1984, 36) notes that, in Callim. *H.* 4, *dsdsd* (9.3%) is slightly more common than *sdddd* (8.7%).

164. I take this from O'Neil 1942, 159; cf. Sens 1997, 43.

165. Cf. Hunter 1999, 20.

4. In *EP* there are eight *spondeiazontes* (i.e., verses with a spondaic fifth foot), namely, vv. 23, 26–27, 60–61, 79, 82, and 101; in every such case the fourth foot is a dactyl, and in all but one case (v. 79) the verse ends in a word of four syllables. That four of these verses are grouped in two pairs is in line with a habit of the third-century mainstream, though this is not in fact a particular characteristic of Theocritus.[166] In at least a majority of the cases in *EP*, a particular effect is intended by the rhythmical oddity; thus v. 23 imitates a rhythmically remarkable *(dsdss)* verse of Homer (*Il.* 2.666), which ends Ἡρακληείης, the name that also creates the spondaic effect in the pointedly parallel vv. 26–27;[167] in vv. 60–61 the spondaic close may express the forced cries of Berenice's birth pangs.

The percentage of *spondeiazontes*, 5.8%, is not far out of line with Homer's 5%, though the figures for both Hesiod (6.4%) and the *Homeric Hymns* (7.4%) are rather higher;[168] *Idyll* 22 (4.9%) is again close to *EP*, whereas *Idyll* 24 (7.9%) again follows the higher figures for Callimachus (7.3%)[169] and the *Argonautica* (9%), in a further indication of the "polished" metrics of that Theocritean poem. The bucolics avoid the fifth-foot spondee (1.3%), in keeping with their marked preference for a dactylic fourth foot.

166. From Kunst (1887, 29–30) I note only 13.42–44 (where see Hunter's note), 15.82–83, 16.76–77, 24.77–78, and the probably non-Theocritean 25.30–31, 98–99.

167. For such effects with proper names cf. 24.2, 61 (both Ἰφικλῆα), 16, 54 (both Ἡρακλῆα).

168. Fusi's figures (cf. n.163) give 5.5% for the *Iliad* and 4.9% for the *Odyssey*.

169. The individual figure for the *Hecale* fragments is, however, 13% (Hollis 1990, 18).

Word Breaks

Every verse in *EP* has either a "masculine" (-|uu) or a "feminine" (-u|u) caesura in the third foot; in keeping with third-century norms, the "feminine" caesura vastly predominates (72.7%); *Idyll* 22 has 74.8% and *Idyll* 24 71.8%. The figures for Callimachus and Apollonius are 74% and 67%, respectively.[170] The Homeric figure of 57% clearly shows how poetic preference developed. The relatively low figure of feminine caesura for Theocritus's bucolics (50.3%)[171] must be considered together with his treatment of the fourth foot in those poems.

Word break after a fourth-foot dactyl (the "bucolic diaeresis")[172] is a striking preference in third-century hexameters. Of Homeric verses, 47% show this feature, but 57% in the *Argonautica* and 63% in Callimachus.[173] The predominance of this caesura in bucolic poetry is a familiar fact: varying ways of counting give between 74% and 80% for Theocritus's bucolics. Other poems, however, are much closer to Homeric norms: thus *Idylls* 13 (47.2%), 16 (40.3%),[174] 18 (43.7%), 22 (46%),[175] 24 (44.2%), and 26 (42.1%). Only two of the five extant verses of the *Berenice* have bucolic diaeresis. *EP* shows the relatively low figure of

170. Cf. West 1982, 153.

171. This is the figure of Kunst (1887, 47) and relates to *Idylls* 1 and 3–11.

172. This is the meaning I shall always give to this term; it is sometimes found applied to any word break after the fourth foot, but this is likely to be misleading.

173. Cf. West 1982, 154.

174. It may be significant that in vv. 90–97 (the "bucolic" passage), five of the seven verses have bucolic diaeresis, including four successive cases (vv. 94–97); note, however, also vv. 44–48 and 70–72.

175. This is based on Sens's figure (1997, 45) of 47% with the subtraction of the three cases of word break after a fourth-foot spondee.

39.7%, which ought perhaps to be interpreted as a particular marker of the "traditional" metrics (and flavor) of this poem; thus only three verses of the twelve-verse proem, which sets the tone for the poem, show this feature. We may contrast the proem of *Idyll* 13, where each of the opening four verses in the "personal" address to Nicias have the "bucolic diaeresis." Similarly, Callimachean metrics demand that a masculine caesura in the third foot should be combined with the bucolic diaeresis; 90% of relevant verses in Callimachus conform to this pattern, and 86% in Theocritus's bucolics, but here again the epicizing poems remain more traditional: *EP*, 59.3%; *Idyll* 22, 57%; *Idyll* 24, 74.3% (another sign of its "polish"); and *Idyll* 26, 68.4%. The figures for *Idyll* 13 (72.2%) and *Idyll* 18 (80%) also reflect the intermediate position of those poems.

Word break after a fourth-foot spondee (a breach of "Naeke's Law") is all but eliminated in Callimachus and his imitators but occurs on average once every 86 verses in the *Argonautica*. Again, there are clear distinctions within the Theocritean corpus.[176] The bucolics all but avoid the license, except for *Idyll* 11,[177] whereas the chatter of the housewives in *Idyll* 15 has an average of one example every 9 verses. *EP* has 6 examples (vv. 36, 45, 85, 87, 90, 133; i.e., one every 22.6 verses); *Idyll* 22 has 8 (i.e., one every 27.8 verses). Once again both *Idyll* 13 (1 example) and *Idyll* 24 (2 examples) are more "modern" than *EP* and *Idyll* 22.

EP is also no particularly firm respecter of the other Calli-

---

176. The evidence is gathered by Kunst (1887, 55–56) and Fantuzzi (1995, 231).

177. Cf. Hunter on 1.130, with bibliography.

machean "rules" for the hexameter;[178] an analysis by Marco Fantuzzi established that Theocritus's bucolics, as a whole, are sharply differentiated from his other poems in their respect for these rules.[179] Thus, for example, *EP* shows seven breaches of "Meyer's First Law," which outlaws word break at the trochee of the second foot after a word that began in the first foot (e.g., v. 64: παῖς ἀγαπητὸς ἔγεντο). These "rules" are in fact the hardening of persistent tendencies within the hexameter from the earliest days, and Theocritus's practice within his "epicizing" poems should be seen in that light.

Prosody

1. "Attic correption" (i.e., counting a syllable as light if it contains a short vowel followed by a combination of a mute and a liquid consonant; e.g., v. 107: ἄτε πλοῦτος) is sparingly used in *EP.* Theocritus's "'epicizing" poems are, in this technique, significantly more traditional than the bucolics and mimes,[180] though there are wide differences from poem to poem, and, even here, Theocritus is considerably freer than are Callimachus and Apollonius. *EP,* in fact, with a figure of only 21.4% correption is the most archaizing of the "epic" poems in this, as in practically every, regard (cf. *Idylls*

178. For these cf. Mineur 1984, 41–45; Hopkinson 1984, 51–55; and Hollis 1990, 15–23.

179. Cf. Fantuzzi 1995. The following statistics are taken from Fantuzzi's account.

180. Cf. Kunst 1887, 64–96; Slings 1993; Fantuzzi 1995, 249–50 (from where the following percentages are taken). Slings's figures differ somewhat (though not significantly), as he and Fantuzzi use slightly different criteria for word end.

13, 35.3%; 16, 29.8%; 18, 48.4%; 22, 36.2%; 24, 32.5%; 26, 22%).
The license is relatively much more common between words than
within an individual word (e.g., ἀπόβλητον, v. 136).[181]

2. *EP* is also archaizing in offering ten examples (vv. 6, 7, 11,
13, 18, 38, 62, 63, 75, 135) of a "Homeric" hiatus before a word
that originally began with a digamma.[182] Of these, hiatus before
dative οἱ (vv. 62, 75) is not rare throughout the corpus, but the li-
cense is otherwise much more common in the "epicizing" poems
than in the bucolics and mimes.

3. ἀπὸ νεφέων, v. 72, imitates a Homeric prosodic license (cf. n.
ad loc.); such features are not uncommon in the "epicizing"
poems.[183]

A NOTE ON THE TRANSMISSION
OF THE TEXT

Some 180 medieval and Renaissance manuscripts containing
Theocritean poems are known. Shared errors demonstrate that
all MSS ultimately go back to a common ancestor, which itself
contained corrections, variant readings, and the like; papyri and
the preserved scholia on *Idylls* 1–18 and 28–29 confirm the pres-
ence of significant textual variation (and not just in matters of di-
alect) from an early date. The MSS fall into three broad families,
though they may change their affiliations from poem to poem.
The representatives of the three families for this edition of *EP* are
as follows:

181. Cf. Modena 1992.
182. Cf. Kunst 1887, 118–20.
183. For Callimachean examples cf. Mineur 1984, 43.

Ambrosian family: K
Laurentian family: LWTr
Vatican family: ASU

Of these families, the Ambrosian tradition of K is generally regarded as the most trustworthy. Two papyri of *EP* are also preserved (see Sigla below). For a detailed account of the MSS and transmission of Theocritus the editions of Gow and Gallavotti should be consulted; there is a brief sketch, with further bibliography, in Hunter 1999, 26–28.

Information in this edition about MSS readings derives from Gallavotti (3d ed.) and Gow. The apparatus is extremely selective, and silence on any reading is not to be interpreted as a sign that the tradition is unanimous; more complete information may be found in the editions of Gallavotti and Gow.

Sigla

PAPYRI

Pap.Ant.   *Papyrus Antinoae* (fifth–sixth century);[1] contains
parts of vv. 1–31, 42–75, 83–88, 101–3, 111–13

POxy. 3551   *Oxyrhynchus Papyrus* 3551 (third century);[2]
contains parts of vv. 95–105

MANUSCRIPTS AND PRINTED BOOKS

K   Ambrosianus 886 (C 222 inf.) (thirteenth
century)

L   Parisinus gr. 2831 (thirteenth–fourteenth
century)

W   Laurentianus Conv. soppr. 15 (fourteenth
century)

1. Cf. Hunt and Johnson 1930.
2. Cf. Parsons 1983, 127–28.

Tr	Parisinus gr. 2832 (fourteenth century)
A	Ambrosianus 390 (G 32 sup.) (thirteenth century)
S	Laurentianus 32. 16 (1280 c.e.)
U	Vaticanus gr. 1825 (fourteenth century)
M	Vaticanus gr. 915 (thirteenth century)
D	Parisinus Anc. Fonds gr. 2726 (fifteenth century)
Non.	Salmanticensis 295 (sixteenth century)[3]
Iunt.	Editio Philippi Iuntae, Florence (1516)
codd.	The reading of all MSS
Ω	The reading of most MSS
l	The reading of LWTr
v	The reading of ASU

ABBREVIATIONS

K a.c.	K before correction
K v.l.	A variant reading in K
K(i)	The first hand in K
K(ii)	The second hand in K

3. Cf. Gow 1: xlvi–ii.

Encomium of Ptolemy Philadelphus

THEOCRITUS

ΘΕΟΚΡΙΤΟΥ ΕΓΚΩΜΙΟΝ
ΕΙΣ ΠΤΟΛΕΜΑΙΟΝ

ἐκ Διὸς ἀρχώμεσθα καὶ ἐς Δία λήγετε Μοῖσαι,
ἀθανάτων τὸν ἄριστον, ἐπὴν† ἀείδωμεν ἀοιδαῖς·
ἀνδρῶν δ᾽ αὖ Πτολεμαῖος ἐνὶ πρώτοισι λεγέσθω
καὶ πύματος καὶ μέσσος· ὃ γὰρ προφερέστατος ἀνδρῶν.
ἥρωες, τοὶ πρόσθεν ἀφ᾽ ἡμιθέων ἐγένοντο,   5
ῥέξαντες καλὰ ἔργα σοφῶν ἐκύρησαν ἀοιδῶν·
αὐτὰρ ἐγὼ Πτολεμαῖον ἐπιστάμενος καλὰ εἰπεῖν
ὑμνήσαιμ᾽· ὕμνοι δὲ καὶ ἀθανάτων γέρας αὐτῶν.
Ἴδαν ἐς πολύδενδρον ἀνὴρ ὑλατόμος ἐλθών
παπταίνει, παρεόντος ἄδην, πόθεν ἄρξεται ἔργου·   10
τί πρῶτον καταλέξω; ἐπεὶ πάρα μυρία εἰπεῖν
οἷσι θεοὶ τὸν ἄριστον ἐτίμησαν βασιλήων.
    ἐκ πατέρων οἷος μὲν ἔην τελέσαι μέγα ἔργον

---

1   Μοῦσαι Pap.Ant.   5   ἁ[μιθέων Pap.Ant. (probably)
2   ἀοιδῆς Pap.Ant.   9   ἐνθών K
4   προφερέστερος l   11   πρᾶτον l

THE ENCOMIUM OF PTOLEMY

From Zeus let us begin and, Muses, cease with Zeus, best of the immortal ones, whenever we raise our voices in song.[1] But of men let Ptolemy be named in the first place, at the end, and in the middle, for he is the greatest of men.

The heroes, who in former times were descended from demigods, performed marvelous deeds and found skilled poets to honor them. I, however, who understand the art of praise, would hymn Ptolemy: hymns are the reward even of the immortals themselves.

When he goes to richly forested Ida, the woodcutter **(10)** gazes around to see where he should start his task in the midst of such plenty; what shall I first set down, for countless to record are the honors that the gods have bestowed upon the best of kings?

---

1. Text is uncertain at the end of the sentence.

Λαγείδας Πτολεμαῖος, ὅτε φρεσὶν ἐγκατάθοιτο
βουλάν, ἃν οὐκ ἄλλος ἀνὴρ οἷός τε νοῆσαι.   15
τῆνον καὶ μακάρεσσι πατὴρ ὁμότιμον ἔθηκεν
ἀθανάτοις, καί οἱ χρύσεος θρόνος ἐν Διὸς οἴκωι
δέδμηται· παρὰ δ' αὐτὸν Ἀλέξανδρος φίλα εἰδώς
ἑδριάει, Πέρσαισι βαρὺς θεὸς αἰολομίτρας.
ἀντία δ' Ἡρακλῆος ἕδρα κενταυροφόνοιο   20
ἵδρυται στερεοῖο τετυγμένα ἐξ ἀδάμαντος·
ἔνθα σὺν ἄλλοισιν θαλίας ἔχει Οὐρανίδηισι,
χαίρων υἱωνῶν περιώσιον υἱωνοῖσιν,
ὅττι σφεων Κρονίδης μελέων ἐξείλετο γῆρας,
ἀθάνατοι δὲ καλεῦνται ἑοὶ νέποδες γεγαῶτες.   25
ἄμφω γὰρ πρόγονός σφιν ὁ καρτερὸς Ἡρακλείδας,
ἀμφότεροι δ' ἀριθμεῦνται ἐς ἔσχατον Ἡρακλῆα.
τῶ καὶ ἐπεὶ δαίτηθεν ἴοι κεκορημένος ἤδη
νέκταρος εὐόδμοιο φίλας ἐς δῶμ' ἀλόχοιο,
τῶι μὲν τόξον ἔδωκεν ὑπωλένιόν τε φαρέτραν,   30

---

14 Λαγείδας Geier: Λαγίδας   20 ἀντία θ' l
    codd. ὅτε Ziegler: ὅκα codd.   24 Κρονίδας υTr
17 θρόνος Bergk: δόμος codd.   25 ἑοὶ Heinsius: θεοὶ codd.
19 αιολομι]τρης Pap.Ant. ⁻μιτραις Non.   30 φαρέτρην LWAU

From his ancestors what a man for bringing to completion
a mighty deed was Ptolemy, son of Lagos, whenever he laid
down in his heart a plan, the like of which no other man could
have conceived. Him the father made equal in honor even to
the blessed immortals, and a golden throne is built for him
in the house of Zeus; beside him, kindly disposed, sits Alexan-
der, the god of the dancing diadem, who brought destruction to
the Persians. (20) Facing them is established the seat of centaur-
slaying Heracles, fashioned from solid adamant; there he joins
in feasting with the heavenly ones and rejoices exceedingly
in the grandsons of his grandsons, for the son of Kronos has
removed old age from their limbs, and his very own descen-
dants are called immortal. Both[2] have as ancestor the mighty
son of Heracles, and both trace their family back in the end to
Heracles. Therefore, whenever, now having drunk his fill of
fragrant nectar, he leaves the feast for the home of his loving
wife, (30) to one he gives his bow and the quiver that hangs

---

2. I.e., Alexander and Ptolemy I.

τῶι δὲ σιδάρειον σκύταλον κεχαραγμένον ὄζοις·
οἳ δ᾽ εἰς ἀμβρόσιον θάλαμον λευκοσφύρου Ἥβας
ὅπλα καὶ αὐτὸν ἄγουσι γενειήταν Διὸς υἱόν.
οἷα δ᾽ ἐν πινυταῖσι περικλειτὰ Βερενίκα
ἔπρεπε θηλυτέρηις, ὄφελος μέγα γειναμένοισι.   35
τᾶι μὲν Κύπρον ἔχοισα Διώνας πότνια κούρα
κόλπον ἐς εὐώδη ῥαδινὰς ἐσεμάξατο χεῖρας·
τῶ οὔπω τινὰ φαντὶ ἁδεῖν τόσον ἀνδρὶ γυναικῶν
ὅσσον περ Πτολεμαῖος ἑὴν ἐφίλησεν ἄκοιτιν.
ἦ μὰν ἀντεφιλεῖτο πολὺ πλέον. ὧδέ κε παισί   40
θαρσήσας σφετέροισιν ἐπιτρέποι οἶκον ἄπαντα,
ὁππότε κεν φιλέων βαίνηι λέχος ἐς φιλεούσης·
ἀστόργου δὲ γυναικὸς ἐπ᾽ ἀλλοτρίωι νόος αἰεί,
ῥηίδιοι δὲ γοναί, τέκνα δ᾽ οὐ ποτεοικότα πατρί.
κάλλει ἀριστεύουσα θεάων πότν᾽ Ἀφροδίτα,   45
σοὶ τήνα μεμέλητο· σέθεν δ᾽ ἕνεκεν Βερενίκα
εὐειδὴς Ἀχέροντα πολύστονον οὐκ ἐπέρασεν,
ἀλλά μιν ἁρπάξασα, πάροιθ᾽ ἐπὶ νῆα κατελθεῖν
κυανέαν καὶ στυγνὸν ἀεὶ πορθμῆα καμόντων,
ἐς ναὸν κατέθηκας, ἑᾶς δ᾽ ἀπεδάσσαο τιμᾶς.   50

34	περικλυτὰ *lv*	42 βαίνηι Iunt.: ⁻νει Ω: ⁻νοι S
36	τῆι *v* κούρη *l*	43 ἀλλοτρίων K αἰὲν *lv*
39	ἐφίλασεν KAU	48 κατενθεῖν K
41	ἐπιτρέποι L: ⁻πει Ω	50 νηὸν Pap.Ant. S

beneath the arm, and to the other his iron club, its surface
pitted with knots; to the ambrosial chamber of white-ankled
Hebe they lead both the weapons and the bearded son of Zeus
himself.

How outstanding among women of sense was renowned
Berenice, a great boon to her parents. The controller of
Cyprus, the powerful daughter of Dione, pressed her delicate
hands upon Berenice's fragrant breast; thus they say that no
woman has ever yet so pleased her husband as Ptolemy loved
his wife. **(40)** Indeed he was much more loved in return. This
is how one might with confidence entrust the whole house to
one's children when going with love to the bed of a loving wife;
the mind of a woman without affection is, however, always
elsewhere, and for her giving birth is a light matter, and the
children do not resemble the father. Supreme in the contest
of beauty, queen among goddesses, Aphrodite, to your heart
was this woman dear; through you fair Berenice did not cross
Acheron, the cause of so much lamentation, but before she
descended to the black boat and the ever-hateful ferryman
of those who have passed on, you snatched her up, **(50)** set her

πᾶσιν δ᾽ ἤπιος ἥδε βροτοῖς μαλακοὺς μὲν ἔρωτας
προσπνείει, κούφας δὲ διδοῖ ποθέοντι μερίμνας.

Ἀργεία κυάνοφρυ, σὺ λαοφόνον Διομήδεα
μισγομένα Τυδῆι τέκες, Καλυδωνίωι ἀνδρί,
ἀλλὰ Θέτις βαθύκολπος ἀκοντιστὰν Ἀχιλῆα   55
Αἰακίδαι Πηλῆι· σὲ δ᾽, αἰχμητὰ Πτολεμαῖε,
αἰχμητᾶι Πτολεμαίωι ἀρίζηλος Βερενίκα.
καί σε Κόως ἀτίταλλε βρέφος νεογιλλὸν ἐόντα,
δεξαμένα παρὰ ματρὸς ὅτε πρώταν ἴδες ἀώ.
ἔνθα γὰρ Εἰλείθυιαν ἐβώσατο λυσίζωνον   60
Ἀντιγόνας θυγάτηρ βεβαρημένα ὠδίνεσσιν·
ἣ δέ οἱ εὐμενέοισα παρίστατο, κὰδ δ᾽ ἄρα πάντων
νωδυνίαν κατέχευε μελῶν· ὃ δὲ πατρὶ ἐοικώς
παῖς ἀγαπητὸς ἔγεντο. Κόως δ᾽ ὀλόλυξεν ἰδοῖσα,
φᾶ δὲ καθαπτομένα βρέφεος χείρεσσι φίλῃσιν·   65
"ὄλβιε κοῦρε γένοιο, τίοις δέ με τόσσον ὅσον περ
Δῆλον ἐτίμησεν κυανάμπυκα Φοῖβος Ἀπόλλων·
ἐν δὲ μιᾶι τιμῆι Τρίοπος καταθεῖο κολώναν,
ἶσον Δωριέεσσι νέμων γέρας ἐγγὺς ἐοῦσιν·
ἶσον καὶ Ῥήναιαν ἄναξ ἐφίλησεν Ἀπόλλων."   70
ὣς ἄρα νᾶσος ἔειπεν· ὁ δ᾽ ὑψόθεν ἔκλαγε φωνᾶι

53	Διομήδην *l*	64	ἰδοῦσα LW
54	μισγομένη Pap.Ant.	Καλυδωνίωι	65	φη Pap.Ant.
	ἀνδρί Hiller: ⁻ιον ἄνδρα codd.	67	Δᾶλον K*l*
57	ἀρίζαλος *v*	68	μιη Pap.Ant. *Τρίοπος* Steph-
59	πράταν *l*		anus: *Τρίοπον* KTr: *τρίοπτον* Ω
61	βεβαρημένα L*v*: βεβαρυμένα KWTr	70	ἐφίλασεν *v*Tr
62	α δε Pap.Ant. εὐμενέοισα KS:	71	νησος Pap.Ant.
	-ουσα *l*AU		

in your temple, and gave her a share in your own honor. In her kindliness to all mortals she inspires gentle loves, and easy to bear are the cares she bestows upon the yearning lover. Dark-browed lady of Argos, you lay with Tydeus, a man of Calydon, and bore bloodthirsty Diomedes; deep-bosomed Thetis bore spearman Achilles to Peleus, son of Aeacus; but you, warrior Ptolemy, are the child of the warrior Ptolemy and glorious Berenice.

When you were a fresh-born infant, Cos received you from your mother when first you saw the light of day and cared for you. (60) For it was there that the daughter of Antigone, wracked by the pains of labor, called upon Eileithyia, the releaser of girdles; the goddess, well disposed, stood beside her and poured painlessness down over her whole body, and the longed-for son, the image of his father, was born. Cos cried aloud at the sight, and, taking the infant in her loving hands, she addressed him: "May you be blessed, my son, and may you honor me as much as Phoebus Apollo honored dark-circled Delos. In like honor too may you hold the hill of Triops, assigning an equal reward to the Dorians who dwell nearby; (70) equally too did lord Apollo love Rhenaia." Thus did the

ἐς τρὶς ἀπὸ νεφέων μέγας αἰετός, αἴσιος ὄρνις.

Ζηνός που τόδε σᾶμα· Διὶ Κρονίωνι μέλοντι
αἰδοῖοι βασιλῆες, ὃ δ᾽ ἔξοχος ὅν κε φιλήσηι
γεινόμενον τὰ πρῶτα· πολὺς δέ οἱ ὄλβος ὀπαδεῖ,   75
πολλᾶς δὲ κρατέει γαίας, πολλᾶς δὲ θαλάσσας.

μυρίαι ἄπειροί τε καὶ ἔθνεα μυρία φωτῶν
λήιον ἀλδήσκουσιν ὀφελλόμενον Διὸς ὄμβρωι,
ἀλλ᾽ οὔτις τόσα φύει ὅσα χθαμαλὰ Αἴγυπτος,
Νεῖλος ἀναβλύζων διερὰν ὅτε βώλακα θρύπτει,   80
οὐδέ τις ἄστεα τόσσα βροτῶν ἔχει ἔργα δαέντων.

τρεῖς μέν οἱ πολίων ἑκατοντάδες ἐνδέδμηνται,
τρεῖς δ᾽ ἄρα χιλιάδες τρισσαῖς ἐπὶ μυριάδεσσι,
δοιαὶ δὲ τριάδες, μετὰ δέ σφισιν ἐννεάδες τρεῖς·
τῶν πάντων Πτολεμαῖος ἀγήνωρ ἐμβασιλεύει.   85

καὶ μὴν Φοινίκας ἀποτέμνεται Ἀρραβίας τε
καὶ Συρίας Λιβύας τε κελαινῶν τ᾽ Αἰθιοπήων·
Παμφύλοισί τε πᾶσι καὶ αἰχμηταῖς Κιλίκεσσι
σαμαίνει, Λυκίοις τε φιλοπτολέμοισί τε Καρσί
καὶ νάσοις Κυκλάδεσσιν, ἐπεί οἱ νᾶες ἄρισται   90

---

72   ἀπὸ K: ἀπαὶ *l*: ὑπαὶ AU: ὑπ᾽ ἐκ S: 78   ὀφελλόμενον D(i): -όμεναι *lv*
    ἀπὸ uel ἀπαὶ Pap.Ant.   αἰετὸς   D(ii): -όμεν K
    αἴσιος Iunt.: αἴσιος αἰετὸς Ω: αἰετὸς   84   ἐνδεκάδες *v*Tr
    ὅσιος K   87   Συρίης Pap.Ant. *v*Tr   Λιβύης
74   αἰδοῖοι Pap.Ant.: -οῖο KLW: -οίου   Pap.Ant. *v*
    *v*Tr   βασιλῆες K(i): -ῆος Ω   88   Παμφύλοισι Schrader: -λοισι codd.
75   ὀπηδεῖ *lv*   89   φιλοπτολέμοισί τε Καρσί K: -μοις
76   γαίας KS: γαίης Ω   θαλάσσας   τε Κάρεσσι Ω
    KAU: -ης *lS*   90   ἄρισται Stephanus: ἄριστοι codd.

island speak, and from the clouds above a huge eagle, a bird of omen, screamed aloud three times. This, no doubt, was Zeus's sign. To Zeus, the son of Kronos, are reverend kings dear, but he whom Zeus loves from the very moment of his birth is pre-eminent; vast is the prosperity that attends him, vast the land over which he rules, and vast the sea.

Countless lands and countless races of men raise their crops with the aid of Zeus's rain, but no land is as productive as low-lying Egypt, **(80)** when the flooding Nile drenches and breaks up the soil; nor does any land have so many towns full of people skilled in crafts. Within are built three hundred cities, and three thousand, and another ten thousand three times over, and three twice, and after them thrice nine: over all of these is lordly Ptolemy king. He takes slices of Phoenicia and Arabia and Syria and Libya and the dark-skinned Ethiopians; all the Pamphyl-ians and the warriors of Cilicia he commands, and the Lycians and the Carians, who delight in war, **(90)** and the islands of the

πόντον ἐπιπλώοντι, θάλασσα δὲ πᾶσα καὶ αἶα
καὶ ποταμοὶ κελάδοντες ἀνάσσονται Πτολεμαίωι,
πολλοὶ δ' ἱππῆες, πολλοὶ δέ μιν ἀσπιδιῶται
χαλκῶι μαρμαίροντι σεσαγμένοι ἀμφαγέρονται.
ὄλβωι μὲν πάντας κε καταβρίθοι βασιλῆας·   95
τόσσον ἐπ' ἆμαρ ἕκαστον ἐς ἀφνεὸν ἔρχεται οἶκον
πάντοθε. λαοὶ δ' ἔργα περιστέλλουσιν ἔκηλοι·
οὐ γάρ τις δηίων πολυκήτεα Νεῖλον ὑπερβάς
πεζὸς ἐν ἀλλοτρίαισι βοὰν ἐστάσατο κώμαις,
οὐδέ τις αἰγιαλόνδε θοᾶς ἐξήλατο ναός   100
θωρηχθεὶς ἐπὶ βουσὶν ἀνάρσιος Αἰγυπτίηισιν·
τοῖος ἀνὴρ πλατέεσσιν ἐνίδρυται πεδίοισι
ξανθοκόμας Πτολεμαῖος, ἐπιστάμενος δόρυ πάλλειν,
ὧι ἐπίπαγχυ μέλει πατρώια πάντα φυλάσσειν
οἷ' ἀγαθῶι βασιλῆι, τὰ δὲ κτεατίζεται αὐτός.   105
οὐ μὰν ἀχρεῖός γε δόμωι ἐνὶ πίονι χρυσός
μυρμάκων ἅτε πλοῦτος ἀεὶ κέχυται μογεόντων·
ἀλλὰ πολὺν μὲν ἔχοντι θεῶν ἐρικυδέες οἶκοι,
αἰεὶ ἀπαρχομένοιο σὺν ἄλλοισιν γεράεσσι,
πολλὸν δ' ἰφθίμοισι δεδώρηται βασιλεῦσι,   110
πολλὸν δὲ πτολίεσσι, πολὺν δ' ἀγαθοῖσιν ἑταίροις.
οὐδὲ Διωνύσου τις ἀνὴρ ἱεροὺς κατ' ἀγῶνας
ἵκετ' ἐπιστάμενος λιγυρὰν ἀναμέλψαι ἀοιδάν,

---

94   ἀμφαγέροντι *lv*   103   ξανθοκόμος *lv*
97   ἔκαλοι POxy. 3551 a.c.   περιστέλ-   109   αἰὲν S   ἀπαρχομένοιο KS: -μενος
      λονται K   LWAU: -μενον Tr
100 ἐξάλλατο Kv   νηός K   112   ἱεροὺς WTrS: ἱερεὺς KAU: ἱερὲς L
101 Αἰγυπτίαισιν Pap.Ant. S   113   ἀοι]δην Pap.Ant.

Cyclades, for his are the finest ships sailing the ocean. All the
sea and the land and the crashing rivers are subject to Ptolemy,
and round about him gather huge numbers of horsemen and
huge numbers of shield-bearing soldiers, burdened with glitter-
ing bronze.

In wealth he would outdo all other kings, so great are the
revenues that come every day and from every direction to his
rich store. Undisturbed, his people tend their fields, for no
foe crosses the swarming Nile to raise by land the cry of battle
in villages that do not belong to him, (100) and no enemy in
armor leaps to the shore from a swift ship to harm the cattle of
Egypt. So great a man is settled in the broad fields, fair-haired
Ptolemy, skilled with the spear, whose principal concern, as is
right for a good king, is to preserve his inheritance from his
father, and he increases the store himself. Gold is not piled up
pointlessly in his rich palace, like the wealth of ants that toil
without pause: much do the glorious houses of the gods receive,
as Ptolemy ever offers firstfruits and other gifts of honor; (110)

ὦι οὐ δωτίναν ἀντάξιον ὤπασε τέχνας.
Μουσάων δ᾽ ὑποφῆται ἀείδοντι Πτολεμαῖον 115
ἀντ᾽ εὐεργεσίης. τί δὲ κάλλιον ἀνδρί κεν εἴη
ὀλβίωι ἢ κλέος ἐσθλὸν ἐν ἀνθρώποισιν ἀρέσθαι;
τοῦτο καὶ Ἀτρείδαισι μένει· τὰ δὲ μυρία τῆνα
ὅσσα μέγαν Πριάμοιο δόμον κτεάτισσαν ἑλόντες
ἀέρι παι κέκρυπται, ὅθεν πάλιν οὐκέτι νόστος. 120
   μοῦνος ὅδε προτέρων τε καὶ ὧν ἔτι θερμὰ κονία
στειβομένα καθύπερθε ποδῶν ἐκμάσσεται ἴχνη,
ματρὶ φίλαι καὶ πατρὶ θυώδεας εἵσατο ναούς·
ἐν δ᾽ αὐτοὺς χρυσῶι περικαλλέας ἠδ᾽ ἐλέφαντι
ἵδρυται πάντεσσιν ἐπιχθονίοισιν ἀρωγούς. 125
πολλὰ δὲ πιανθέντα βοῶν ὅγε μηρία καίει
μησὶ περιπλομένοισιν ἐρευθομένων ἐπὶ βωμῶν,
αὐτός τ᾽ ἰφθίμα τ᾽ ἄλοχος, τᾶς οὔτις ἀρείων
νυμφίον ἐν μεγάροισι γυνὰ περιβάλλετ᾽ ἀγοστῶι,
ἐκ θυμοῦ στέργοισα κασίγνητόν τε πόσιν τε. 130

---

117 ἢ κλέος Tr: κλέος Ω   126 ὅγε Tr(ii): ὅτε Ω: ὅδε SM
121 τε καὶ ὧν Briggs: τεκέων K: 127 μησὶ Ahrens: μασὶ codd.
      τοκέων Ω   κονία K: -ίη Ω   128 ἀρείων KTr: ἀρείω Ω

much too he bestows upon powerful kings, much upon cities,
and much upon his brave companions. Nor does any man,
skilled in raising aloud tuneful song, enter the sacred contests
of Dionysus without receiving a gift worthy of his art. The
intermediaries of the Muses sing of Ptolemy in return for his
benefactions. What finer thing could a wealthy man win than
good renown among men? This remains for the sons of Atreus
also; but the countless treasure that they gained by sacking
the great palace of Priam, (120) this is hidden somewhere
in darkness, in a place from which there is no way back.

This man, alone of men of the past and of those whose still
warm footprints mark the trodden dust, has established fragrant
shrines to his loving mother and father; within, he has set them
glorious in gold and ivory to bring aid to all upon the earth.
Many are the fattened thighs of cattle that he burns upon the
bloodied altars as the passage of months proceeds, both he
and his noble partner, than whom no better wife embraces her
young husband in the halls, (130) loving with all her heart her

ὧδε καὶ ἀθανάτων ἱερὸς γάμος ἐξετελέσθη
οὓς τέκετο κρείουσα Ῥέα βασιλῆας Ὀλύμπου·
ἐν δὲ λέχος στόρνυσιν ἰαύειν Ζηνὶ καὶ Ἥρηι
χεῖρας φοιβήσασα μύροις ἔτι παρθένος Ἶρις.

χαῖρε, ἄναξ Πτολεμαῖε· σέθεν δ᾽ ἐγὼ ἶσα καὶ ἄλλων
μνάσομαι ἡμιθέων, δοκέω δ᾽ ἔπος οὐκ ἀπόβλητον
φθέγξομαι ἐσσομένοις· ἀρετήν γε μὲν ἐκ Διὸς αἰτεῦ.

137 αἰτεῦ ᵃKl: ἔξοις v

brother and her husband. In this manner too was accomplished the sacred marriage of the immortals whom Queen Rhea bore as kings of Olympus: it is one bed that Iris, to this day a virgin, prepares for Zeus and Hera, when she has cleansed her hands with perfumes.

Farewell, Lord Ptolemy! You, no less than the other demigods, will I remember, and what I say shall not, I believe, be rejected by those who come after. For virtue make your request from Zeus.

Commentary

1–12 Proem. The twelve-verse proem falls into three quatrains, demarcated by the absence of connecting particles in vv. 5 and 9, which gives the sense of three fresh starts:

> 1–4 Zeus and Ptolemy hold analogous positions on heaven and on earth <and should therefore hold similarly analogous positions in song>;
>
> 5–8 The great deeds of the heroes of old were celebrated by excellent poets, but I will hymn Ptolemy [i.e., rather than the heroes of old];
>
> 9–12 The woodcutter on Mount Ida does not know where to begin. Where shall I begin, as there is so much material?

Each quatrain, however, is also centrally divided into two couplets, in a pattern that allows both the central hierarchy and the way it is to be blurred to emerge clearly:

1–2 Zeus, best of *gods* and a potential subject of song.

3–4 Ptolemy, best of *men* and a potential subject of song.

5–6 The archaic *heroes* have already been suitably celebrated.

7–8 I shall hymn Ptolemy, in the form of song appropriate also to the gods.

9–10 The woodcutter on Mount Ida.

11–12 Where do I begin?

Already, then, as the proem establishes apparently discrete categories of being, vv. 7–8 test the boundary (as indeed does Ptolemy) between analogy and identity through a self-conscious acknowledgment that the language and mode of praise, the *hymnos* (cf. above, p. 8, 8n.), has been transferred from god to man.

"Likeness" and analogy, difference and similarity, are central to the progress of the proem and of the poem as a whole: How is Philadelphus "like" Zeus? How was his birth like Apollo's? (Cf. Hunter 1996, 79–82.) Though similar patterns of composition by couplet are found also in the shorter openings of *Idylls* 11, 13, and 16 (cf. Legrand 1898, 388–95; Hunter 1996, 155–56), the asyndetic juxtaposition of verse units and the "paratactic" comparison of vv. 9–12 (cf. 9–10n.), which forces the reader to construct the nature of the similarity or analogy or identity rather than relying on the poet's guiding "and in just the same way . . . ," give these notions structural, as well as thematic, prominence in the opening of *EP.* The poem will proceed by suggesting a whole series of models by which Ptolemy's position may be understood: his father, Soter; Alexander; Agamemnon; Achilles; Alcinous; and Odysseus are among the most prominent; so, too, Arsinoe is "like" her mother, Berenice (who herself is "like" Aphrodite); Arete; and Hera. It is, however, the analogy and affinity between Zeus, the king in heaven (cf. v. 132), and earthly kings, an analogy familiar from Homer and, particularly, Hesiod onward (cf. esp. *Theog.* 68–103; Nisbet and Hubbard on Hor. *Carm.* 1.12.50), but now given a new urgency in changed political circumstances (cf. above, pp. 3–6), which carries—as it does in Callimachus's *Hymn to Zeus*—the greatest weight; the proem is framed by "Zeus" (v. 1) and "the best of kings" (v. 12), by ἀθανάτων τὸν ἄριστον (v. 2) ~ τὸν ἄριστον . . . βασιλήων (v. 12), in a "ring composition" that pushes analogy ever closer to identity.

In Egyptian tradition the pharaoh was not only the son of the Sun-god, but also his "living image" (cf., for example, Lichtheim 1976, 26 [Hatshepsut]; Assmann 1975, no. 237.34–35; Peden 1994, 21 [Ramses II]; Goodenough 1928, 80–82; Hornung 1957, 130; Hornung 1967; Otto 1971), or in the Greek of the Rosetta Stone, the "living εἰκών of Zeus" (*OGIS* 90.3). In the Hesiodic language of "Zeus-nurtured kings," Greek tradition offered poets a pattern comfortably "analogous" to this Egyptian mode, and while the scholars of the Museum fretted about the relationship of Homer's similes, εἰκόνες, to the narrative in which they were embedded (cf. Clausing 1913), and epic poets experimented with the boundaries of inherited simile technique (cf., for example, Hunter 1993, 129–38), "likeness to the divine" was exploited by the Ptolemies as a powerful political idea.

The priamel is a poetic form in which analogy and likeness play a central role (cf. Race 1982; Fantuzzi 2000, 136–38). The structure of the opening of *Idyll* 17 has an important affinity with (and difference from) the priamels that open Pindar's *Ol.* 1 (ἄριστον μὲν ὕδωρ κτλ.) and particularly his *Ol.* 2 (ἀναξιφόρμιγγες ὕμνοι, | τίνα θεόν, τίν᾽ ἥρωα, τίνα δ᾽ ἄνδρα κελαδήσομεν; κτλ). Horace indeed seems to have combined elements of *Idyll* 17 with *Ol.* 2 for *Carm.*

1.12 *(quem uirum aut heroa)*, which perhaps suggests that he too recognized a special relationship between Theocritus and Pindar. Certainly, Theron's wealth ($\pi\lambda o\hat{v}\tau o\varsigma$ and ὄλβος), which is stressed throughout *Ol.* 2, foreshadows the praise of Ptolemy, and the glorious afterlife on the Island of the Blessed, which Pindar seems to hold out to Theron, is here rewritten as the life of Olympian ease, now led by Alexander and Soter, which certainly awaits Philadelphus; whereas the great heroes of the archaic age (Peleus, Kadmos, Achilles, *Ol.* 2.78–79; cf. Hes. *WD* 167–73) were transported to the Island, the new "demigods" will go one better, feasting with Zeus rather than, as in Pindar (*Ol.* 2.76–77), with his father.

T.'s emphatic stress on the "categories" of existence itself finds analogies not merely in the position of Hellenistic kings in general (cf. Weber 1993, 219–20), but specifically in writing about Egypt. Hecataeus of Abdera (Diod. Sic. 1.11–13) divided the rulers of Egypt since the beginning of time into gods who were physical properties (e.g., fire as Hephaestus), mortals "who because of their wisdom and benefactions to all mankind achieved immortality" (e.g., Osiris-Dionysus, Isis-Demeter), and then mortal kings; so too T.'s contemporary Manetho seems to have divided the kings into gods, men, and an intermediate class of ἥρωες or νέκυες ἡμίθεοι (frr. 2–6; cf. Murray 1970, 168). Both historians of Egypt thus show a suggestive interest in kings and queens who move between "mortal" and "divine" status, and this shared concern with division and categorization suggests that more lies behind T.'s insistence than merely an emphatic restatement of the inherited Hesiodic order.

1 T. positions himself within a very familiar bardic tradition, so that the rhetorical novelty of his undertaking may emerge more

clearly. That poems should "begin from/with Zeus" is a standard idea of the rhapsodic and lyric tradition (cf. Terpander, *PMG* 698, Ζεῦ πάντων ἀρχά, πάντων ἀγήτωρ, | Ζεῦ σοὶ πέμπω ταύταν ὕμνων ἀρχάν; Alcman, *PMG* 29, ἐγὼν δ' ἀείσομαι | ἐκ Διὸς ἀρχομένα; Pind. *Nem.* 2.1–3, ὅθεν περ καὶ Ὁμηρίδαι | ῥαπτῶν ἐπέων τὰ πόλλ' ἀοιδοί | ἄρχονται, Διὸς ἐκ προοιμίου κτλ; 5.25–26 [the Muses themselves], πρώτιστον μὲν ὕμνη-| σαν Διὸς ἀρχόμεναι σεμνὰν Θέτιν | Πηλέα θ'; Kidd on Aratus *Phain.* 1; Bömer on Ovid *Fasti* 5.111). The opening injunction to the Muses to sing of Zeus may, however, evoke the opening of Hes. *WD*, Μοῦσαι Πιερίηθεν ἀοιδῆισι κλείουσαι, | δεῦτε Δί' ἐννέπετε κτλ. (cf. further below on Aratus). So, too, the combination of "beginning" and "ceasing" is a traditional poetic motif (cf. Hes. *Theog.* 34 [the Muses bid Hesiod], σφᾶς δ' αὐτὰς πρῶ- τόν τε καὶ ὕστατον αἰὲν ἀείδειν [with West's note]; 47–49 [the Muses], δεύτερον αὖτε Ζῆνα, θεῶν πατέρ' ἠδὲ καὶ ἀνδρῶν, | * ἀρχόμεναι θ' ὑμνε- ῦσι θεαὶ λήγουσαί τ' ἀοιδῆς* | ὅσσον φέρτατός ἐστι θεῶν κάρτει τε μέγισ- τος; fr. 305 M-W; *Hymn. Hom. Dion.* [1] 17–18, οἱ δέ σ' ἀοιδοὶ | ᾄδομεν ἀρχόμενοι λήγοντές τ'; Virg. *Ecl.* 8.11 [to a patron], *a te principium, tibi desinam*); *Idyll* 17 will actualize the motif by quite literally beginning (v. 1) and ending (v. 137) with Zeus. A particularly suggestive example of this motif is the first of the alternative proems to the *Theognidea* (vv. 1–4), ὦ ἄνα Λητοῦς υἱέ, Διὸς τέκος, οὔποτε σεῖο | λήσομαι ἀρχόμενος οὐδ' ἀποπαυόμενος, | ἀλλ' αἰεὶ πρῶτόν τε καὶ ὕστατον ἔν τε μέσοισιν | ἀείσω; T. adopts this strengthened three-part assertion in order to suggest, without actually making explicit, that Ptolemy will be an even more persistent theme of song than Zeus. An archaic model for such an address to a king is *Il.* 9.96 ff. (Nestor to Agamemnon, ἐν σοὶ μὲν λήξω, σέο δ' ἄρξομαι κτλ.), a passage in which the relationship between rulers and Zeus is central; in view of the importance of the Agamemnon-model throughout *EP* and the fact that it concludes with an echo of another speech of Nestor to Agamemnon (cf. 135–37n.), the similarity may not be accidental (note *Il.* 9.103, αὐτὰρ ἐγὼν . . .).

The openings of two roughly contemporary poems seem related to the beginning of *EP.* Callimachus's *Hymn to Zeus* literally "begins from" Zeus, Ζηνὸς ἔοι τί κεν ἄλλο κτλ., and as the close of *Idyll* 17 seems plainly related to the close of that Callimachean hymn (cf. 135–37n.), it is likely enough that the two poems are also related in their openings. If Callim. *H.* 1 is indeed earlier (cf. above, p. 5), then T. has framed his poem εἰς Πτολεμαῖον with echoes of Callimachus's poem εἰς Δία in one more parallelism between earthly and heavenly kings; Callimachus's poem itself constructs a set of shifting analogies between Zeus and kings on earth. (On *EP* and Callim. *H.* 1 cf. further 13n., 135–37n.) ἐκ Διὸς ἀρχώμεσθα are also the opening words of Aratus's *Phainomena*, and it is with Aratus's poem that they are constantly associated throughout antiquity (cf. Σ 1–4a; Kidd on *Phain.* 1; Fantuzzi 1980, 165). Virg. *Ecl.* 3.60–61, *ab Ioue principium Musae: Iouis omnia plena;* | *ille colit terras, illi mea carmina curae,* combines the Aratean and Theocritean openings (with a brilliant transposition of Μοῦσαι into the syntactically ambiguous *Musae*); the context within the *Eclogues* suggests that Virgil here constructs T. as having imitated Aratus, rather than vice versa. The switch from first to second person, ἀρχώμεσθα to λήγετε, may indeed mark the opening words as a quotation or opening "motto' (for this technique cf. 29.1; Cavarzere 1996). The echo of Aratus, if such it is (cf. Vahlen 1907, 1: 303–11, for the skeptical case), at the head of a very "Hesiodic" proem has been interpreted as a way of marking T.'s turning back from the Stoicized Zeus of Aratus to the all-powerful divine king of Aratus's Hesiodic model (cf. Perrotta 1978, 145–52; Fantuzzi 1980;

Fantuzzi 1993, 166–67), in a kind of "window reference" that alludes both to a model and to the model's model. For possible borrowings from Aratus elsewhere in T. cf. 22.8–22; 7.139–40; Pendergraft 1986; Sens 1994, 66–69; Kidd 1997, 40–41.

Gutzwiller (1996, 142) notes that the injunction to "begin and end" with Zeus would fit the closing poem of a collection, as the Antinoopolis papyrus perhaps suggests that *EP* might at one time have been.

Μοῖσαι: The choice between this Aeolic and Pindaric form and Μοῦσαι is hardly possible without greater certainty concerning the dialect of the poem as a whole (cf. above, p. 54); for the evidence of the variant forms in T. cf. Nöthiger 1971, 93; Molinos Tejada 1990, 55–58. *Pap.Ant.*, which here has Μοῦσαι, has Μοῦσαι at 1.104 and Μοῖσα at 7.82.

2 **ἀθανάτων τὸν ἄριστον** is most probably in apposition to Δία (so the paraphrase in Σ 1–4c), rather than the object of the verb of the ἐπήν clause: Zeus is the beginning and end of every song without qualification. (Cf. Latte 1968, 530–31.)

At verse end the required sense is "whenever we turn our hands to song"; ἀείδωμεν probably arose from an incorrect anticipation of the following word rather than as an error for, say, ἄιδωμεν (which is adopted by Schechter 1965; and Rossi 1989). If ἀοιδῆς (or -ᾶς) is correct, then Latte's μνασθῶμεν is attractive, but κλείωμεν ἀοιδαῖς (Schaefer) would appropriately evoke Hes. *WD* 1 (and cf. *Theog.* 44).

3–4 **ἀνδρῶν . . . ἀνδρῶν** frames the couplet. For the division into "gods—men—heroes" cf. 1–12n.

ἐνὶ πρώτοισι: This and μετὰ πρώτοισι are often used in Homer of fighting "in the front ranks"; there is thus already here a suggestion of the heroic status that the poem will construct for Ptolemy, with some resonance of π(τ)όλεμος > Πτολεμαῖος. Callim. *H.* 4.16 (Delos), ἀλλά οἱ οὐ νεμεσητὸν ἐνὶ πρώτῃσι λέγεσθαι, uses the phrase in a different sense. ἐνί does not occur in the "bucolic poems" but is found at 2.26, 14.49 (high style?), and 18.33, as well as in *Idylls* 22 (vv. 94, 190) and 25 (v. 163) (cf. above, p. 59).

λεγέσθω: No strong difference between "singing" and "speaking" is here implied, and λέγειν is commonly used of hexameter verse (cf. vv. 7, 11 [εἰπεῖν]; Hes. *Theog.* 27 [the Muses!], etc.), but the completely general verb stresses that Ptolemy should be praised in every single utterance concerning men.

The order "first—last—middle" is standard (cf. Theognis 1–4 [1n. above]; Hunter 1983, 90); Ptolemy is in fact named in the third and third-to-last verses, and the story of his birth occupies the central section of the poem. No other "mortal" of the present generation is in fact even named in the poem (not even Arsinoe, v. 128), for Soter and Berenice have now passed to another realm of being.

ὁ γάρ: This substantive use of the article with γάρ, frequent in Homer, occurs in T. elsewhere only at fr. 3.4 (from the *Berenice*) and in *Idyll* 25 (vv. 5, 44, 197) (cf. Leutner 1907, 28; above, p. 63).

προφερέστατος: The adjective only here in T., and Homer has this superlative only at *Od.* 8.128; T. may have in mind Hes. *Theog.* 79, where Kalliope, who has a special relationship with kings, is προφερεστάτη . . . ἁπασέων (sc. the Muses) (cf. 12n.).

5 ἥρωες: As a third category, somewhere between "gods" and "men," it is not surprising that the "heroes" are named last (cf.

3–4n.), but the positioning is also determined by the fact that, unlike for Pindar at *Ol.* 2.1–4, the heroes are no longer a potential subject for song, because of the quality of those who have sung of them in the past. In T. the ἥρωες are the great figures of the Homeric and pre-Homeric generations (cf. 13.28 [the Argonauts]; 22.78 [the Argonauts], 163 [the Dioscuri, addressed by an ignorant Lynceus], 216 [the Greeks at Troy]); at 16.80 Hieron is προτέροις ἴσος ἡρώεσσι, and the context suggests that these are such as Achilles and Ajax (v. 74; cf. 15.138).

ἡμιθέων: Elsewhere T. (and Greek poetry generally) uses this term synonymously with ἥρωες (cf. 13.69 [the Argonauts]; 15.137 [Adonis]; 18.18 [Menelaos and his peers]; 24.132 [Kastor and his peers]); some of these heroes did indeed, like Achilles (Pl. *Ap.* 28c2, etc.), have one divine parent (cf. *Arg.* 3.919–21; 4.1773, with Fränkel's text; Cat. 64.23), but poetry did not treat this as a necessary criterion for inclusion in the group (cf. Hes. *WD* 159– 60 [the warriors who fought at Thebes and Troy], ἀνδρῶν ἡρώων θεῖον γένος, οἳ καλέονται | ἡμίθεοι, προτέρη γενεὴ κατ᾽ ἀπείρονα γαῖαν [with West's note]). (The only Homeric instance of ἡμίθεος is *Il.* 12.23, where ΣbT observe that the usage is not normal for Homer.) So, too, some "heroes" did indeed have parents who themselves had one divine parent, and Isocrates (*Panath.* 81) distinguishes among the Greeks at Troy "descendants of the gods" (οἱ ἀπὸ θεῶν) from "sons of gods" (οἱ ἐξ αὐτῶν τῶν θεῶν γεγονότας), but T.'s specification "heroes who were descended from *hemi-theoi*" seems chosen to reflect the circumstances of the poem: Soter and Berenice have now become (at the very least) ἡμίθεοι in a rather different sense, and Ptolemy's "ultimate" ancestor, Heracles, was, in the strictest sense of the term, ἡμίθεος (cf. also 20n.). By the end of the poem, Philadelphus himself will openly have achieved this status (vv. 135–36). Fantuzzi (2000, 140–41; 2001) suggests that T. took his cue from ἡμιθέων ὠκύμορον γενε-ήν, "short-lived generation of *hemitheoi*" in Simonides' "Plataea" elegy (fr. 11.17–18 W), in a passage about the power of Homer's poetry to confer *kleos*, which T. clearly echoes at 16.45–46; Simonides' phrase refers to the generation of Achilles, but on this reading T. interprets it (allusively but "wrongly") as "offspring of *hemitheoi*."

6 Cf. 16.73–74, ἔσσεται οὗτος ἀνὴρ ὃς ἐμοῦ κεχρήσετ᾽ ἀοιδοῦ | ῥέξας ἢ Ἀχιλεὺς ὅσσον μέγας ἢ βαρὺς Αἴας κτλ; *Il.* 10.281–82 (Odysseus prays to Athena), δὸς δὲ πάλιν ἐπὶ νῆας ἐυκλεῖας ἀφικέσθαι, | ῥέξ-αντας μέγα ἔργον, ὅ κε Τρώεσσι μελήσῃ; 22.304–5 (Hector's wish to die gloriously), μέγα ῥέξας τι καὶ ἐσσομένοισι πυθέσθαι, where poetry's power to confer this *kleos* is at least implicit.

καλὰ ἔργα: For the hiatus cf. above, p. 70. Homer does not use this combination for "great deeds," but it is very common in Pindar (cf. *Pyth.* 7.18–19, τὸ δ᾽ ἄχνυμαι, | φθόνον ἀμειβόμενον τὰ καλὰ ἔργα; *Nem.* 6.30, ἀοιδαὶ καὶ λόγοι τὰ καλὰ σφιν ἔργ᾽ ἐκόμισαν; Slater 1969 s.v. καλός 1).

σοφῶν . . . ἀοιδῶν: σοφός is standardly applied to good poets and poetry from the archaic period on (cf. 15.145; *Epigr.* 10.3; Hes. fr. 306; Solon fr. 13.52; Pind. *Ol.* 1.9; Ar. *Frogs* 882; Massimilla on Callim. fr. 1.17–18); what follows suggests that ἀοιδῶν is from ἀοιδός rather than ἀοιδή. T. is primarily of course thinking of Homer, but the plural is to be taken literally; whether Homer is here joined by, for instance, the poets of the "epic cycle" (cf. Hes. *WD* 159–60 [5n. above]) or by "lyric epic" poets such as Stesichorus can hardly be determined, but the plu-

ral emphasizes that there is no need for T. to enter that over-
crowded field.

7 The temptation, strengthened by the fact that the first six verses
have all been end-stopped, to take Πτολεμαῖον as the object of καλὰ
εἰπεῖν (LSJ s.v. λέγω III.3; so apparently Griffiths 1979, 72) sug-
gests again that Ptolemy is the only possible subject of song.

αὐτὰρ ἐγὼ: A very common formula for transition, particu-
larly within hymns, from proem to narrative proper, from one sub-
ject to another, or from narrative to epilogue (cf. *Hymn.Hom.Ap.*
177, 546; Simonides fr. 11.20 [where see Parsons 1992, 32; Ob-
bink 2001, 69]; Callim. fr. 112.9; Poseidippos, *SH* 705.21). Here,
at the head of the second half of the proem, the transition is from
past poets and their subject to the present day; at 16.66 the phrase
is rather part of a movement away from the hopeless pursuit of
mean patrons to the prospect of a better future.

ἐπιστάμενος: The language is Homeric (cf. *Il.* 4.404 [Diomedes
to Agamemnon], μὴ ψεῦδε᾽ ἐπιστάμενος σάφα εἰπεῖν), and the thought
picks up σοφῶν: the poet has to be fitted for and worthy of the sub-
ject (cf. v. 113; *Od.* 11.367–68 [ἐπισταμένως]; *Hymn. Hom.Herm.* 479
[Apollo], καλὰ καὶ εὖ κατὰ κόσμον ἐπιστάμενος ἀγορεύειν). So, too,
ἐπιστάμενος καλὰ εἰπεῖν, "being a skillful encomiast," is bound to
the preceding verse by the repetition of καλά, the repeated hiatus
before an originally digammated word (cf. above, p. 70), and by the
fact that epic verse, which is alluded to in v. 6, was itself taken to
be encomiastic (cf. Arist. *Poet.* 1448b27–30; *ΣIl.* 1.1; Koster 1970,
115, etc.); there is no sharp distinction between *hymnos* and epic
(cf. 16.2, 50; 22.219), and T. can thus present himself as the mod-
ern Homer, as well as the modern Pindar. The phrase is of course

generically loaded (see following n., and cf. above, p. 8), but that does not necessarily make it an ironic "wink" to the reader to suggest that the following poem is simply a meaningless exercise in encomium (so Effe 1995, 115–16).

8 The repeated *hymnos* carries a generic charge (cf. 16.2, 103; 22.1, 214; Nicander fr. 104.2 [to Attalos], κέκλυθι μηδ᾽ ἄμνηστον ἀπ᾽ οὔατος ὕμνον ἐρύξῃς). ὑμνεῖν is used of praise for mortal subjects from a comparatively early date (cf., for example, Pind. *Isthm.* 3.7; Critias fr.eleg. 4.1–2 West, καὶ νῦν Κλεινίου υἱὸν Ἀθηναῖον στεφανώσω | Ἀλκιβιάδην νέοισιν ὑμνήσας τρόποις; Pl. *Leg.* 7.802a), but a stricter application of *hymnos* to praise of the divine was always available (cf. Pl. *Rep.* 10.607a4, *Leg.* 3.700b1–2; Färber 1936, 28–30; Harvey 1955, 165–68; Hunter 1996, 50; Pulleyn 1997, 43–55). Later rhetorical theory formalized the early distinction between ἐγκώμια to men and ὕμνοι to gods (Ammon. *Diff.* 482 Nickau; Men. Rhet. I 331–32 R-W and passim, etc.), and v. 8 seems to prefigure such scholarly categorization: the nuanced distinctions between god, hero, and man, which the very existence of the Ptolemies had thrown into sharp relief, are linked by the poet to the scholastic distinctions of song type being forged in Ptolemy's own library (cf. 1–12n.). T. exploits, indeed plays with, the semantic breadth of ὑμνεῖν to bring Ptolemy closer to the gods. "I shall hymn Ptolemy; hymns are what even the immortals receive"; here is one more likeness between the two.

9–10 The abundance of trees on Ida causes the woodcutter uncertainty as to where to begin. These verses offer a parallel to the countless available topics for Ptolemy's encomiast, but in form they are a "paratactic simile," that is, an illustrative exemplum that is not linked to the main narrative by an introductory ὡς or other term (cf. 13.62–63; 14.41–42; Vahlen 1907, 1; 305–11; Bernsdorff 1996). Here, moreover (contrast 13.64, 14.41), the poet draws no explicit link at all between the woodcutter's position and his own: similarity and difference are to be constructions of the reader (cf. 1–12n.).

Behind this couplet seems to lie the expedition to Ida to cut wood for Patroclus's funeral at *Il.* 23.114 ff., but the felling of trees on Ida perhaps also evokes the beginning of the story of Paris and Helen—that is, the beginning of the whole story of the Trojan War. Having in vv. 6–7 suggested a parallelism between himself and Homer, T. now suggests that he faces one of the same problems as Homer, namely, where to begin, a problem that, in the view of ancient literary critics, Homer had solved triumphantly (cf. Hor. *Ars p.* 140–42, with Brink's notes). The application of the woodcutter simile to poetry is eased by the familiar use of ὕλη (Lat. *silua*) for the "material" or "subject matter" of a work (cf. LSJ s.v. III.3; Coleman 1988, xxii–iv; Hinds 1998, 11–14). Whether or not vv. 2–3 of Simonides' "Plataea" poem, the death of Achilles compared to woodcutters felling a great tree, are relevant here (cf. Fantuzzi 2001) must remain uncertain in view of the fragmentary state of that text; Virgil (*Ecl.* 4.1–3) may have read T.'s woodcutter as a bucolic marker of Theocritean authorship (cf. the δρυτόμος at 5.64).

Ἴδαν: This has sometimes been understood as a noun for "a wood" (cf. LSJ s.v. ἴδη), or referred to a later grammatical idea that Ida could be used to mean any mountain (cf. Σ 9–12a; *Suda ι101*), but πολύδενδρον (cf. 11.47), varying the standard Homeric epithet for Ida, πολυπίδαξ, seems to make the reference to the mountain in the Troad certain (and cf. *Il.* 21.449,Ἴδης ... πολυπτύχου ὑληέσσης; Bacchyl. 5.65–67 [the countless leaves on Mount Ida]).

ἐλθών: The choice of this form rather than Doric ἐνθών depends merely upon a general assessment of the language of the poem, and no confidence is possible (cf. above, p. 54).

παπταίνει suggests confusion and uncertainty.

ἄδην: An epic word occurring only here in T.

11 Alleged embarrassment before the richness of potential material is a familiar hymnic and rhetorical trope (cf. *Hymn. Hom. Ap.* 19 ff., 207 ff.; Eur. *El.* 907–8; [Andoc.] *Alcib.* 10; Isoc. *De bigis* 39; Dem. 60.15; Men. Rhet. 368.21–69.17 = p.76–78 R-W; Bundy 1972, 58–77). T. has in mind Odysseus at *Od.* 9.14–15, τί πρῶτόν τοι ἔπειτα, τί δ' ὑστάτιον καταλέξω; | κήδε' ἐπεί μοι πολλὰ δόσαν θεοὶ οὐρανίωνες: by evoking the passage but omitting any equivalent for the second half of Odysseus's question, T. suggests again that there can be no end to the praise of Ptolemy.

καταλέξω: The compound suggests 'a methodically ordered account" (Heubeck on *Od.* 9.14). The second half of the compound causes a momentary surprise: τί πρῶτον κατατεμῶ; could have been the first (unmetrical) words of the woodcutter.

μυρία tops Odysseus's πολλά but also introduces the motifs of counting and enumeration that are to become very important (cf. vv. 77–85; Hunter 1996, 80); the "Grand Procession" (above, p. 2) shows how Ptolemy made a virtue out of multiplied excess.

12 An echo of the opening couplet seals the analogy between Zeus and Ptolemy, and the verse reverts to Hesiod's famous passage on "reverend kings," which lies at the heart of so much Hellenistic encomium (cf. Bing 1988, 76–83, on Callim. *H.* 1) and is echoed again at vv. 73–75 (cf. *Theog.* 81–82, the Muses "honoring" a 'Zeus-nurtured king"). Cf. further Hunter 1996, 81.

οἶσι: This epic form occurs nowhere else in the Theocritean corpus except in the probably spurious *Idyll* 25 (vv. 33, 45); cf. above, p. 58.

ἐτίμησαν: Gods commonly "honor" mortals for their qualities or good services, in Egyptian no less than in Greek tradition (cf. West on Hes. *Theog.* 81), and the possession of great wealth itself may be a sign of such honor. In the priestly decrees for later Ptolemies (above, p. 3), it is a standard motif that the gods reward the king's services with victory, health, stability in the kingdom, etc. (cf. "Canopus decree" for Euergetes, *OGIS* 56.20 = Austin 1981, 366; Simpson 1996, 229; "Memphis decree" for Epiphanes, *OGIS* 90.35 = Austin 1981, 376; Simpson 1996, 266–67).

13 Despite the alleged *aporia* of vv. 11–12 and the startling asyndeton with which the main part of the poem now begins, an effect that wryly suggests that the poet could have started in innumerable other ways, T. in fact begins in the expected place, with the honorand's family (cf. *Rhet. Alex.* 1440b24, μετὰ τὰ προοίμια πρώτην τὴν γενεαλογίαν τάξομεν; Xen. *Ages.* 1.2; Isoc. *Euag.* 12, *Busiris* 10, *De bigis* 25, etc.). As the first verse-paragraph began ἐκ Διός, so the second begins ἐκ πατέρων; Zeus, father of Heracles and Dionysus, is indeed the beginning of the Ptolemaic line. πατήρ of Zeus in v. 16 (where see n.) exploits this same rhetoric.

ἐκ πατέρων has been taken as an answer to the question of v. 11 ("from Philadelphus's parents"), but the following pause would then be extremely awkward; better (so Gow) to take ἐκ πατέρων with what follows: "Through [his heritage from] his ancestors what a man was…" (cf. 16.33; 24.108). Despite the past tense ἔην, Λαγείδας comes as a surprise, because the "natural" tendency at first reading is indeed to suppose that v. 13 refers to Philadelphus. What is said of Soter is, of course, at one level also said of his son, but T. constructs this surprise precisely because the Ptolemaic claim to divine ancestry rested upon Soter's parentage. Through his mother Arsinoe, Soter traced his line back to Heracles and Dionysus and thus ultimately to Zeus (cf. Satyros, *FGrHist* 631 F1); this lineage also placed Soter firmly in the Macedonian royal house, which traced its ancestry to Heracles, and thus made him rightful heir to Philip and Alexander, as vv. 26–27 (where see n.) emphasize. Later we find Philadelphus's (adopted) son Euergetes proclaiming in an official document that he is "the descendant on his father's side of Heracles, son of Zeus, and on his mother's side of Dionysus, son of Zeus" (*OGIS* 54.4–5); whether it can be inferred from this and v. 27 that Soter claimed descent from Heracles through his father Lagos, as well as through his mother, must remain uncertain. It is at any rate extremely improbable (pace, for example, Herz 1992, 72–73) that either text alludes to a story found in later sources (Paus. 1.6.2) that Soter's real father was Philip, not Lagos.

ἔην: Elsewhere only at 24.133 and 25.218 (cf. Hunter 1996, 41; above, p. 57).

τελέσαι: Cf. *Od.* 2.270–77 (Athena, disguised as Mentor, addresses Telemachus), "Telemachus, in your life hereafter you will be no coward and no fool, if indeed your father's fearless spirit has been instilled in you, sure as he was in accomplishing all that he said or put his hand to (οἶος κεῖνος ἔην τελέσαι ἔργον τε ἔπος τε). Then this journey will not be vain or fruitless. But if you are no true son of Odysseus and Penelope, I cannot hope you should reach fulfilment (τελευτήσειν) of your desires. Few children are quite like their father . . ." (trans. Shewring, adapted). The themes of the whole passage become very important later in the poem, but here the Homeric triangle of Odysseus—Telemachus—Athena/Mentor is replayed as Soter—Philadelphus—Theocritus (the wise counselor). Telemachus is a paradigm of a wise young ruler in Philodemos's *On the Good King According to Homer* (22.35 Dorandi), and Hazzard (2000, 46) speculates about the influence of the figure of Telemachus upon Philadelphus (cf. further 23n., 34–35n., 62–64n., 117n.).

The motif of bringing one's desires to fulfillment (τελεῖν) is a very important one in the discourse of Ptolemaic kingship; cf. Callim. *H.* 1.57, ἀλλ' ἔτι παιδνὸς ἐὼν ἐφράσσαο πάντα τέλεια; 87–88, ἑσπέριος κεῖνός γε τελεῖ τά κεν ἦρι νοήσηι· | ἑσπέριος τὰ μέγιστα, τὰ μείονα δ', εὖτε νοήσηι. These passages are not close enough to T. to make a connection necessary (pace, for example, Meincke 1965, 183), though it might be thought likely. An Egyptian parallel for Callimachus's verses has been identified in a text praising Ramses II: "You are like Re in all things which you have done; whatever your heart wishes, happens. If you conceive a plan in the night, in the morning it is already brought to accomplishment" (Assmann 1975, no. 237.1–4 = Davies 1997, 237; cf. Reinsch-Werner 1976, 53), and it is clear that this was a prominent pharaonic idea (cf. Lichtheim 1973, 119 [Sesostris III], "What my heart plans is done by my arm"; Peden 1994, 121 [Ramses III]; Posener 1960, 42–49; Koenen 1977, 59–60). Isis declares: "Whatever I decide, this is also brought to fulfilment (τελεῖται)" (1.46 Totti); and another hymn to the goddess declares: "Whatever comes forth from her mouth is accomplished immediately" (Zabkar 1988, 69).

μέγα ἔργον: Cf. 6n. The Homeric phrasing establishes Soter as an epic figure, just as his son is to be.

14–15 Λαγείδας: The expected Λαγίδας with short middle syllable cannot be used in hexameters (cf. Callim. fr. 384.40; Pfeiffer on fr. 734).

ὅτε: Cf. above, p. 56.

φρεσὶν ἐγκατάθοιτο: The image of laying something down in a store suggests the godlike king as a source of wise thought to which only he has access. Like Zeus's (*Il.* 1.5), Soter's βουλή, a word found only here in T., is both private and something within his capabilities alone.

16–33 A picture of Olympian feasting, which owes some of its tone and position in the poem to the opening of the *Homeric Hymn to Apollo*, a poem that will be a very important model later in *EP.* In the archaic hymn, the gods feast, sitting on θρόνοι, with Apollo's parents, Leto and Zeus, sitting beside each other; Leto relieves Apollo of his bow and quiver and leads her son to a seat (cf. 17.30–33); Zeus greets his son, offers him nectar (cf. 17.29) in a golden cup, and Leto "rejoices" (cf. v. 23) in her great son (*Hymn. Hom. Ap.* 2–13; cf. also 204–6, the pleasure Zeus and Leto take in their son). The representation of a peaceful symposium, quite the opposite of the drunken and murderous brawls with which Greek tradition often associated Macedonia, promotes the civilized Hellenic values that Ptolemy sought to promulgate as characteristics of his rule (cf. Murray 1996). Here, even Heracles behaves well (28–33n.).

16 τῆνον: Cf. above, p. 55.

πατήρ: That is, Zeus (cf. 13n.). Following so soon after the patronymic *Λαγείδας*, "father" perhaps hints that, like his companions on Olympus, Heracles and Alexander, Soter had two "fathers," one of whom was Zeus. Soter's quasi-divine status has in fact been established both by his "father" and his son (v. 123). For representations of Soter with the attributes of Zeus cf. Tondriau 1948b, 128–29.

μακάρεσσι . . . ὁμότιμον: Soter is an *ἀνήρ* (v. 15) but has been made "equal in honor to the blessed immortals." At one level he is like a positive version of Tantalus, upon whom the gods bestowed singular honor and wealth and with whom they dined, but who then abused their favor (Pind. *Ol.* 1.54–66). In another way the honor that Zeus, here acting in his Hesiodic role of distributor of *τιμαί*, has bestowed upon Soter reflects the kinds of honors that Soter and other early Hellenistic kings in fact received in their lifetimes: *ἰσόθεοι τιμαί* are a standard part of the system of rewards with which cities thanked and/or sought to conciliate powerful rulers (cf. Habicht 1970, 196–97). Soter had received such honors from the Island League (*SIG* 390), and Philadelphus was similarly honored "equally to a god" by the Byzantines (Dion. Byz., *GGM* II 34; Habicht 1970, 116). It is this intellectual structure, as much as reference to specific details of cult—for example, the placing of Soter's statue as *σύνναος* in the shrines of other gods (cf. 17n., 50n., 121 ff., with nn.)—that informs T.'s image.

ὁμότιμος occurs in Homer only at *Il.*15.186, where Poseidon claims to be *ὁμότιμος* with Zeus. It is attested as a court title in Persia (Xen. *Cyr.* 2.1.9, 7.5.85), and *ὁμότιμοι τοῖς συγγενέσι*, "of equal rank with [the king's] relations," is known as a grade at the Ptolemaic court, but only from the second century B.C.E. on (Mooren 1975, 232–33), and it is perhaps improbable that T.

wishes to suggest that Soter has been introduced as a "lower-grade" divinity.

17 χρύσεος: Treatment of the first syllable as short (cf. 18.28; McLennan on Callim. *H.* 1.48) may have originated in "misunderstood" Homeric synizesis—in other words, χρυσέωι regarded as an anapaest rather than as a spondee.

θρόνος: The transmitted δόμος is very awkward. In the *Iliad* the gods do have individual δώματα, built by Hephaestus, to which they retire after feasting (1.605–8); we also hear of Hera's own θάλαμος (14.166–68), and this spatial arrangement is followed in the Olympian opening scene of *Arg.* 3 (cf. 3.9, θαλαμόνδε κιοῦσαι [sc. Hera and Athena]), where Aphrodite has a μέγα δῶμα (3.36). Such palaces and chambers were no doubt golden (cf. *Il.* 4.2; Pind. *Nem.* 10.88), and Pind. *Isthm.* 4.76–78 describes the Olympian life of Heracles in a passage that is very suggestive for *EP*: νῦν δὲ παρ᾽ Αἰγιόχωι κάλλιστον ὄλβον | ἀμφέπων ναίει, τετίμα- | ταί τε πρὸς ἀθανάτων φίλος, Ἥβαν τ᾽ ὀπυίει, | χρυσέων οἴκων ἄναξ καὶ γαμβρὸς Ἥρας. If δόμος is retained, the *figura etymologica* (δόμος ... δέδμηται) would find parallels in *Arg.* 3.36–37 and perhaps Callim. fr. 50.81 M. Nevertheless, δόμος ἐν Διὸς οἴκωι is a very unhappy juxtaposition, even if ἐν Διὸς οἴκωι just means "on Olympus" (cf., for example, Pind. *Ol.* 1.42 [Poseidon takes Pelops], ὕπατον εὐρυτίμου ποτὶ δῶμα Διός), and the clear implication of vv. 19–20 is that seating arrangements at the (perpetual) Olympian banquet are being described. As in the *Iliad*, therefore, the gods feast in Zeus's palace, where each god will have a place (*Il.* 1.533–34, 8.438–43; cf. *Hymn. Hom. Aphr.* 203–4; Callim. *H.* 3.168–69), and after dinner Heracles is escorted back to another δῶμα (cf. 29n.). T. has sharpened the Homeric picture somewhat by insisting on the fixed and stable seating arrangements where each god has an (unmovable) chair (cf. v. 18, δέδμηται; v. 21, ἵδρυται). Some have understood ἐν Διὸς οἴκωι to refer not to Olympus but to an Alexandrian temple of Zeus (so LSJ s.v. δόμος I.2, interpreted as a "chamber" within the temple; and Rice 1983, 117, reading θρόνος); that T.'s Olympus should be made to resemble an Alexandrian temple of Zeus is a plausible literary conceit, but there is no evidence for this view, and it is not easy to reconcile with vv. 22 ff.

In Homer, Zeus has a golden θρόνος on Olympus (*Il.* 8.442; cf. *Aen.* 10.116–17), Hera bribes Sleep with such a gift (*Il.*14.238–39), and χρυσόθρονος is a standard epithet of goddesses (cf. further Braswell on Pind. *Pyth.* 4.260–61[c]; West 1997, 112). Anti-Alexander traditions reported that the great ruler conducted business in Babylon on "a golden throne and silver-footed couches" (Ephippus, *FGrHist* 126 F4) and that he slept on a golden couch (Polycleitos, *FGrHist* 128 F1). Thrones are important symbols of power in both Macedonian and Egyptian traditions (cf. Quint. Curt. 10.6.4 [the death of Alexander]; Thompson 2000, 378–79; and for Philadelphus, Roeder 1959, 116), and in the "Grand Procession" (above, p. 2) there were chryselephantine thrones (cf. 123–25n.), one of which was "the throne of Ptolemy Soter" (Ath. 5.202a–b; cf. Rice 1983, 116–17). Alexander's corpse is said by later sources to have been placed by Soter in a golden sarcophagus (Strabo 17.1.8); if the same was done by Philadelphus for his father, the golden thrones of the afterlife will have been foreshadowed in contemporary royal death-ritual.

18 φίλα εἰδώς: "With friendly feelings [toward Soter]" (cf. *Od.* 3.277 [Nestor and Agamemnon], φίλα εἰδότες ἀλλήλοισιν; LSJ s.v. οἶδα B1). Alexander's favor will be not just the result of the closeness of Alexander and Soter while the former was alive, but will also reflect Soter's establishment of the cult of Alexander in the city named after him (cf. 19n.) and the Ptolemies' control of Alexander's body. Thus T. represents Alexander himself acknowledging the Ptolemies as his true heirs. For the "Homeric" hiatus cf. 25.37; *Od.* 3.277 (above), 15.557; above, p. 70.

19 Cf. Stat. *Achil.* 1.713–17, *ambiguo sub pectore pridem | uerso quid . . . Baccheaque terga mitrasque | huc tuleris uarioque aspersas nebridas auro. | hisne grauem Priamo Phrygibusque armabis Achillem?*

ἐδρίαει: An epic verb to match an epic practice: Hellenistic scholarship was familiar with the fact that Homeric heroes sat, rather than reclined, at dinner (cf. Ath. 1.17 f.). Alexander was believed sometimes to have imitated this tradition (Ath. loc. cit. = Douris, *FGrHist* 76 F49); T.'s Olympus thus looks very Macedonian.

Πέρσαισι βαρὺς θεὸς: Cf. 3.15, *νῦν ἔγνων τὸν Ἔρωτα· βαρὺς θεός.* Alexander's destruction of the Persian empire is stressed, not just because this was the central achievement of his career and at the heart of his divine status in the empire, but because the "Persians" are no less the standard enemy of Egyptian tradition than of Greek. The Ptolemies continued, for example, the pharaonic tradition of proclaiming that they had recovered for Egypt temple statues stolen by the hated Persians (cf., for Philadelphus, the "Pithom Stele" = Roeder 1959, 119; and for Euergetes, *OGIS* 54.21; Winnicki 1994; Hölbl 2001, 81).

Alexander was a θεός in Alexandria—Soter had established the dynastic cult in his honor (cf. Fraser 1972, 1: 215–26)—and so θεός cannot be limited solely to Πέρσαισι, "a god for the Persians" (as, for example, Meincke 1965, 98; Levi 1975, 203).

αἰολομίτρας: A Homeric *hapax* (*Il.* 5.707), "with glittering girdle [i.e., front armor]" (LSJ), is here revised to refer to the headband or diadem adopted by Alexander, which subsequently became a badge of power for Hellenistic kings of all dynasties (cf. Callim. *H.* 4.166–67; Phoenix fr. 1.24 Powell; Ritter 1965; Brandenburg, 1966, 154–59; Smith 1988, 34–38; Stewart 1993, 352–57). The origin of Alexander's innovation is disputed—one tradition has it as Persian (Diod. Sic. 17.77.5; Curt. Ruf. 6.6.4)—but some connection with Dionysus, whether constructed before or after Alexander's adoption of the diadem, seems certain. Some indeed traced the royal diadem back to a *mitra* invented by Dionysus as a protection against hangovers, from which the god had the epithet μιτρηφόρος (Diod. Sic. 4.4.4). At all periods Dionysus is portrayed wearing a headband (cf. *LIMC*); the Dionysiac *mitra* seems to have been worn on the forehead below the hairline, whereas the royal diadem was worn farther up in the hair, but certain coin portraits of Alexander, minted under Soter, show him wearing the Dionysiac band (cf. Stewart 1993, 233–39). Although Dionysus may have been an influential model for the world-conquering Alexander (cf., for instance, Bosworth 1996, 119–27), the god's importance for the Ptolemaic royal house certainly intensified from Philadelphus on; in the Dionysiac section of the "Grand Procession" the statues of Alexander and Ptolemy wore golden ivy crowns (Ath. 5.201d), perhaps evoking the diadem. Thus Alexander here takes a role elsewhere played by Dionysus, namely, that of Heracles' drinking partner (cf. *LIMC* s.v. Herakles 1500–10; Lada-Richards 1999, 201–4).

αἰολο- is a productive element for Homeric compound adjectives, and αἰόλος itself is commonly glossed as ποικίλος (*LfgrE* s.v.). Gow indeed took it here as "particoloured": Demetrius Poliorcetes is reported to have worn a "gold-spangled *mitra* with purple *kausia*" (Douris, *FGrHist* 76 F14), and Curtius (6.6.4) reports that Alexander's diadem was purple and white, in imitation of the Persian king; other sources also give the headwear of Alexander and the successors as the Macedonian felt *kausia* worn with a headband around it (Ephippus, *FGrHist* 126 F5; Plut. *Ant.* 54.5). It is perhaps less important that Curtius is mistaken—the diadem was white—than that such associations seem out of place here. The meaning of the epithet must remain uncertain, though there is some attraction in the idea that the reference is to the "dancing" ends of the headband (αἰόλος, "darting, quick-moving"), which hung over the neck and would move as the king exerted himself (so Rossi 1989). In view of the close association of the *mitra* with Alexander and Dionysus, αἰολομίτραις or -ηις (cf. *Pap.Ant.*), referring to the Persians, is an unconvincing alternative.

20 ἀντία δ': Adverbial, "facing them."

Ἡρακλῆος: Cf. 13n. The Argead royal house of Macedonia traced itself back to the Argive Temenidai, that is, the descendants of Temenos, whose ancestor was Heracles. For Alexander, Heracles was, with Achilles, the most important model after whom he fashioned himself (cf. Huttner 1997, 86–123); Heracles was clearly important also in Ptolemaic ideology (*Idyll* 24; Huttner 1997, 124–45), though his cult had little prominence in Alexandria, and only one representation of Philadelphus as Heracles has been found (Kyrieleis 1975, Taf. 9; Stewart 1993, 261). His prominence in *EP* is due in part to the fact that he is the model par excellence for a great "hero" whose prowess has earned him a place in heaven; in a poem that is centrally concerned with what it might mean to be ἡμίθεος or μακάρεσσι ὁμότιμος, Heracles, whom

Pindar strikingly designates ἥρως θεός (*Nem.* 3.22), is the category-breaking figure by which all others are judged. Herodotus's discussion of the cults of Heracles throughout the Mediterranean shows the centrality of Heracles to this discussion: "I think those Greeks act most correctly who have established and maintain double temples of Heracles (Ἡράκλεια), and sacrifice (θύουσι) to one as to an immortal and give him the name Olympian, and to the other they make offerings (ἐναγίζουσι) as to a hero" (2.44.5, where see Lloyd's notes; and West on Hes. *Theog.* 947–55).

κενταυροφόνοιο: Heracles is associated with two "centaur-killing" stories. He killed Nessos during the centaur's attempt to rape his wife, Deianeira, who herself is part of the Ptolemaic royal line as mother of Hyllos (Satyros, *FGrHist* 631 F1), and he was involved in a drunken fracas with all of the centaurs in the cave of Pholos, during or after which he accidentally killed Cheiron (cf. 7.149–50, with Gow and Hunter ad loc.). It is this latter story that is evoked by ἀηδών . . . κενταυροκτόνος of the Sirens at Lycoph. *Alex.* 670. Both Heracles and Alexander (like Ptolemy) spread civilized Hellenic virtues by the defeat of the forces of darkness, whether they be Persians or centaurs (who are frequently cast in this role in monumental sculpture, as on the Parthenon, the Zeus temple at Olympia, and the Apollo temple at Bassae); it might be thought that the Nessos story sets forth this lesson more clearly than the sad fate of Cheiron, but centaurs are paradigmatic disturbers of banquets (cf. the story of the battle of the centaurs and the Lapiths), and it is the blessings of the peaceful symposium that are on show on this Olympus.

21 στερεοῖο . . . ἀδάμαντος: Heracles' seat reflects himself (cf. 13.5, Ἀμφιτρύωνος ὁ χαλκεοκάρδιος υἱός) and is strong enough to hold his great bulk. "Adamant" was a wondrously hard metal of the poetic imagination, used particularly for the attributes of gods (cf. Troxler 1964, 19–21; West on Hes. *Theog.* 161).

τετυγμένα ἐξ: For the hiatus at the "bucolic diaeresis" cf. 3.30, πάχει ἐξεμαράνθη; 24.135, τετυγμένα ἀγχόθι πατρός; Gow on 2.83.

22 A reworking of *Od.* 11.602–3 (Heracles), αὐτὸς δὲ μετ᾽ ἀθανάτοισι θεοῖσι | τέρπεται ἐν θαλίης καὶ ἔχει καλλίσφυρον Ἥβην (cf. *Arg.* 1.1319 [Glaukos prophesies Heracles' future], ναίειν δ᾽ ἀθανάτοισι συνέστιον; Hor. *Carm.* 4.8.29–30, *sic Iouis interest* | *optatis epulis impiger Hercules*). The eternal "symposium of the gods" is of particular interest to Heracles, who has a great love of food and drink. For the iconography of Heracles as symposiast cf. *LIMC* s.v. Herakles 1483–1523.

Οὐρανίδηισι: "Dwellers in heaven" (cf. Pind. *Pyth.* 4.194, with Braswell's note), rather than specifically "sons of Ouranos," though the form emphasizes the grandeur of the divine company that Heracles and Alexander now keep. This word occurs in this verse position at Callim. *H.* 1.3, a poem with close links to *EP* (above, p. 5).

23 There is a close verbal model in *Il.* 2.665–66, οἱ ἄλλοι | υἱέες υἱωνοί τε βίης Ἡρακληείης; T.'s four-word *spondeiazon* (cf. 60–61n.) imitates the metrical pattern of the Homeric verse. T. also has in mind, however, *Od.* 24.514–15 (Laertes watching Telemachos and Odysseus), τίς νύ μοι ἡμέρη ἥδε, θεοὶ φίλοι; ἦ μάλα χαίρω· | υἱός θ᾽ υἱωνός τ᾽ ἀρετῆς πέρι δῆριν ἔχουσι. Once again (cf. 13n.) the family of Odysseus functions as a paradigm for the Ptolemies, here in the matter of *arete*.

χαίρων . . . περιώσιον: Cf. *Hymn. Hom. Pan* 41 (Hermes rejoicing at the sight of his son, Pan), χαῖρεν δὲ νόωι περιώσια δαίμων.

24 The true epic mark of divinity is to be "immortal and ageless" (ἀθάνατος καὶ ἀγήρως) forever; the story of Eos and Tithonus (*Hymn. Hom. Aphr.* 218–40) shows, however, that in the case of those who make the transition from earthly to divine status, the two qualities could be granted separately by Zeus. Heracles' resistance to debilitating old age is secure, for he has actually married Hebe, the "prime of life" (cf. Hes. *Theog.* 955, Heracles lives forever on Olympus ἀπήμαντος καὶ ἀγήραος; see further 33n.). Alexander died young, and the preservation of his body at Alexandria might well be represented poetically as the granting of eternal agelessness, whatever Greek or Egyptian methods of preservation were actually employed on the corpse (cf. Hunter 1996, 132–34). When he died in 282, Soter was an old man (eighty-four, according to Lucian *Macr.* 12); T. may just mean that Soter will not die (v. 25), but it is much more likely that the Olympian Soter has been returned to prime adulthood, so that he resembles Alexander in more than just divine privilege.

σφεων: An epic form found elsewhere only at 22.10 (where see Sens's note); in both places it is scanned as a monosyllable with synizesis.

μελέων ἐξείλετο γῆρας: A close revision of *Od.* 11.200–201 (a passage about the miseries of old age and sorrowing for one's children), νοῦσος . . . μελέων ἐξείλετο θυμόν.

25 καλεῦνται: Cf. above, p. 56.

ἑοὶ: This third-person possessive is not found in the bucolics or mimes (cf. v. 39; 12.33, 22.147, 24.59); as a second-person it is confined to 17.50 and 22.173 (cf. Rengakos 1993, 117; above, p. 59).

νέποδες: "Descendants," a word of high Hellenistic poetry originating in a Homeric *hapax* at *Od.* 4.404, φῶκαι νέποδες καλῆς ἁλοσύδνης (cf. Callim. fr. 222; Pfeiffer on fr. 533; Livrea on *Arg.* 4.1745; Rengakos 1994, 117).

γεγαῶτες: Such epic perfects occur in T. elsewhere only at 22.176.

26–27 Successive *spondeiazontes* give great emphasis to Heracles' place in the joint lineage of Alexander and Soter; the anaphora of ἄμφω . . . ἀμφότεροι (cf. 8.3–4) stresses that Soter belongs to the same family as Alexander and thus was his true and rightful heir. As in a sequentially ordered prose genealogy, we move from a "descendant of Heracles" back to Heracles himself.

ἄμφω: Elsewhere in T. this form is always nominative or accusative, and, like the dual in general, it is largely restricted to the "epic" poems (cf. Hatzikosta 1981); for ἄμφω in the oblique cases cf. *Arg.* 1.165, 1011, 1169. At 2.143 and 6.3 ἄμφω emphasizes the "unity" of a pair of individuals.

σφιν: Elsewhere in T. only at 13.34 (where see Hunter's note), 16.40, and *Epigr.* 13.4.

Ἡρακλείδας: A surprise for Ἡρακλῆς, particularly after ὁ καρτερός, which has a clear epic resonance (cf. 22.140, with Sens's note; Campbell on Quint. Smyrn. 12.315); at 25.176 Heracles' slaying of the Nemean lion is a χειρῶν καρτερὸν ἔργον. The legendary first king of the Macedonian royal house was Karanos, a tenth-generation descendant of Heracles (cf. Theopompus, *FGrHist* 115 F393; Satyros, *FGrHist* 631 F1; Diod. Sic. 7.15; Plut. *Alex.* 2.1). Karanos is very probably T.'s "mighty descendant of Heracles," though Heracles'

· son Hyllos (so Bousquet 1988, 40 n. 53) or even an unknown (to us) alternative cannot be ruled out (cf. Huttner 1997, 142–43).

ἀριθμεῦνται: Cf. Men. fr. 835.5 K-A, ἀριθμοῦσίν τε τοὺς πάππους ὅσοι. For the form cf. above, p. 56.

ἐς ἔσχατον Ἡρακλῆα: Heracles was perhaps the favorite "ancestor" for elite families to claim; and Pl. *Tht.* 175a comments on this habit (cf. Xen. *Ages.* 1.2, ἔτι καὶ νῦν τοῖς προγόνοις ὀνομαζομένοις ἀπομνημονεύεται, ὁπόστος ἀφ᾽ Ἡρακλέους ἐγένετο κτλ; Pl. *Alc.* I 120e; above, p. 12, on Pl. *Lysis*). The family of Attalos offers another such example from Hellenistic royalty (cf. Nicander fr. 104). The unusual ἔσχατος (cf. *Aen.* 7.49, *tu sanguinis ultimus auctor*) is probably influenced by the use of this word to indicate the final element of a series or place on a journey (LSJ s.v. I.4).

28–33 In an Olympian version of the *komos* scenes so familiar in vase painting (cf. Lissarrague 1990, 29–31), Alexander and Soter escort Heracles, not on a drunken revel in pursuit of an adulterous affair, but to the loving arms of his wife; though echoes of the traditional Heracles may still be heard (note κεκορημένος), the Olympian Heracles is now a reformed and much quieter character. Zeus-Hera, Heracles-Hebe, and Soter-Berenice are all divine paradigms for the marriage of Philadelphus and Arsinoe: in these marriages the mutual affection and desire of the wedding night continues endlessly. That Heracles is taken to Hebe's δῶμα (cf. 17n.), rather than "his own," not merely evokes the *komos* pattern but also probably reflects the fact that, as a daughter of Hera, she had a residence or chamber on Olympus before Heracles' arrival (cf. perhaps 24.169).

28 δαίτηθεν: A *hapax* taken from *Od.* 10.216–17, ὡς δ᾽ ὅτ᾽ ἂν ἀμφὶ ἄνακτα κύνες δαίτηθεν ἰόντα | σαίνωσ᾽ · αἰεὶ γάρ τε φέρει μειλίγματα

θυμοῦ. The transference of this image from dogs fawning on their master to Alexander and Soter fussing around the tipsy Heracles is a light touch in keeping with the tone of the whole passage.

29 A mannered verse consisting of a prepositional phrase and two noun-adjective pairs in the genitive, chiastically arranged; rhyme links the closing noun with the adjective that closes the first half of the verse (cf. 24.9; Hunter on 7.62) in such a way that εὐόδμοιο colors ἀλόχοιο as well as its own noun. Hebe was certainly "fragrant" as well as "dear" (cf. vv. 32, 37 [Berenice's fragrance]). The breach of "Naeke's Law" (above p. 68; Hunter on 1.130) is a weak one, as ἐς δῶμ᾽ may be treated as a single unit.

νέκταρος: The traditional drink of the Olympians (cf. *Il.* 1.598; *Hymn. Hom. Aphr.* 206; Hor. *Carm.* 3.3.12; Onians 1954, 296–99). For the iconography of Heracles after too much to drink cf. *LIMC* s.v. Herakles 875–910.

30 To be entrusted with Heracles' weapons is a mark of singular closeness indeed (cf. *Hymn. Hom. Ap.* 6–9 (Leto and Apollo, a passage in T.'s mind here; cf. 17–33n.). On vase paintings, Heracles' bow and quiver are normally hung up or lying against the couch when the hero is at a symposium.

ἔδωκεν: Aorist of repeated action.

ὑπωλένιον: Best explained as "which hangs/is carried under the arm," that is, a kind of fabricated "formulaic" epithet (for a noun that does not have one in archaic epic), rather than one particularly appropriate for the moment of narration. The quiver is normally slung over the back and hangs down below the elbow; cf. Pind. *Ol.* 2.83–84, πολλά μοι ὑπ᾽ ἀγκῶνος ὠκέα βέλη | ἔνδον ἐντὶ φαρέτρας, where a scholiast (I p. 97 Drachmann) quotes this Theocritean phrase to illustrate ὑπ' ἀγκῶνος. Another scholiast on the same Pindaric passage notes that this mode of carrying the quiver is typical of Scythians, whereas Cretans carry it "over the shoulders" (κατὰ τῶν ὤμων); artistic portrayals of Heracles do indeed show (broadly) two alternative positions—either roughly upright on the back or slung low across the back, in which case the top of the quiver may indeed seem to be "under the elbow" (cf., for example, *LIMC* V2 s.v. Herakles 2457, 2822, etc.). At 13.56 T. gives Herakles a "Scythian" bow.

31 Probably a principal model for Virg. *Ecl.* 5.90, *[pedum] formosum paribus nodis atque aere.* Heracles is given both wooden and, though more rarely, metal clubs in art and literature, though nowhere else one of iron (for which cf. *Il.* 7.141); in *Arg.* he has a χαλκοβαρὲς ῥόπαλον. (Cf. further Vox 1989.) The knots (ὄζοι) are a common feature in art: here the surface of the club has been fashioned (κεχαραγμένον, lit. "scratched, worked") uneven, thus leaving raised "knots."

σκύταλον: Not the usual word for Heracles' club (ῥόπαλον, κορύνη), but cf. Pind. *Ol.* 9.30.

32 ἀμβρόσιον: "Fragrant (with feminine scents)" (cf. *Il.* 14.170–72, where Hera, preparing to seduce Zeus, cleanses herself with ambrosia and anoints her body ἐλαίωι | ἀμβροσίωι ἑδανῶι, τό ῥά οἱ τεθυωμένον ἦεν; *LfgrE* s.v. BI.1; Onians 1954, 292–95). At one level the word varies εὐώδης, a standard epic epithet of θάλαμος (*Il.* 3.382, etc.), but the connection with "ambrosia," the sweet-smelling Olympian oil, is still strongly felt after νέκταρος in v. 29.

λευκοσφύρου: In archaic epic Hebe is standardly καλλίσφυρος (*Od.* 11.603; *Hymn. Hom. Heracles* [15].8; Hes. *Theog.* 950). -σφυρος was a productive suffix, though "white-ankled" is not found elsewhere.

33 ὅπλα καὶ αὐτὸν κτλ: Despite Hesiod fr. 33(a).28–29 (Pericly-menos), οὐδ' ἔδδεισε Διὸς ταλασίφρονα παῖδα, | αὐτὸν καὶ κλυτὰ τόξα, this is an amusing pairing, perhaps suggestive of ὅπλοις αὐτοῖς, "weapons and all," and one pointed by the slight zeugma with ἄγουσι (one would expect φέρειν of the weapons). The zeugma highlights the fact that the tipsy Heracles would be unable to make it unaided to Hebe. Representations of Heracles and Hebe together regularly show the ὅπλα, even in bedroom settings (cf. *LIMC* s.v. Herakles 3340).

γενειήταν: In different contexts a beard may function as a sign of physical, social, or intellectual maturity (cf. 10.40, 14.28; *Od.* 18.269), but here it is likely to be one sign that, despite his marriage to Ἥβη, Heracles is on Olympus rather older than the eternally young Alexander and Soter. He has resigned his role to them and takes pleasure in their youth (v. 23), while he devotes himself to banqueting. Hellenistic art regularly portrays Heracles as a bearded man, past his prime, whereas Alexander and Soter (like Philadelphus himself) are standardly clean-shaven (cf. Kyrieleis 1975, 4–20; Stewart 1993 passim; I withdraw the interpretation of γενειήταν offered at Hunter 1996, 12).

Διὸς υἱόν forms a ring with ἐκ πατέρων (v. 13) to enclose the verse-paragraph.

34–40 For all that the picture of Berenice has been fashioned to accord with particular Ptolemaic themes, she also embodies very traditional values. The passage may be instructively compared with the description of the only type of woman to win the praise of the archaic iambist Semonides of Amorgos, namely, the "bee woman": "Under her management her husband's livelihood flourishes and increases, and she grows old in love with a loving husband, the mother of a handsome and distinguished family (φίλη δὲ σὺν φιλέοντι γηράσκει πόσει | τεκοῦσα καλὸν κὠνομάκλυτον γένος). She stands out among all women and a divine grace surrounds her. She takes no pleasure in sitting among women in places where they talk about sex. Such women are the best and the most sensible whom Zeus bestows as a favor on men" (fr. 7.85–93, trans. Gerber).

34–35 οἷα δ' picks up οἷος μέν (v. 13) but perhaps also suggests the Hesiodic ἢ οἵη formula by which the *Catalogue of Women* was structured.

πινυταῖσι: In the *Odyssey* a standard epithet for Penelope, thus continuing the Odyssean paradigm for the Ptolemaic family (cf. 13n.).

περικλειτά: This form occurs first here and in an epigram on T., *AP* 9.434.3 (= *Epigr.* 27.3 Gow, third century?), where we need not assume a borrowing from this passage. Homer has περικλυτός, and Ibycus (*PMG* 282.2) and Apollonius περικλεής.

θηλυτέρηις: Archaic epic uses θηλυτέρη as an epithet of γυνή, but here the adjectival form is used substantivally (a not uncommon phenomenon in Hellenistic epic). There seems to be no certain earlier example with this word; ἁ θήλεια at 15.145, whatever the tone, is unlikely to be epic in flavor. For this form of the dative plural cf. above, p. 58.

ὄφελος μέγα γειναμένοισι: It was a standard Greek idea that children were supposed to "benefit" their parents, whether by looking after them in their old age or by increasing the wealth of the

oikos (cf. Ar. *Thesm.* 469, οὕτως ὀναίμην τῶν τέκνων; Philemon fr.
143 K-A, ἔτεκές με, μῆτερ, καὶ γένοιτό σοι τέκνων | ὄνησις, ὥσπερ
καὶ δίκαιόν ἐστί σοι). The duty of care for one's parents is also a
standard motif of Egyptian wisdom and afterlife texts (cf. the boast
of a pharaonic courtier of the early first millennium: "No one re-
viled my parents on account of me, | They were much honoured
owing to my worth. | They found me helpful while they were on
earth, | And I supply them in the desert vale," Lichtheim 1980,
15). Pharaohs were always of service to their divine "parents" (cf.
Peden 1994, 153 [Ramses IV]: "I am beneficial to you [Osiris] like
your son Horus"). Berenice has indeed "benefited" her parents,
both by the "royal" marriage she made and by the glorious grand-
children (Philadelphus and Arsinoe) she bore for them. Here again
Berenice uncannily foreshadows the virtues of her daughter, Ar-
sinoe, who certainly was "a great blessing to her parents." (Cf. fur-
ther 123–25n. below.)

Berenice was the daughter of a Macedonian noblewoman,
Antigone (cf. v. 61), and (perhaps, cf. Σ 34) a Cyrenean called Ma-
gas. The apparently pointed allusion to Berenice's parents may
have a political significance at which we can only guess; by her
first husband (a Macedonian called Philip) Berenice was mother
of Magas I of Cyrene, who was probably estranged from, if not
actually at war with, Philadelphus at the time of *EP* (cf. 87n.).

36–37 Two more carefully wrought verses where style and sub-
ject match: Aphrodite is described in a grand hymnic periphra-
sis, and the chiastic arrangement of nouns and adjectives in v. 37
juxtaposes the feminine qualities of Berenice and Aphrodite to em-
phasize their similarity. At the first level these verses are not so
much in fact about Berenice's deification (for which see 50n.), but

about how Berenice's beauty and grace were like an emanation from Aphrodite herself (cf. τῶι, "therefore," v. 38); she was in the truest sense ἐπαφρόδιτος (though there is no reason, pace Tondriau 1948a, 14 n. 1, to think that T. alludes to a cult title Ἐπαφροδίτη). Nevertheless, the ideas of divinity and of divine beauty easily slide into one another, as the similarity of these verses to the description of how Aphrodite made Berenice immortal at 15.108 shows: ἀμβροσίαν ἐς στῆθος ἀποστάξασα γυναικός. While on earth Berenice was like an earthly version of Aphrodite, after death she has come to share the goddess's cult and prerogatives (vv. 50–52). It can hardly be doubted that Berenice was indeed closely associated in her lifetime with Aphrodite, though some of the emphasis that T. gives to this here and elsewhere (15.106–8; the lost *Berenike?*) may be a retrojection from the very close association of Arsinoe and Aphrodite, as part of the fashioning of the first two Ptolemies and their wives as absolutely identical pairs. The link between Berenice and "the queenly daughter of Dione" is here reinforced by the fact that both are presented in relation to their parents. For possible representations on coins of Berenice as Aphrodite cf. Koch 1924, 72–76 (and cf. further Visser 1938, 80; Gutzwiller 1992, 364–65; Weber 1993, 253–54).

Κύπρον: Ptolemaic possession of Cyprus, finally established by Soter in 294, meant that the Ptolemies almost "possessed" the island's goddess. For Cyprus under the Ptolemies cf. Bagnall 1976, 38–79.

εὐώδη picks up the fragrances of heaven (vv. 29, 32) to mark Berenice as "another" Hebe, just as Soter was "another" Heracles.

ῥαδινάς: A common epithet in high poetry for Aphrodite or parts of her body (cf. Hes. *Theog.* 195; Sappho fr. 102.2 Voigt; *Arg.* 3.106 [below]).

ἐσεμάξατο: Perhaps "wiped," rather than just "impressed" (ἐσ-μάσσειν). The closest parallel is a fragmentary epitaph from Priene (Gaertringen 1906, no. 287 = *SGO* 0/01/03): Ἡγησὼ φθιμ[ ]ης ῥοδόπηχυς ι Ἠὼς μαξαμέ[ ]σατο· ι καὶ χάρις ἔστιλ[βεν κτλ. Here too divine "impressing" yields female grace. The idea is perhaps of a marvelous fluid passing from immortal to mortal (cf. Crinagoras, *APlan*. 273 = *GP* 2070–77 on Apollo's gifts to a doctor: αὐτός σοι Φοίβοιο πάις λαθικηδέα τέχνης ι ἰδμοσύνην, πανάκηι χεῖρα λιπηνάμενος, ι Πρηξαγόρη, στέρνοις ἐνεμάξατο); as Apollo's hair drips Πανάκεια (Callim. *H*. 2.38–41), and the Graces can immortalize Callimachus's poems by wiping their oil-rich hands upon them (fr. 9.13–14 M), so Aphrodite passed on to Berenice beauty and the power to arouse affection. *Arg.* 3.106 (Hera and Aphrodite), τὴν δ' Ἥρη ῥαδινῆς ἐπεμάσσατο χειρός, is in language and subject close enough to the present verse to suggest some connection between them, although Apollonius's verb is presumably ἐπιμαίεσθαι, rather than (the unattested) ἐπιμάσσεσθαι.

38–39 These verses suggest two models for Berenice and Soter: (1) Arete and Alcinous, the rulers of Homer's Phaeacians; cf. *Od.* 7.66–71: "Arete, whom Alcinous made his wife and honoured ever since as no other wife in the world is honoured, of all wives who at present (νῦν γε) rule a household under their husband's eye. Such has always been, and such still is, the honour paid to Arete by Alcinous and by her children and by the people, etc." (trans. Shewring, adapted). *Od.* 7.66–77 as a whole seems to look forward uncannily to the Ptolemaic themes of intrafamilial affection and the power of great women. Through reminiscence of this passage of the *Odyssey* T. forges one more bond between the current rulers and their parents, for elsewhere Arete and Alcinous, whom Hesiod (at least) made brother and sister (fr. 222 M-W), foreshadow Arsinoe and Philadelphus themselves: the Phaeacians lie behind the praise of Ptolemaic sea power at vv. 90–91 (see n. ad loc.), and when in *Idyll* 15 Gorgo and Praxinoa gape at the marvels of the Ptolemaic palace, they play out a low-life version of Odysseus looking in wonder at the marvels of Alcinous's palace (*Od.* 7.81–135). The Alcinous and Arete of *Arg.* 4 may also be poetic analogues of the brother-sister rulers in Alexandria (cf. Hunter 1993, 161–62). (2) Alcmene and Amphitryon, the parents of Heracles; cf. Hes. *Scut.* 3–10: "Alcmene . . . surpassed all human women (γυναικῶν . . . θηλυτεράων) in appearance and stature; in intelligence, she was not rivaled by any woman born of mortal parents. From her head and dark eyes wafted such beauty as comes from golden Aphrodite. She honored her husband in her heart as no mortal woman has yet done." This paradigm figures Philadelphus as a new Heracles, like Alexander and Soter before him, but particularly suggests an "equation" between Soter and the Olympian Soter, namely, Zeus, the "real" father of Heracles.

Both a Greek and an Egyptian background may be invoked for this emphasis upon marital devotion (cf. Koenen 1983, 160–65; Schmitt 1991). In the great inscribed Isis-text of self-presentation (1 Totti), the goddess proclaims ἐγὼ στέργεσθαι γυναῖκας ὑπὸ ἀνδρῶν ἠνάγκασα (§27). The theme subsequently became a standard motif of Hellenistic ruler-ideology. Thus Attalus III describes his mother as εὐσεβεστάτη μὲν γενομένη πασῶν, φιλοστοργοτάτη δὲ διαφερόντως πρός τε τὸν πατέρα μου καὶ πρὸς ἐμέ (Welles, *RC* 67), as Antiochus III proclaims the mutual φιλοστοργία of himself and Queen Laodice (Welles, *RC* 36). For the theme in later imperial rhetoric cf. Men. Rhet. 376 (= p. 90 R-W). (Cf. further 131–32n.).

These verses may have contributed to Cat. 64.334–36, *nulla domus tales umquam contexit amores, | nullus amor tali coniunxit foedere amantes, | qualis adest Thetidi, qualis concordia Peleo.*

οὔπω: This leaves the way open for the future (cf. *Od.* 7.68; Hes. *Scut.* 10), without, of course, implying that Arsinoe and Philadelphus currently fall short of their parents' standard (cf. vv. 128–30).

φαντί: Public report is indeed important: the mutual affection of Berenice and Soter is something the people still talk about, which is itself a sign of their regard for their former rulers. Another representation of this affectionate interest by the public in their rulers is found in *Idyll* 15.

ἀδεῖν: The "inversion" (Gow) of the following verse, "No wife has so pleased her husband as Ptolemy loved Berenice," is explained by the use of ἀνδάνειν, "be pleasing to," as "be loved/found sexually attractive by" (cf. *Od.* 5.153 [Odysseus and Calypso], κατείβετο δὲ γλυκὺς αἰὼν | νόστον ὀδυρομένωι, ἐπεὶ οὐκέτι ἥνδανε νύμφη, where there is the same hiatus after -τι before the verb; there is a related use at *Od.* 2.114). Roman elegy freely uses *placere* in this way (cf. Prop. 2.7.19, *tu mihi sola places: placeam tibi, Cynthia, solus;* Pichon 1902, 234). The grammatical "inversion" also suggests the mutuality of the love, even before it is made explicit in v. 40.

ἐὴν: Cf. 25n.

40 ἀντεφιλεῖτο: Cf. 12.16, 28.6; the compound is not found in early poetry, but note Xen. *Symp.* 8.3 (teasing), ὁ Νικήρατος ... ἐρῶν τῆς γυναικὸς ἀντερᾶται. Here again we may sense that Berenice and Soter are being fashioned on the pattern of their children, whose mutual love became an important plank of royal ideology (cf. 130n.).

41–42 Mutual marital affection allows the king to sleep peacefully, because he knows that his wife is not committing adultery, that "his" children really are his and have his best interests at heart, and that he can safely entrust affairs to them. Soter obviously had this confidence in the future Philadelphus when he made him co-regent in 285 B.C.E.. The principal verbal model is *Od.* 2.225–27, Μέντωρ, ὅς ῥ᾿Ὀδυσῆος ἀμύμονος ἦεν ἑταῖρος, | καί οἱ ἰὼν ἐν νηυσὶν ἐπέτρεπεν οἶκον ἅπαντα, | πείθεσθαί τε γέροντι καὶ ἔμπεδα πάντα φυλάσσειν, but note also *Od.* 7.148–50 (Odysseus's prayer for the Phaeacians), θεοὶ ὄλβια δοῖεν | ζωέμεναι, καὶ παισὶν ἐπιτρέψειεν ἕκαστος | κτήματ᾿ ἐνὶ μεγάροισι γέρας θ᾿ ὅ τι δῆμος ἔδωκεν. Berenice and Soter certainly enjoyed this good fortune (cf. vv. 104–5).

σφετέροισιν: Elsewhere T. uses this pronominal adjective for the third person only at 12.4, 13.53 (plural), 22.209, and 24.60, and for the second person singular at 22.67; at 25.163 it is used for the first person. There are no examples in the bucolics or mimes (cf. above, p. 58).

ἐπιτρέποι: The indefinite subject (Eng. "one") is not expressed (cf. K-G I 35–36).

φιλέων . . . φιλεούσης: Cf. Semonides fr. 7.86–87 (34–40n. above).

43 ἀστόργου: In other words, without the φιλοστοργία of a Berenice or an Arsinoe (v. 130); almost any of Semonides' female types, other than the bee woman (34–40n.), would fit the bill, but sexual promiscuity brings her closest to the ass woman (Semonides fr. 7.43–49). It is an old idea that T. has a specific woman in mind and/or that his readers could not fail to associate vv. 43–44 with particular women from recent history. The favorite candidates are usually Soter's first wife, Eurydice, mother of Philadelphus's half brother Ptolemaios Keraunos (here condemned by implication as "not like his father" and thus unworthy of rule); and Arsinoe I, Philadelphus's first wife (cf. Prott 1898, 468–74; Rostropowicz 1982; Meincke 1965, 104; Weber 1993, 233–34). Griffiths (1979, 78–79) observes that Philadelphus followed his father in "coming late to a faithful, loving, and indeed divine wife worthy of himself"; the emphasis, however, is upon Berenice as a positive paradigm, here set off by contrast to a nonspecific negative model.

ἐπ᾽ ἀλλοτρίωι: "On another"; the use of ἐπί with the dative here resembles the use with verbs of love and desire (Page 1955, 276). Two interpretations are possible: (1) The bad woman thinks of another man while making love to her husband (cf. v. 42); hence the children resemble the former not the latter, by a familiar ancient model of conception (cf. Reeve 1989). (2) The bad woman is always thinking of another man, and, if not actually promiscuous, might as well be. The children will not resemble their "father," either because they are in fact not his children (cf. [Phocylides] 178, οὐ γὰρ τίκτει παῖδας ὁμοίους μοιχικὰ λέκτρα) or because such resemblance is possible only in, and is a sure sign of, a well-ordered society, which itself, in the model T. constructs, depends upon a loving parental relationship.

44 ῥηΐδιοι δὲ γοναί: Both Leto and Berenice experienced sharp birth pains before release (cf. 60–61n.), as presumably also did Rhea, who contrasts her suffering with the ὠδῖνες ἐλαφραί of the earth (Callim. *H.* 1.29); Callimachus's Artemis indeed boasts that her own birth was painless (*H.* 3.24–25), but that is a miraculous aetiology for the goddess's identification with Eileithyia. "Easy births" here are probably those into which little thought has gone and that happen all too frequently when the mother is promiscuous; for ἄστοργοι γυναῖκες giving birth is "no big deal," and equally little thought goes into the succession. Bing (1988, 117) adduces Niobe as such an example—a woman who valued quantity over quality. Koenen (1983, 162) compares Archilochus fr. 196A West (the "Cologne Epode"), where the narrator apparently rejects one woman because she is promiscuous, and any children are therefore likely to be τυφλὰ κἀλιτήμερα, and Merkelbach (1981, 32) proposed βαρδεῖαι δὲ γοναί.

τέκνα κτλ.: From Hesiod on, the resemblance or lack of it between children and parents was a sure sign of good order or its reverse in a state (cf. *WD* 182, 235, with West's note; Aeschin. 3.111; Callim. *H.* 4.170 [Soter and Philadelphus]; Hor. *Carm.* 4.5.23; and see 63n.). The Hesiodic motif prepares for the presentation of Egypt as the Hesiodic "Just City" writ large (vv. 77 ff.).

45 κάλλει ἀριστεύουσα θεάων: Such a more or less explicit allusion to the Judgment of Paris (for ἀριστεύειν cf. 15.98) might be thought unwise in the context of marital bliss, but the Ptolemaic Aphrodite is a bestower of harmony, not a wrecker of marriages (cf. vv. 50–52), as Helen also is refashioned (15.110; probably *Idyll* 18; Hunter 1996, 163–65, with bibliography). Aphrodite is among goddesses what Berenice was on earth, a point reinforced by the two prosodically identical names concluding successive verses. θεάων is taken more naturally with ἀριστεύουσα (cf. LSJ s.v. ἀριστεύω I.2) than with πότν'.

Ἀφροδίτα: This name can be used in hexameters only by treating the first syllable as open ("Attic correption"); Callimachus and

Apollonius avoid the license entirely, and T. restricts it to verse end (cf. Fantuzzi 1988, 155–63).

46 τῆνα: Cf. above, p. 55.

μεμέλητο: μέλειν is commonly used of a divinity's special interest in a particular human or institution (cf. v. 73; Eur. *Hipp.* 60, Ἄρτεμιν ἃ μελόμεσθα; *Rh.* 647, μέλει δ᾽ ὁ σός μοι [Athena pretending to be Aphrodite] πόλεμος; Callim. *H.* 1.72–73, ἀλλὰ τὰ μὲν μακάρεσσιν ὀλίζοσιν αὖθι παρῆκας | ἄλλα μέλειν ἑτέροισι; Virg. *Ecl.* 3.61, *illi [sc. Ioui] mea carmina curae*; Hor. *Carm.* 1.12.50–51, *orte Saturno, tibi cura magni | Caesaris fatis data*).

σέθεν: This high form is excluded from the bucolics and mimes, except for 4.38 (cf. Hunter 1996, 42).

47 Ἀχέροντα: Used also as the boundary of the Underworld at 15.136 and Callim. fr. 191.35. In the *Odyssey* it is probably conceived as a lake into which the rivers Pyriphlegethon and Kokytos flow (10.513–14), but later poetry varies between a lake (e.g., Ar. *Frogs* 137) and a river (e.g., Pl. *Phd.* 112e8–13a2, which also has a lake called "Acherousia"; Virg. *Aen.* 6.298).

πολύστονον: The primary sense is probably "which causes many lamentations" rather than "ringing with the wails of the dead." The compound epithet may point to an etymology of Ἀχέρων, which is variously connected with ἄχος and α-χαρά (cf. Cornutus p. 74.22–23 Lang; *Etym. Magn.* 180.47–48 Gaisford; Servius on *Aen.* 6.107); *Σ Od.* 10.514 seems to connect the name with ἰαχή.

48–49 The "hateful ferryman" is also used as an image of irreversible death at 16.40–41 (and cf. Hermesianax fr. 7.3–6 Powell) and is a feature of genuine epitaphic poetry (cf. *CEG* 2.680 [Cyrenaica, fourth century?], πορθμῖδος εὐσέλμου μεδέων γέρον ὃς διὰ πάντα | νυκτὸς ὕπο σκιερᾶς πείρατα πλεῖς ποταμοῦ κτλ). T. may, however, have chosen this particular way of describing death because it evokes aspects of Egyptian funerary practice and conceptions, while closely following a very familiar Greek idea. The "ferryman" is a familiar figure in the Egyptian voyage across water to the afterlife (cf., for example, Lichtheim 1973, 35; Kees 1961, 97–98; Barthelmess 1992), and for a Greek view of Egyptian practice cf. Diod. Sic. 1.92.1–2: "When the body is ready to be buried the family announce the day of burial . . . and affirm that the deceased is about to cross over the lake (διαβαίνειν μέλλει τὴν λίμνην) . . . the boat (βᾶρις) is launched . . . which is in the charge of the boatman whom the Egyptians call in their own language *charon*" (cf. 1.96.8–9). If it is correct that T.'s image has an Egyptian resonance, and some color is lent to the idea by the fact that the other description of Aphrodite's blessing to Berenice also seems to offer a Greek reading of Egyptian practice (15.106–8; cf. Hunter 1996, 132–34), the *interpretatio Graeca* is of course misleading, as no Egyptian would wish to be rescued from "the ferryman"; it is, however, suggestive evocation, rather than ethnographic accuracy, that is at issue.

ἁρπάξασα: The traditional language of divine abduction (e.g. *Hymn. Hom. Dem.*3 [Hades and Persephone]; *Hymn. Hom. Aphr.* 203 [Zeus and Ganymede]; Pind. *Ol.* 1.40 [Poseidon and Pelops]) was adapted by Ptolemaic poets to the apotheosis of members of the royal house (cf. Callim. fr. 228 [above, pp. 50–52]).

κυανέαν: The color of death and hence of Charon's boat (cf. Aesch. *Sept.* 856–57; Leonidas, *AP* 7.67.2 = *HE* 2332; *GV* 1536.2 Peek [Miletos, third century], κυανέαν πορθμῖδ' . . . νεκύων; Virg.

Aen. 6.303). The treatment of the first syllable of κυανέος as long is not uncommon in dactylic verse.

στυγνὸν ἀεὶ: Hades is στυγερός at *Il.* 8.368 and *Arg.* 3.810, and στυγνός is often associated with death in later poets (cf. Fantuzzi on Bion, *EA* 51–52). The name of the Underworld river, Styx, is associated with στυγεῖν and στυγερός, and that connection resonates here (cf. Henrichs 1989; at *SGO* 04/13/01 the dead travels στυγερὸν πορθμὸν . . . νεκύων).

πορθμῆα· Charon first occurs in extant literature in the epic *Minyas* (fr. 1 Davies, sixth century?); there he is already old, as literature and art standardly portray him (cf. 16.41; Ar. *Frogs* 139). On this figure cf. *LIMC* s.v.; Kurtz 1975, index s.v.; Sourvinou-Inwood 1995, 303–61; and for other cultures, Lincoln 1980.

50 Berenice's deification "by Aphrodite" is also described at 15.106–8. When this actually happened is unclear (presumably early 270s, but apparently after the Ptolemaia of 279/8), but more seems to have been involved than the mere drawing of Berenice into the cult of her husband to form the pair of Theoi Soteres. A "shrine of Berenice" existed in Alexandria at the time of the "Grand Procession" (Ath. 5.202d; cf. above, p. 2), but we hear nothing further of this. This verse itself suggests that Berenice became a σύνναος θεός with Aphrodite, that is, an image of her was placed in Aphrodite's temple. Here too, Berenice foreshadows the fate of her daughter, and not just in a close association with Aphrodite (cf. 90–91n.), for after Arsinoe's death Philadelphus decreed that images of her be placed in all Egyptian temples as σύνναος (cf. Nock 1930; Quaegebeur 1971, 242–43); the practice becomes standard with later Ptolemies (including the Theoi Adelphoi). Outside Alexandria, there is evidence of a joint shrine

of Aphrodite-Berenice and "the Syrian goddess" in the Fayum (*PEnteux*. 13; Rowlandson 1998, 28–30).

κατέθηκας: A further rewriting of epic motifs: in *Il*. 16 Sleep and Death carry the body of Sarpedon to Lycia where they "deposit" it (κάτθεσαν, 16.683) for burial. Here Berenice is "established" in Aphrodite's temple.

ἑᾶς . . . τιμᾶς: Interpretation as genitive, rather than accusative plural (ἑᾶς . . . τιμάς), is probably to be preferred (cf. Callim. *H*. 4.9, Δήλωι νῦν οἴμης ἀποδάσσομαι, and contrast Hes. *Theog*. 885 [Zeus and the other gods], ὃ δὲ τοῖσιν ἐὺ διεδάσσατο τιμάς; for ἑᾶς cf. 25n.).

51–52 The love that Berenice-Aphrodite inspires is a gentle one, not the torturing *eros* of poetic tradition, and she eases the cares of those who already feel *pothos*; κούφας is predicative. She has some of the qualities of a healing god (cf. Pind. *Pyth*. 3.6 τέκτονα νωδυνίας ǀ ἥμερον γυιαρκέος Ἀσκλαπιόν), and the verses describe blessings for which many worshippers doubtless prayed.

ἤπιος: Here of two terminations (cf. Hes. *Theog*. 407; Eur. *Tro*. 53).

προσπνείει: Divine breath is always powerful (cf. Richardson on *Hymn. Hom. Dem*. 238), but the idea is very often associated with Aphrodite and Eros (cf. 12.10; *Arg*. 3.937, 972; Tib. 2.1.79–80, *a miseri, quos hic grauiter deus urget! at ille ǀ felix cui placidus leniter adflat Amor*; [Lucian] *Amores* 37 [in an extended use of the image], ἤπια ταῖς ἑκάστου διανοίαις ἐμπνεῖ).

κούφας . . . μερίμνας: A quasi oxymoron that catches the novelty of the idea that *pothos* can be made "light" (cf. 11.3); the Aphrodite of poetic tradition is responsible for πόθον ἀργαλέον καὶ γυιοβόρους μελεδώνας (Hes. *WD* 66; and cf. βαρύς at 1.100, 3.15), but the divine Berenice, like the Ptolemaic Aphrodite herself, offers balm. For the noun cf. Sappho fr. 1.25–26, χαλέπαν δὲ λῦσον | ἐκ μερίμναν; Lat. *curae. Arg.* uses μελεδήματα and μεληδόνες (3.4, 471, 752, 812). If there is an echo of Hes. *WD* 178 (the fifth age), χαλεπὰς δὲ θεοὶ δώσουσι μερίμνας (cf. Reinsch-Werner 1976, 378), the point will be that Berenice's divinity has eased the otherwise universally painful mortal condition.

53–58 The relation between Philadelphus and his parents is compared to that of Diomedes and Achilles and their parents; in form the passage is a kind of priamel (cf. Meincke 1965, 108), but the terms of the comparison are left unexpressed—it is for us to draw (out) the conclusions. All three sons resembled their fathers in the approved Hesiodic mode; as Gow notes, "The doubled αἰχμητὰ . . . αἰχμηταῖ [shows] that datives λαοφόνωι and ἀκοντισταῖ are implied in the preceding clauses." The rhetoric of the passage, however, suggests that the closeness between Philadelphus and Soter is of a special kind: the Ptolemies are in fact a Hesiodic "limit case," in which the son, who (unusually) bears the same name as the father, is *very* like, perhaps identical with, the father (cf. 56–57n.). So, too, the chiastic arrangement of vv. 53 and 55 is replaced in vv. 56–77 by a parallel order of epithet and name to suggest sameness, rather than difference. Greek tradition would in fact have accounted both Diomedes and Achilles as surpassing their fathers in heroic prowess, but T.'s rhetoric works to shut off that possibility in the case of the Ptolemies; for a different view cf. Gerber 1981. Griffiths (1979, 76) notes that we move from a purely mortal hero to Achilles whose mother was a goddess to Philadelphus both of whose parents are now divine; the sequencing certainly suggests that as Achilles surpassed Diomedes, so Philadelphus surpasses both of them. Gerber (1981) notes that both Diomedes and Achilles were the object of divine or hero cult in various places— Diomedes in fact on the Ptolemaic island of Cyprus—and suggests that this too holds out promise for the future to Philadelphus (cf. Farnell 1921, 285–93).

53 Ἀργεία κυάνοφρυ: The identity of this "dark-browed Argive lady" is mysterious until the end of the verse. The immediately preceding verses tempt us to interpret this as a hymnic address to Berenice, with "Argive" as a reference to the connections between the Macedonian royal house (the "Argeads") and Argos. Just as Achilles is chosen in part because of his importance as a model for Alexander and his successors (cf., for example, Stewart 1993, 78–86), so Diomedes is, after Heracles himself, the greatest Argive hero.

Diomedes' mother was Deipyle, an Argive princess. As Deipyle had a sister called Argeia (Apollod. 3.6.1; Σ Eur. *Phoen.* 135, 137), T. may here be playing with mythological identities.

κυάνοφρυ: The short scansion of the first vowel varies the prosody of κυανέαν in v. 49. This is a high-style adjective, used parodically at 3.18 and 4.59; it occurs in a mid-third century list of poetical compound adjectives (*PHibeh* 172.10).

λαοφόνον: A variation of the Homeric ἀνδροφόνος, which is used of Hector, Ares, and Achilles. Diomedes does indeed rejoice in slaughter in the *Iliad* (esp. book 5), but it is his father, Tydeus, who was notoriously bloodthirsty (cf. *Il.* 4.396–97; and esp. Aesch. *Sept.* 377–96). Correction to λαοφόνωι is, however, unnecessary: the explicit application of the word to the son rather than the father marks the likeness across the generations. The relation with his father is in fact central to Homer's presentation of Diomedes:

at *Il.*5.115–26 Diomedes prays to Athena to aid him "if ever she aided his father," and in response the goddess inspires in him μένος πατρώιον . . . | ἄτρομον, οἷον ἔχεσκε σακέσπολος ἱππότα Τυδεύς; at 4.364 ff. Agamemnon succeeds in rousing Diomedes by rebuking him with failing to match his father's prowess, which is narrated at some length; Athena then uses a similar ploy at 5.800–813, "Indeed Tydeus's son is little like his father; Tydeus was small in stature, but a fighter . . . ; you are not then the offspring of fierce Tydeus, son of Oineus."

Καλυδωνίωι ἀνδρί: The transmitted accusative is difficult. Tydeus was the son of Oineus, king of Kalydon, and was taken in by Adrastos of Argos, Deipyle's father, after he went into exile from his homeland (according to Apollod. 1.8.5 for killing a member of his family). Thus it is Tydeus, not his son, who is the "Kalydonian man/husband," particularly in the context of marriage to an Argive princess; "Kalydonian" will thus be a variant of the Homeric Τυδεὺς Αἰτώλιος (*Il.* 4.399), and for the warlike reputation of the Aitolians cf. Mastronarde on Eur. *Phoen.* 134. The few Latin examples of *Calydonius* applied to Diomedes (Ovid *Met.* 15.769, with Bömer's note) might ultimately derive from this passage but cannot be decisive for the text here. Wilamowitz (1924, 2: 133 n. 2) understood "Kalydonian" of Diomedes to mean "riesig" on the model of the famous boar; Com. Adesp. *354 K-A, which Wilamowitz cites, however, lends no real support to this interpretation.

55 ἀλλά: Progressive (Denniston 21–22), rather than adversative, which would yield no obvious sense.

βαθύκολπος: Used at *Hymn. Hom. Dem.* 5 of the daughters of Ocean, and appropriate generally to a marine goddess.

ἀκοντιστὰν: At *Il.* 21.233 Achilles is δουρικλυτός, but the parallel of Diomedes and Tydeus suggests that particular qualities of Peleus are relevant here. In the *Iliad* Achilles has a heavy wooden spear, given to him by Peleus (who had received it from Cheiron), and which he alone of the heroes at Troy could use (16.140–44, 19.387–91; see Janko on the former passage). Homer calls the spear Πηλιάδα μελίην and seems to associate this formula with Peleus, πάλλειν ("to wield"), and Pelion. Grammatical tradition later etymologized Πηλεύς from πάλλειν (*Etym. Magn.* 669.54 Gaisford), and this is likely the point of T.'s otherwise rather colorless praise. For Peleus's skill with the spear cf. *Arg.* 2.829. Achilles' most famous use of his spear is the killing of Hector.

56–57 The hymnic second-person address to Philadelphus changes the order of the previous examples, so that Soter and Berenice, the model couple, together compose a remarkable four-word verse (cf. 61n.).

αἰχμητὰ Πτολεμαῖε: Cf. 16.103 αἰχμητὴν Ἱέρωνα; the common Iliadic word "heroizes" these latter-day kings. The term has, however, embarrassed critics who feel that, whatever Philadelphus's achievements, he was not a "spearman" to match his military father, and Strabo 17.1.5 (cf. Ael. *VH* 4.15) reports his "bodily lack of strength" (cf. Weber 1993, 232–33). Be that as it may—and Philadelphus's military achievements have in fact often been underestimated (for the indictment cf., for example, Hazzard 2000, 106–8)—the Hesiodic pattern is here reinforced by an inherited pharaonic conception of kingship in which the son (Horus) is indeed "identical" to the father (Osiris), because both successively play out the same role as protector of Egypt. What is true of one is true of the other; repetitiveness across the generations is the hallmark of the self-representation of the pharaohs in art and inscriptions, and something of that ideology colors T.'s presentation here and in vv. 86–94 (where see nn.). (Cf. further Stephens 2003, 129.)

ἀρίζηλος: Used of Soter at Callim. fr. 734 (where see Pfeiffer's note) and of a Berenice in Callim. *Epigr.* 51 Pf. (= *HE* 1121–24, where see Gow and Page); the latter could be Soter's wife but seems more likely to be Berenice II (note the epigram's concern with perfumes). These three texts are likely to be interrelated in ways that we can no longer recover. ἀρίζηλος is partly explained by the parallelism with περικλειτά (v. 34): the two phrases demarcate the section of the poem concerned with Berenice's virtues. Homer uses ἀρίζηλος of the brilliant gleam of lightning and stars (*Il.* 13.244, 22.27; cf. [T.] 25.141; Pind. *Ol.* 2.55; *Arg.* 3.958) and of the golden representations of Ares and Athena on the Shield of Achilles (καλὼ καὶ μεγάλω σὺν τεύχεσιν, ὥς τε θεώ περ | ἀμφὶς ἀριζήλω· λαοὶ δ' ὑπολίζονες ἦσαν, *Il.*18.518–19); such numinous shining well suits the deified Berenice, herself now a star, as her successors also were to be.

58–76 Philadelphus was born on Cos in 308 ("Marmor Parium," *FGrHist* 239 F19). For Ptolemaic relations with this island, which enjoyed freedom from Ptolemaic taxes and the imposition of a governor cf. Bagnall 1976, 103–5; Sherwin-White 1978, 90–108; Cos was finally lost to Antigonos Gonatas in 261/0. Sherwin-White notes that behind the present passage may lie "some particular benefaction" by Philadelphus to the site of his birth (cf. esp. vv, 66–69), but, if so, we can only guess at its nature. It is a reasonable conclusion from *Idyll* 7 that T. himself had close connections with Cos (cf. above, p. 30) and perhaps lived there for a time, and this too may have contributed to the prominence of this episode in the encomium. It is, of course, not impossible that *EP* was written for a Coan festival (cf. Prott 1898, 476; below, on v. 70).

The birth story reworks the birth of Apollo on Delos in *Hymn. Hom. Ap.*, where Cos is among the islands that were too scared to give Leto shelter (*Hymn. Hom. Ap.* 42; cf. Pretagostini 2000); there is also a clear intertextual relation with Callimachus's *Hymn to Delos*, where, as here (vv. 62–70), Cos is the subject of the central verses of the poem (vv. 160–70). The starting point for this poetic elaboration is the fact that Delos was the religious and political center of the Island League, which existed under Ptolemaic protection and which had paid cult honors to Soter from an early date (*SIG* 390 = Austin 1981, no. 218; Habicht 1970, 111–12); an annual Delian Ptolemaia, funded by Philadelphus, celebrated the link between islands and king (Durrbach 1921, no. 21 = *IG* XI 1038). The League had also dedicated statues of Philadelphus on Delos, almost certainly before *EP* was composed (Durrbach 1921, no. 17 = *OGIS* 25). At the probable date of composition of *EP* Philadelphus's control of Delos amounted to "a state of dependence . . . a true hegemony involving a protectorate" (Bagnall 1976, 154; cf. Durrbach 1921, 25; Reger 1994, 17–47 [some modifications to too simple a view of Ptolemaic control]). As such, Philadelphus was not merely the defender of the preeminent Aegean cult site of Apollo, but in the poetic imagination a true *alter Apollo*, to whose favor the island owed its prosperity. The importance for Alexandrian poets of the *Homeric Hymn to Apollo*, which is rewritten three times by Callimachus (*H.* 2–4), presumably reflects this position; Aratus too seems to have written a version of the archaic hymn (cf. *SH* 109, Delos addresses Leto), but the circumstances and context of that poem are unknown. It is also worth noting that, from Philadelphus on, the birth stories of each new ruler, which had already been a prominent means of royal legitimation in the pharaonic period, gained new iconographic significance, expressed in the decoration of "mammisi" or "birth-houses" attached to temples (cf. Daumas 1958; Brunner 1964); that poets also gave prominence at this time to royal birth-narratives is unlikely to be a coincidence (cf. Stephens 2003, 56–57).

58 Κόως: This form with epic diectasis (*Κόος > Κῶς > Κόως) is found already in Homer (cf. Janko on *Il.* 14.255). A cult personification of the island is attested only from the late second to early first century (Sherwin-White 1978, 332), but here we are already well on the way to this. The eponymous heroine of the island was the daughter of Merops, the indigenous founding hero (cf. Hunter on 7.4–7). In *Hymn. Hom. Ap.* Delos speaks (vv. 61–82) and rejoices in the promised honors (v. 90), and the infant Apollo is fed on nectar and ambrosia by Themis (vv. 123–25). Callimachus exploited the explicit statement of the archaic poet (v. 123) that Leto did not suckle her son to turn Delos into the god's wet nurse (*H.* 4.10, 264–76). In T. this seems also to be the situation, though less explicitly than in Callimachus (and such coyness in the case of a living king with a deified mother is understandable): ἀτιτάλλειν neither necessarily involves (cf., for example, Pind. *Nem.* 3.58) nor excludes breast-feeding, but T. may have exploited or created a connection between the very rare (*Od.* 12.86; Isaeus fr. V Thalheim) νεογιλλός and both νέος and γάλα (cf. *Σ Od.* ad loc.). (See also next note.)

Meleager may (or may not) have this passage in mind at *AP* 7.418.3 (= *HE* 3996), <ἃ> καὶ Δία θρεψαμένα Κῶς, where "Zeus" is most obviously understood as Philadelphus.

59 δεξαμένα: In Callimachus Delos is the first to pick Apollo up from the ground and address him (*H.* 4.264–65). Here Cos "receives" the baby as Demeter "received" Demophoon in order to act—as his parents thought—as a wet nurse (*Hymn. Hom. Dem.* 226, 231), and as the nymphs "received" Dionysus (*Hymn. Hom. Dion.* 26.3–4, [Διόνυσον] ὃν τρέφον ἠύκομοι νύμφαι παρὰ πατρὸς ἄνακτος | δεξάμεναι κόλποισι καὶ ἐνδυκέως ἀτίταλλον). A specific echo of the latter passage would be very appropriate, given the importance of Dionysus for Philadelphus.

πρώταν . . . ἀώ: ἀώς is not uncommonly used of "the light of day," rather than specifically "dawn" (cf. Hunter on 7.35), but there is an obvious appropriateness in the usage for the first light ever seen by a baby. The verse alludes to the fears Delos expresses to Leto in *Hymn. Hom. Ap.* about allowing her to give birth there: δείδοικα . . . μὴ ὁπότ᾽ ἂν τὸ πρῶτον ἴδηι φάος ἠελίοιο | νῆσον ἀτιμήσας κτλ. (*Hymn. Hom. Ap.* 70–72); in that poem, Leto swears an oath to allay the island's fears, but in the encomium no such hesitation is possible.

ὅτε: Cf. above, p. 56.

60–61 Successive *spondeiazontes* (cf. above, p. 66) mark Berenice's pain and cries. V. 61 is a stately four-word hexameter (cf. Bassett 1919) appropriate to the dignity of the occasion. Eileithyia is the goddess of childbirth, commonly identified or associated with Artemis Λοχία (cf. Callim. *H.* 3.20–25; fr. 79); her absence from Delos, as a result of Hera's opposition, delayed Apollo's birth in *Hymn. Hom. Ap.* (vv. 97–116). Here, however, there will be no delay or divine opposition, and Eileithyia answers the call at once. Callimachus too took over the motif from *Hymn. Hom. Ap.* (cf. *H.* 4.132, 257).

ἐβώσατο: For such forms (= ἐβοήσατο) cf. Gow on 12.35.

λυσίζωνον: "Undoing the girdle (ζώνη, μίτρη)" is in poetry a standard prelude to childbirth (cf. Pind. *Ol.* 6.39; Callim. *H.* 1.21; 4.209, 222 [the birth of Apollo on Delos]; *Arg.* 1.288, etc.). A scholion on this last passage says that there was a temple of Artemis Λυσίζωνος in Athens.

Ἀντιγόνας θυγάτηρ: The periphrasis, rather than merely playing with the "birth" etymology of Berenice's mother's name, may be used here to suggest that Berenice is about to give birth to a genuine Macedonian ruler; Σ on this verse informs us that Antigone was Antipater's niece. It is also worth noting how easy it is to forget, when reading this passage, that in 308 Berenice was in fact not a young girl giving birth to her first child but was over thirty and had already had at least three children.

βεβαρημένα: This is to be preferred to βεβαρυμμένα, because the present participle of βαρύνομαι would be expected, as at Callim. *H.* 4.202; for the common perfect passive use of βαρέω cf. LSJ s.v. II.

62–64 After the "labored" *spondeiazontes* come three purely dactylic verses to mark the speed of the birth and of the release from pain. So, too, in *Hymn. Hom. Ap.* things move very rapidly once Eileithyia is on the scene (vv. 115–19).

νωδυνίαν κατέχευε: "Painlessness," like sleep, is conceived as a kind of mist (cf. *Od.* 7.41–42) that floods (or can be poured) over the body. At *Hymn. Hom. Ap.* 97 and 115 Eileithyia is given the epithet μογοστόκος; this was standardly understood as "easing the pains of childbirth" (cf. 27.30; Σ *Il.* 11.270; *LfgrE* s.v.), and T.'s phrase is a verbal expression of this function.

πατρὶ ἐοικώς: The theme of vv. 40–44 is picked up with the implication that one could tell at once that this baby was the son of Soter.

ἀγαπητὸς: This standard description of Telemachos (*Od.* 2.365, etc.; cf. 13n.) was particularly used for only sons (μονογενεῖς) or sons who had arrived late in their parents' life (cf. Poll. 3.19; *LfgrE* s.v. ἀγαπάζω). Berenice and Soter both already had other children by previous unions and at least one common daughter (Arsinoe), but Philadelphus was their first son, and the description is thus quite appropriate.

ἔγεντο: T. uses this syncopated poetic form in 1.88 and 14.27, as well as in *Idyll* 13 (vv. 2, 9), but he may have felt it as particularly appropriate to the high style of this poem and the grand subject of Ptolemy's birth.

ὀλόλυξεν: A standard reaction to divine epiphany (cf. Deubner 1941; Fraenkel on Aesch. *Ag.* 597). Here T. closely reworks *Hymn. Hom. Ap.* 119 (ἐκ δ' ἔθορε πρὸ φόως δέ, θεαὶ δ' ὀλόλυξαν ἅπασαι); Callimachus's reworking at *H.* 4.255–58 is much further from the archaic model (ὁ δ' ἔκθορεν, αἱ δ' ἐπὶ μακρόν | νύμφαι Δηλιάδες, ποταμοῦ γένος ἀρχαίοιο, | εἶπαν Ἐλειθυίης ἱερὸν μέλος, αὐτίκα δ' αἰθήρ | χάλκεος ἀντήχησε διαπρυσίην ὀλολυγήν; cf. above, p. 6; Griffiths 1977–78, 100).

65 In Callimachus also the island is the first to address the new infant (cf. 59n.).

χείρεσσι φίλῃσι: A Homeric verse ending (*Il.* 17.620), here given new meaning, as the "loving hands" are no longer those of a warrior in the heat of battle, but of a woman cradling a newborn child. For the ending -ῃσι cf. above, p. 58.

66 ὄλβιε: The predicate adjective is attracted into the vocative of the subject (cf. Callim. fr. 127 M [= 599 Pf.], ἀντὶ γὰρ ἐκλήθης"Ιμβρασε Παρθενίου; K-G 1: 50). Griffiths (1977–78, 99) sees here a Theocritean response to the unborn Apollo's address to Ptolemy in Callimachus, ἐσσόμενε Πτολεμαῖε (Callim. *H*. 4.188).

τίοις δέ με κτλ: The verses rework and explicitly allude to a prominent motif of the principal model text (cf. *Hymn. Hom. Ap.* 65 [Delos], ὧδέ δέ κεν περιτιμήεσσα γενοίμην; 88 [Leto's oath], τίσει δέ σέ γ' ἔξοχα πάντων; 146, ἀλλὰ σὺ Δήλωι Φοῖβε μάλιστ' ἐπιτέρπεαι ἦτορ). Callimachus's version is *H*. 4.268–73 (Delos speaks while holding the infant god): "From me will Apollo be called Delian, and no other land will be so loved by another god, not Kerchnis by Poseidon who rules Lechaion, not the Kyllenian hill by Hermes, not Crete by Zeus, as I by Apollo."

67 κυανάμπυκα: Appropriate to an island surrounded by the sea (cf. *Hymn. Hom. Ap.* 26–27, . . . κραναῆι ἐνὶ νήσωι | Δήλωι ἐν ἀμφιρύτηι; ἑκάτερθε δὲ κῦμα κελαινὸν κτλ; Callim. *H*. 4.13–14 [the sea around Delos], ὁ δ' ἀμφί ἑ πουλὺς ἑλίσσων |'Ικαρίου πολλὴν ἀπομάσσεται ὕδατος ἄχνην). Before T., this compound occurs as an epithet of Thebe in Pindar's *Hymn to Zeus* (fr. 29.3 M), and in the same poem Delos is described as τηλέφαντον κυανέας χθονὸς ἄστρον (fr. 33c.6); Pindar's hymn was an important model for Callimachus in both *H*. 1 and *H*. 4.

68–70 Cos prays that the new king will favor not just herself, but also "the Triopian hill," that is, the headland (Cape Crio) lying to the southeast of Cos, site of Knidos and a temple of "Triopian Apollo." The verses plainly show that Philadelphus was interested in the area (a fact on which Σ elaborates), and we know that Knidos enjoyed good relations with him, but we can only guess at the detailed history that lies behind this passage (cf. Bagnall 1976, 98).

The temple was the center of the Dorian pentapolis of Lindos, Ialysos, Kamiros, Cos, and Knidos (Hdt. 1.144), which in classical times celebrated a "Dorian festival" there; the importance of both the pentapolis and the festival seems to have declined by the third century (cf. *RE* 7A.174–75; Tarn 1910, 214; Sherwin-White 1978, 30), but Ptolemaic interest would suit the parallelism with Apollo's patronage of the Ionians on Delos (cf. below on Δωριέεσσι). (For a quite different approach to the text and its interpretation cf. White 1981; 1982.)

ἐν δὲ μιᾶι τιμῆι: The similarity to Achilles' famous complaint at *Il.* 9.319, ἐν δὲ ἰῆι τιμῆι ἡμὲν κακὸς ἠδὲ καὶ ἐσθλός, has no obvious significance, though ἶσον . . . γέρας in v. 69 seems also to evoke the quarrel of Achilles and Agamemnon (cf. *Il.* 1.163).

Τρίοπος: The transmitted Τρίοπον is puzzling, as the adjective is elsewhere always Τριόπιος, and "of Triops," the eponymous hero of the area, seems preferable. Triops (or Triopas) was in legend the Thessalian ancestor of the earliest settlers at Knidos and is also found associated with Cos (cf. Callim. *H.* 6.24–25; Wilamowitz 1924, 2: 35–40; Hopkinson 1984, 30).

κατθεῖο: "Set down in equal *time*" may have a specific subtext: both Cos and Knidos were free of Ptolemaic taxation (a real γέρας) (cf. Sherwin-White 1978, 93), so that we are tempted to understand "set down at the same assessment."

Δωριέεσσι: Namely, Knidos and the Triopian temple. The prominence given to "Dorian solidarity" is the counterpart to the extended description in *Hymn. Hom. Ap.* of the Ionian festival on Delos in which Apollo delights (vv. 147, 152) and evokes Ptolemy himself as a "Dorian" (cf. above, pp. 62–63). Thus in an exchange of texts between Kytenion and Xanthos at the very end of the third century (*SEG* xxxviii 1476) the Dorian ancestry of Ptolemy IV is used as a powerful argument for a particular course of action. (Cf. further above, p. 62.)

'Ρήναιαν: The island close to Delos that in the late 520s Polycrates of Samos dedicated to Apollo and bound to Delos with a chain (Thuc. 1.13.6, 3.104.2); there it was said the Delians gave birth and buried their dead (Strabo 10.5.5). Rhenaia is the final place mentioned in the catalogue of islands that would not accept Leto (*Hymn. Hom. Ap.* 44), but the apparently forced analogy between it and the Triopian peninsula perhaps suggests that more is at stake here than just another allusion to the archaic model. Thucydides cites *Hymn. Hom. Ap.* as evidence for the Ionian festival on Delos in the same chapter (3.104) in which he records Polycrates' chaining of Rhenaia, and Burkert (1979) has attractively suggested that the composite nature of *Hymn. Hom. Ap.* reflects this same occasion when, according to late sources, Polycrates celebrated on Delos "Delian and Pythian Games" on the instructions of the Delphic oracle. It seems unlikely that T. and Callimachus did not know of Polycrates' unique celebration, though no ancient source makes the link that Burkert has suggested. It may, however, be worth speculating that T. here relies on a known connection between Rhenaia and his principal model text to reinforce the analogy between his poem and *Hymn. Hom. Ap.*; whether or not there was also an analogy between the Ionian festival of the archaic hymn and the context of performance of *EP* we can only guess.

71–72 Cf. Callim. *H.* 4.274 (the conclusion of the island's address to the newborn Apollo), ὧδε σὺ μὲν κατέλεξας· ὁ δὲ γλυκὺν ἔσπασε μαζόν.

A bird omen promises the fulfillment of Cos's wishes; this is a regular pattern of archaic poetry (cf. *Il.* 8.245 ff. [an eagle, τελειό-

τατον πετεηνῶν from Zeus]; 13.821–22, ὡς ἄρα οἱ εἰπόντι ἐπέπτατο
δεξιὸς ὄρνις, | αἰετὸς ὑψιπετής; Pind. *Isthm.* 6.49–50 [an eagle again]),
and here the appearance of Zeus's eagle is paralleled by the musical
swans that herald Apollo's birth in Callim. *H.* 4.249–54; miraculous
events are, of course, no surprise at the birth of the great (cf. Isoc.
Euag. 21, φῆμαι καὶ μαντεῖαι καὶ ὄψεις ἐν τοῖς ὕπνοις; Philostr. *Her.*
35.6, an eagle [ἀετός] brings "Aias" his name and signals Zeus's
granting of a prayer; Men. Rhet. 371.4 ff. [p. 80 R-W]). Just as Cal-
limachus's swans are appropriate to Apollo, so is the eagle to Ptole-
my. Through their association with Zeus, eagles had long been as-
sociated with kingly power, but the image takes on new significance
for the Ptolemies: an eagle on a thunderbolt was the standard badge
of Ptolemaic coins (cf. Head 1911, 847–52; Mørkholm 1991 pas-
sim), and huge gilt eagles perched on the *skene* for Philadelphus's
symposium (Ath. 5.197a). Callimachus (*H.* 1.68–69) specifically
notes the role of the eagle in a passage that T. may have in mind
here (cf. Perrotta 1978, 154–55; above, p. 5): θήκαο δ' οἰωνῶν μέγ'
ὑπείροχον ἀγγελιώτην | σῶν τεράων· ἅ τ' ἐμοῖσι φίλοις ἐνδέξια φαί-
νοις. In Callimachus also we move from the eagle to Zeus's care for
kings, and the identity of Callimachus's φίλοι is perhaps made clear
by T.'s praise for the Ptolemaic royal house. So, too, Poseidippos
notes that the kings of Macedon had always been attended by vic-
tory omens of "an eagle from the clouds and lightning" (*P.Mil.Vogl.*
VIII 309, col. V 20–25 = Bastianini and Gallazzi 2001, 53).

νᾶσος: We realize with a shock that we have been listening to
an island.

ἔειπεν: T. uses this lengthened epic form elsewhere only at
22.153 and 26.18, 19 (and cf. 25.77, 179); cf. above, p. 57.

ἔκλαγε: The verb is commonly used of bird and animal sounds,
which can in context be ominous or prophetic (cf. *Il.* 10.276 [a

bird sent by Athena], κλάγξαντος ἄκουσαν; Aesch. *Ag.* 201, μάντις ἔκλαγξε; Soph. *OT* 966 [sarcastic], κλάζοντας ὄρνεις).

φωνᾶι: Though it is not uncommon of animal noises (LSJ s.v. I.2), the noun is perhaps chosen to indicate that this cry was meaningful (cf. *Hymn. Hom. Herm.* 544, φωνῆι τ' ἠδὲ ποτῆισι τεληέντων οἰωνῶν).

ἐς τρὶς: Three is always a number of great potency (but cf. esp. *Il.* 8.170–71, τρὶς δ' ἄρ' ἀπ' Ἰδαίων ὀρέων κτύπε μητίετα Ζεὺς | σῆμα τιθεὶς Τρώεσσι). Callimachus's swans circle Delos and sing seven times (another magical number; see J. Gwyn Griffiths on Apul. *Met.* 11.1), and Callimachus (*H.* 4.249–54) draws an aetiological lesson from this (the number of strings on a lyre); whether there is also an aetiology concealed in T.'s verse, as at 13.58–60 (where see Hunter), we do not know. Griffiths (1977–78, 98) sees an argument for Callimachean priority in the "perfunctory" three cries after the seven songs of Callimachus's swans.

ἀπὸ νεφέων: The final syllable of ἀπό is lengthened in imitation of a Homeric license (cf. *Il.* 11.664, ἀπὸ νευρῆς, and 23.874, ὑπὸ νεφέων, both in the same *sedes*); "correction" to ἀπαί or ὑπαί is a common manuscript resort in such cases, but the license is here perfectly at home in a decidedly epic context.

αἴσιος ὄρνις: A variation of the Homeric verse end δεξιὸς ὄρνις (*Il.* 13.821; *Od.* 15.160, 525, 531).

73–76 The Hesiodic theme of the proem now returns before the central division of the poem (cf. *Theog.* 80 ff., ἥ γὰρ [sc. Καλλιόπη] καὶ βασιλεῦσιν ἅμ' αἰδοίοισιν ὀπηδεῖ· | ὅντινα τιμήσουσι Διὸς κοῦραι μεγάλοιο | γεινόμενον τ' ἐσίδωσι διοτρεφέων βασιλήων κτλ, and 96–97, ἐκ δὲ Διὸς βασιλῆες· ὅ δ' ὄλβιος, ὅντινα Μοῦσαι | φιλῶνται κτλ). As is appropriate to Ptolemy, ὄλβος here, as at Callim. *H.* 1.84, consists of great prosperity and extensive territory. The special relationship between Ptolemy and the land over which he rules (77 ff. nn.) gives the similarity between these verses and the *Homeric Hymn to the Earth* (v. 30) particular suggestiveness: ὁ δ᾽ ὄλβιος ὅν κε σὺ θυμῶι | πρόφρων τιμήσηις· τῶι τ᾽ ἄφθονα πάντα πάρεστι. | βρίθει μέν σφιν ἄρουρα φερέσβιος, ἠδὲ κατ᾽ ἀγροὺς | κτήνεσιν εὐθηνεῖ . . . ὄλβος δὲ πολὺς καὶ πλοῦτος ὀπηδεῖ. For ὄλβος ὀπηδεῖ at verse ending cf. also Hes. *WD* 326.

που: An amusingly disingenuous touch from the poet who has just told the story.

μέλοντι: Cf. 46n. The verb also occurs in the seventy-third verse of Callim. *H.* 1 (quoted in 46n.), at the head of a 'Hesiodic' passage on Zeus and kings; this may or may not be coincidence. For the Doric form in –οντι cf. above, p. 56.

ἔξοχος picks up the opening theme of Ptolemy as the "best" of kings.

γεινόμενον τὰ πρῶτα: The same phrase of Aphrodite at Hes. *Theog.* 202 and of Artemis (with singular τὸ πρῶτον) at Callim. *H.* 3.23; related expressions occur at *Il.* 6.345; *Od.* 4.13, 19.355; Callim. *H.* 5.105. Pace Reinsch-Werner (1976, 258), it hardly seems possible to build a relative chronology for T. and Callimachus on these similarities.

πολὺς . . . πολλᾶς . . . πολλᾶς: The anaphora (cf. 75–76, 110–11n.) rounds off the "Apolline" section by associating Ptolemy with a standard etymology for Apollo's name, and one particularly favored by Callimachus (cf. *H.* 2.34–35, 69–70, etc). For Ptolemy's territory cf. 86–92n.

77–85 The praise of lands and cities is a very old theme in Greek poetry (cf., for example, *Od.* 13.237–49), and it came eventually to form a stock subject in the rhetorical schools (cf. Men. Rhet. 344.16 ff. [= pp. 28–42 R-W]; Hendriks, Parsons, and Worp 1981, 74–75). Hor. *Carm.* 1.7 plays with the familiarity of the theme in a generically conscious way (cf. the notes of Nisbet-Hubbard), and, like T., Horace leads up to the place that he actually wishes to praise in a quasi priamel (cf. also Soph. *OC* 694–701; Virg. *Georg.* 2.136–39; Hunter 2001). As at 53 ff., the priamel is here used to mark a new direction for the poem (cf. Meincke 1965, 125). More specifically, praise of the homeland of the *laudandus* is an integral part of epinician poetry and encomiastic rhetoric (cf. Pind. *Nem.* 1.14–15 [Zeus and Persephone], κατένευ- | σέν τέ οἱ χαίταις, ἀριστεύοισαν εὐκάρπου χθονός | Σικελίαν πίειραν ὀρθώ- | σειν κορυ- φαῖς πολίων ἀφνεαῖς κτλ). Isoc. *Bus.* 12–14 is a rhetorical *laudes Aegyptiae* that shares many motifs with the present passage; for a (very probably) later Sotadean encomium of Alexandria or Egypt, which also employs some of these same ideas cf. Hendriks, Parsons, and Worp 1981. Herodas 1.26–35 is a comical version of the "praises of Alexandria" theme (cf. above, pp. 36–37).

The wealth of Egypt had been proverbial in Greek literature ever since Achilles stated that he would not yield to Agamemnon, however much the latter offered him: "Not even if he offered me ten times or twenty times all he possesses now, and others' wealth besides, not even all the riches that pour into Orchomenos, or Thebes in Egypt, where the houses are piled high with treasure, and the city has a hundred gates, and through each gate two hundred men drive out with horses and chariots: not even if he offered me gifts unnumbered like the sand or dust..." (*Il.* 9.379–85, trans. Hammond). This passage, with its interest in counting, offers epic authority to the "census" that T. gives in vv. 82–84. (Cf. *Od.* 3.301, 14.285–86; 79–80n.)

77 ἄπειροι: "Regions of dry land" (cf. Hes. *Theog.* 964, νῆσοί τ᾽ ἤπειροί τε καὶ ἁλμυρὸς ἔνδοθι πόντος). This rare meaning of the word, in juxtaposition to the repeated μυρίαι, allows the etymology "without limit (πέρας)" to resonate (cf. Eur. fr. 1010 N², ἤπειρον εἰς ἄπειρον ἐκβάλλων πόδα; *Etym. Magn.* 433.54–55 Gaisford).

ἔθνεα μυρία φωτῶν: The language is epic; cf. *Od.* 11.632, ἔθνεα ... μυρία νεκρῶν; *Arg.* 2.1204–5, Κόλχων | ἔθνεα ... ἀπείρονα; 4.646, ἔθνεα μυρία Κελτῶν. As the examples from the *Arg.* show, such language would normally be applied to the "vast hordes" of non-Greek peoples; here, however, it denotes all the world *except* the inhabitants of Egypt, and this is a mark of the adaptation of traditional attitudes and ideologies to a new situation.

τε καὶ: The τε is postponed, as not infrequently (Denniston 517).

78 λήϊον ἀλδήσκουσιν: "Raise up crops, bring them to ripeness" (Gow). The only occurrence of ἀλδήσκω before T. (*Epigr.* 511 Kaibel seems certainly later) is in a famous simile at *Il.* 23.599, λήϊου ἀλδήσκοντος, "of the growing crop"; T. has copied Homer's *hapax* but used the verb transitively, instead of the more usual ἀλδαίνω.

ὀφελλόμενον: ὀφελλόμεναι is accepted by Gow as "sharpening the contrast between the rain-fed countries and Egypt dependent on the Nile" and may be correct.

Διὸς ὄμβρωι: The rainlessness of Egypt and its dependence upon the Nile flood was one of the most commented upon of that country's paradoxical reversals (cf. Hdt. 2.13.3, 22.3; Eur. *Hel.* 1–3; *Arg.* 4.269–71; Tib. 1.7.25–26; Bonneau 1964, 129).

79–80 Hiatus within a fifth-foot spondee (cf. 22.174, if ἀποσχομένω ὑσμίνης is read) may here throw particular emphasis on the proud name of "low-lying Egypt."

The fertility and richness of πολυλήϊος Egypt (*Arg.* 4.267) had long been proverbial (cf., for example, Bacchyl. fr. 20B.14–16 M; Ar. fr. 581.15 K-A). The cause was the annual flood of miraculously productive Nile water (cf. Callim. fr. 384.27, θηλύτατον καὶ Νεῖλος ἄγων ἐνιαύσιον ὕδωρ; Strabo 15.1.22–23 [citing Aristotle on the subject]; *GLP* 124.6–8 [Hellenistic?], "Great is the flood of Nile, and great [πολλὴ . . . πολλὴ] the abundance that is spread over the corn, and smiles, and brings fertility; the fruits thereof go forth to every land" [trans. Page]; and an [early imperial?] "Nile hymn" [Cribiore 1995], in which the river's water is σταχυητόκον [vv. 21–22]); "flowing with gold" later became a stock epithet for the river (Ath.5.203c; "Nile hymn" 8; Bonneau 1964, 130). This age-old pharaonic topic acquired a particular significance under the Ptolemies, for whom the advertisement of wealth was a prominent ideological weapon (cf. below 95–97n.). The link between the two ideas has, again, both a Greek and an Egyptian background, which fit together smoothly. On one hand, Ptolemaic Egypt is a macrocosmic version of the Hesiodic "Just City" (*WD* 225–37; cf. *Od.* 19.109–14) in which peace and prosperity now depend not upon the justice of the inhabitants (though that might be thought implicit in v. 97), but upon the fact of rule by a just king who derives his authority from Zeus; the idea passed into the stock themes of Hellenistic kingship theory (cf. Philodemos *On the Good King* cols. iv–v Dorandi). So, too, from an Egyptian perspective, the king, as preserver of good order throughout the land, was responsible for the Nile flood and for the country's prosperity (cf. Merkelbach 1981, 27–28; Koenen and Thompson 1984, 120–25). For a hieroglyphic example in honor of Philadelphus cf. Sauneron 1960, 87: "Ses greniers atteignent jusqu'au ciel; toute graine . . ."

Αἴγυπτος | Νεῖλος: The juxtaposition suggests the importance of the latter for the former and also puts together the Homeric (*Od.* 4.477, etc.) and the modern names of the river. Kees (1961, chap. 2) offers a useful introduction to the importance of the Nile for Egyptian agriculture (cf. Bowman and Rogan 1999).

διερὰν . . . βώλακα: The basic sense of the adjective is "wet," but διερὸς βροτός (*Od.* 6.201) was understood as "a living man" (cf. *LfgrE* s.v.; Williams on Callim. *H.* 2.23; Zinato 1974), and "quickened with life" would not be inappropriate here; the "Nile hymn" speaks of the land as τραφερὴν . . . μετὰ χεύματα Νείλου (vv. 21–22) (cf. Virg. *Georg.* 4.291, *[Nilus] et uiridem Aegyptum nigra fecundat harena;* Dion. Perieg. 227–29: "[The Nile] enriches the fertile soil of Egypt with its waters. No river is like the Nile, either for the production of mud or for increasing the prosperity (ὄλβος) of the land"). One view held that the Nile flood not merely made the earth fertile but actually generated new life-forms, in a replay of the primeval flood (cf. Diod. Sic. 1.10.6–7; Bonneau 1964, 121–22; Vian on 4.681). Williams (1981, 87–88) suggests that T. is playing with a believed connection between διερός and Ζεύς (cf. *Arg.* 2.1098–99; Σ *Arg.* 1.184).

βῶλαξ is a rare form of βῶλος, "soil, land" (LSJ s.v. 2). Dioscorides, *AP* 9.568.3 (= *HE* 1679) seems to use βῶλος to refer to Egyptian farmland (cf. also Diod. Sic. 1.10.2).

81 From agricultural plenty we move to the towns and villages, which are equally productive. ἔργα δαέντες is here "people skilled in crafts," the activities that are traditionally under the protection of Athena and Hephaestus (cf. *Hymn. Hom. Heph.* 20.5; Solon fr. 13.49–50; and 95–97n. below). For this theme cf. Isoc. *Bus.* 17 (because each Egyptian works only at a single craft): "We shall find that in the crafts (τέχνας) the Egyptians surpass those who work at the same skilled occupations elsewhere more than artisans in general (τοὺς ἄλλους δημιουργούς) excel the layman." Hecataeus of Abdera, who divided Egyptian citizens into "herdsmen," "farmers," and "craftsmen" (τεχνῖται or δημιουργοί), makes the same point as Isocrates (Diod. Sic. 1.74.6–7), and it is likely that this explains T.'s emphasis here.

82–84 The figure of 33,333 πόλεις (i.e., in fact, "villages," κῶμαι) probably derives from Hecataeus of Abdera (cf. Diod. Sic. 1.31.7–8; ΣbT *Il.* 9.383; Wilamowitz 1962, 4: 31–32). Hdt. 2.177.1 gives Egypt 20,000 πόλεις in the time of Amasis in the sixth century (cf. Lloyd 1975 ad loc.).

The three-verse catalogue is framed by τρεῖς ... τρεῖς and amusingly evokes the Egyptian and Ptolemaic passion for counting and census-making; a document of 258 B.C.E. reveals a census ordered by Philadelphus of every field and its revenue, animal by animal and tree by tree, in Egypt (cf. Bresciani 1978; Turner 1984, 135–36; Burstein 1985, no. 97). For another good example of such census practices cf. Burstein 1985, no. 101. The well-ordered and controlled world of Egypt is thus opposed to the chaotic ἔθνεα μυρία φωτῶν of less fortunate places. The number is not, however, to be given too much credence: "three" is a common element in fictional magnitudes (cf. Scheidel 1996), and we might compare a later temple-inscription from Edfu that gives the amount of arable land in Egypt as 27,000,000 arouras, that is, 3 x 3 x 3 million (Schlott 1969, 160–69).

μέν οἱ: The μέν is treated as long in imitation of a Homeric feature, the result of the original digamma before οἱ (cf. Gow on

15.112; above, p. 70). The same license accounts for the hiatus ἐπεί οἱ in v. 90.

σφισιν: Cf. above, p. 58; 26–27n.

85 For the breach of "Naeke's Law" cf. above, p. 68.

ἀγήνωρ: The epithet is only rarely used of persons in a good sense in early epic ("manly, kingly"; cf. *LfgrE* s.v. a), and the only occurrences of the adjective (2.2) and noun (2.150, 481) in *Arg.* are pejorative; T. may have wanted to evoke a connection with ἄγειν (cf. Eust. *Hom.* 1280.4, 1396.44), and also perhaps with the interpretation of Λαγός as "leader of the people." Grammarians normally etymologize the adjective as ἀπὸ τοῦ ἄγαν τῆι ἠνορέηι χρῆσθαι (cf. Σ *Il.* 9.699; *Etym. Magn.* 9.42).

ἐμβασιλεύει: The compound, here constructed with the genitive on the pattern of the simple βασιλεύειν, distinguishes the seat of Ptolemy's *basileia* (Egypt) from territories with which he enjoys a different relationship; see next note, and cf. Isocrates' advice to Philip: Ἕλληνας εὐεργετεῖν, Μακεδόνων δὲ βασιλεύειν, τῶν δὲ βαρβάρων ὡς πλείστων ἄρχειν (*Ad Phil.* 154).

86–92 After Egypt the catalogue moves to regions under "foreign" control, where Philadelphus extends his borders by encroachment (ἀποτέμνεται), and then to states where his power is transmitted through agents of one kind or another (σαμαίνει), whether these be governors (*strategoi*, a military term like σημαίνειν, which Σ gloss as ἐπιτάσσειν) or simply those able to make his desires known to nominally free states. In all these areas, as in Egypt, Ptolemy "reigns" (ἀνάσσειν, v. 92); as the list of areas moves from the specific to the general ("all the seas and lands and rivers . . ."), so do the verbs (cf. *LfgrE* s.v. ἀνάσσω). The careful patterning of verbs may in fact be modeled on *Il.* 1.287–89 (Agamemnon complaining about Achilles), ἀλλ᾽ ὅδ᾽ ἀνὴρ ἐθέλει περὶ πάντων ἔμμεναι ἄλλων, | πάντων μὲν κρατέειν ἐθέλει, πάντεσσι δ᾽ ἀνάσσειν, | πᾶσι δὲ σημαίνειν, ἅ τιν᾽ οὐ πείσεσθαι ὀίω; ΣbT ad loc. preserve an attempt to distinguish between the synonyms: . . . ἐκτὸς εἰ μὴ τὸ κρατεῖν σημαίνει τὸ νικᾶν, ἄρχειν δὲ τὸ ἀνάσσειν, ἐπιτάσσειν δὲ τὸ σημαίνειν; and cf. *Il.* 16.171–72 of the organization of Achilles' fleet: πέντε δ᾽ ἄρ᾽ ἡγεμόνας ποιήσατο τοῖς ἐπεποίθει, | σημαίνειν· αὐτὸς δὲ μέγα κρατέων ἤνασσε. T.'s passage puts such epic distinctions into contemporary practice, but Ptolemy has gone one better than both Agamemnon and Achilles: as the true heir of Alexander, whom Dio later portrays quoting *Il.* 1.288 (above) with approval (Dio Chrys. 2.5), he really does rule τὰ πάντα (cf. 91–92n.).

The spatial ordering of the first part of the catalogue is from the east (Phoenicia, Arabia, Syria) to the west (Libya) and finally to the south (Ethiopia). These lands are grouped together as (broadly conceived) sharing boundaries with "Egypt" and hence available for partial annexation through military operations (ἀποτέμνεται): the second, "Greek," part of the catalogue, where Ptolemy's control is peaceful, moves west from Pamphylia (and, to its east, Cilicia) to Lycia and then Caria, before embracing the Cyclades. A broadly similar patterning is observable in Euergetes' list of the lands he inherited from his father (*OGIS* 54.6–8): Αἰγύπτου καὶ Λιβύης καὶ Συρίας καὶ Φοινίκης καὶ Κύπρου καὶ Λυκίας καὶ Καρίας καὶ τῶν Κυκλάδων νήσων. In giving prominence to the extension of Egypt's boundaries T. associates Ptolemy with a fundamental kingly duty upon which the safety of the land depended; thus in the "Letter of Aristeas" one of the Jewish sages tells Philadelphus that whereas ordinary men are naturally inclined to

food, drink, and pleasure, kings are rather inclined to the acqui-
sition of territory ("Letter of Aristeas" 220). The successful ex-
tension of boundaries is in fact a standard pharaonic claim, seen,
for example, in a poem about Sesostris I in "The Story of Sinu-
he" (Lichtheim 1973, 226 = Assmann 1975, 476): "Enlarger of
frontiers, he will conquer southern lands, while ignoring north-
ern lands, though made to smite Asiatics and tread on Sand-
farers"; Sesostris functioned as a model both for Alexander and
the Ptolemies, and for his conquests see Diod. Sic. 1.55; and for
further examples of this pharaonic pattern cf. Peden 1994, 215:
"I [Ramses III] advanced the boundaries of Egypt on all sides";
Hornung 1957, 125–26; Huss 1994, 103 n. 160; Selden 1998,
331–37. Cat. 66.35–36 (from Callimachus), *is [sc. Euergetes] haut
in tempore longo | captam Asiam Aegypti finibus addiderat*, offers an-
other Ptolemaic example of the pattern. The habit of territorial
annexation was not, of course, limited to the pharaohs and
Ptolemies, but it is perhaps worthy of note that Isocrates' ideal-
ized Nikokles preaches a very different form of behavior: "I am
so far from coveting what belongs to others that while rulers of
a different kind, if they have the slightest advantage in power over
their neighbors, annex some of their land (ἀποτέμνονται τῆς γῆς) and
seek to aggrandize themselves (πλεονεκτεῖν), I did not think it right
to take even the land that was offered to me, but prefer rather to
hold through just means what is my own than to acquire through
base means territory many times greater than that which I now
possess" (*Nic.* 34). Ptolemaic ideology, as here represented by T.,
could not be more different than the "philosophical" ideal pro-
moted by Isocrates.

The "boundaries" of Egypt, like the catalogue of Egypt's ene-
mies, had long been fixed. Herodotus records that "in the time of

Psammetichos guard posts were established at Elephantine toward the Ethiopians, in Daphnai at Pelusium toward the Arabians and Syrians, and at Marea toward Libya" (2.30.2). So, too, Ptolemaic catalogues, such as those of T., may be seen as an accommodation to Greek conceptions and geography of the traditional list of the enemies of Egypt, the so-called Nine Bows, over whom a pharaoh would claim to have triumphed; the meaning of such lists does not reside in their historicity, as narrowly understood, but in their message that the king on the throne is doing what kings must do to preserve the well-being of Egypt (cf. *LdÄ* s.v. Neunbogen; Loprieno 1988; Zabkar 1988, 63–67; Valbelle 1990). An excellent example is the "Victory Hymn" of Thutmose III (*ANET* 373–75 = Assmann 1975, no. 233), which celebrates the king's universal power in an extended catalogue.

In keeping with a central strategy of the whole poem (above, pp. 141–42), Philadelphus is here described as emulating not just an inherited pharaonic pattern, but also his father who campaigned against both Syria and Phoenicia (cf. Diod. Sic. 18.43) and who passed on to his son much of the control that is here catalogued. In the original division of the empire after Alexander's death, Soter received "Egypt, Libya [i.e., everything to the west of the Nile Valley], and all Arabia that bordered Egypt" (Arrian, *FGrHist* 156 F1.5–7); this territory was essentially confirmed in the subsequent settlements of 320 (Arrian, *FGrHist* 156 F9.34; Austin 1981, no. 24) and 311 (Diod. Sic.19.105.1; Austin 1981, no. 30).

In view of the traditional patterns that lie behind these verses, it is extremely difficult, and perhaps misguided, to use them to identify the limits of an absolute chronology for the poem (cf. Perrotta 1978, 76–79; Fraser 1972, 2: 933–34; Weber 1993, 213, 312–13). In particular, the omission of Cyprus and the relation between these verses and the "First Syrian War" between Philadelphus and Antiochus have given rise to very considerable discussion, most of which is inconclusive, both because of the absence of much external information about that war (cf. Tarn 1926; Hölbl 2001, 38–40) and because the conventionality of the verses has too often been ignored. That there is a connection between the passage and "real historical facts" is hardly to be doubted—thus (at the simplest level) Philadelphus did indeed control a vast swathe of Asia Minor; and cf. the catalogue of Ptolemaic possessions at Polyb. 5.34.6–9—but the nature of that connection is more than usually slippery. Philadelphus clearly did pursue an active, even aggressive foreign policy, which finds a fair reflection in these verses (cf. Tarn 1928; Burstein 1989), but their formulaic quality and the reticence, typical of Ptolemaic poetry, in specifically naming rival kings remain obstacles to any historical reconstruction based upon them. Nor can chronological conclusions safely be drawn from the tense of ἀποτέμνεται; that Philadelphus "*is* cutting slices off . . ." merely shows that he is acting as a proper warrior-king should.

86 Φοινίκας: Philadelphus controlled important sections of the Phoenician and Syrian coasts, though many of the details are disputed (Bagnall 1976, 11–13); these areas were particularly important sources of timber for shipbuilding. Together "Phoenicia" and "Syria" make up roughly the whole area between Egypt and Cilicia.

Ἀρραβίας: "Arabia" was traditionally all the desert east of the Delta and Nile Valley (Hdt. 2.8, etc.), from where "for millenia [nomads] had infiltrated the E. Delta" (Lloyd 1975 on Hdt. 2.30.2). Philadelphus's activity in the east is proclaimed on the

"Pithom Stele," and his reign was in fact marked by very active trade investigation of the Red Sea area (cf. Tarn 1929; Burstein 1989; Fraser 1972, 1: 176–80). For bibliography on Ptolemaic activity at the Red Sea cf. Burstein 1989, 3 n. 1.

87 Συρίας: That is, Coele Syria, essentially modern Lebanon and northern Israel, a central site of military operations for both Soter and Philadelphus (cf. Winnicki 1989b, 1991; Walbank on Polyb. 5.34.6; Lorton 1971).

Λιβύας: Traditionally conceived as everything to the west of the fertile Delta and Nile Valley (cf. *LdÄ* s.v. Libyen, Libyer; the name is etymologized from λίψ, the west or southwest wind, at Dion. Perieg. 231; Servius on *Aen.* 1.22). There may be a specific reference to Cyrenaica, which was ruled by Philadelphus's half brother Magas; Magas had controlled Cyrene for Soter, but after the latter's death, relations with Alexandria broke down, and Magas declared himself an independent king. An attack upon Egypt in the "First Syrian War" was aborted because of trouble at home (cf. Chamoux 1956). Relations with Cyrene are, therefore, a very fragile dating criterion for the poem, but if any weight is given to them, this factor points to the same period in the 270s as the other evidence (above, p. 7). "Libya" is, however, a very loose concept, as well as being one of the "traditional" enemies of Egypt, and in part its presence is dictated by the need for geographical all-inclusiveness.

κελαινῶν τ' Αἰθιοπήων: The Ethiopians are dark because they live near the sun's eastern home, according to a very common Greek conception (cf. *Od.* 1.22–23; Hes. *WD* 527–28; Eur. *Phaethon* 1–5, with Diggle's notes); Αἰθίοψ was etymologized as "burnt face." Greeks regarded Egyptians as darker than themselves

(Aesch. *Supp.* 154–55, 719–20, etc.), but "Ethiopians" from south of Elephantine were, from both Egyptian and Greek perspectives, "black" (cf. Cameron 1995, 233–35). κελαινῶν Αἰθιοπήων ends a hexameter at Dion. Perieg. 179.

The southern border of Egypt was conventionally placed at Elephantine (Aswan) (cf. Hdt. 2.29.4, with Lloyd's note; Strabo 1.2.25), but at various periods Egyptian control had extended deep into Nubia (cf. Zibelius-Chen 1988). Philadelphus's activity in the south is in fact clear from both the historical and the archaeological records: Diod. Sic.1.37.5 (cf. Pliny *NH* 6.183) records a campaign "with Greek forces" of Philadelphus into "Ethiopia" (cf. Fraser 1972, 1: 175–76; Steinmeyer-Schareika 1978; Burstein 1989, 6–7, 32–33; Hölbl 2001, 55–58), and the archaeological record clearly shows that Egyptian activity, territorial expansion, and temple building in Nubia reached a peak in this reign (cf. Préaux 1952; Burstein 1993; Dietze 1994; below, 124n.). The principal purposes of this activity were to secure control over the Nubian gold mines and hunting grounds, but there is no reason to doubt also genuine geographical and zoological curiosity. Philadelphus's "Grand Procession" was filled with marvelous *paradoxa* from the south (Ath. 5.201a–c). (Cf. further 124n.)

88 Παμφύλοισί τε πᾶσι: The jingle stresses the universality of Philadelphus's rule over "all tribes." Pamphylia was indeed under Philadelphus's control through the 270s and 260s (Bagnall 1976, 110–14; Hölbl 2001, 38; Cohen 1995, 335–36), and many Pamphylians are known to have been active in the Ptolemaic administration (cf. Robert 1963, 418–20).

αἰχμηταῖς Κιλίκεσσι: A recently published inscription has confirmed the presence of a Ptolemaic *strategos* in Cilicia under

Philadelphus, in whose reign the Cilician towns of Arsinoe and Berenike were probably founded (cf. Kirsten and Opelt 1989; Jones and Habicht 1989; Cohen 1995, 363–65).

89 For Ptolemaic control of extensive areas of southern Asia Minor cf. Bagnall 1976, 89–110; Wörrle 1977, 1978; Mastrocinque 1979; Robert and Robert 1983, 118–32; there were well-established communities of Ionians and Carians in Egypt during the pharaonic period (cf. the "Hellenomemphites" and the "Caromemphites"), and these two regions had long been important sources of mercenaries in Egypt (cf. Archilochus fr. 216 West; Hdt. 2.152–54; Austin 1970, 15–34; Lloyd 1975, 14–23), and the recruiting of both soldiers and administrators from these areas intensified under Soter and Philadelphus.

90–91 Ptolemaic control over the Island League was firm throughout this period; Philadelphus (and later Arsinoe), like Soter before them (*SIG* 390 = Austin 1981, no. 218), enjoyed cult honors in the islands (cf. Durrbach 1921, nos. 17, 21; Reger 1994, 16–47; 58–76n. above). The Ptolemaic navy, particularly under the admiral Sostratos of Knidos, was exceptionally large and powerful: Ath. 5.203d notes that Philadelphus owned some very large ships, and places the total navy at "more than four thousand vessels" (cf. App. *Praef.* 10). (Cf. in general Hauben 1970; Van't Dack and Hauben 1978.) The theme is again a traditional one, for the might of the ruler's ships is a common topos of pharaonic inscriptions, but here it has particular encomiastic point in the light of Arsinoe's special relationship with the navy, through her association with the marine Aphrodite and Aphrodite Euploia (cf. Satyrus,

POxy. 2465 fr.2, col. II 19; Poseidippos, *HE* 3120–25; Robert 1966; Gutzwiller 1992a, 1992b).

ἐπεί οἱ: Cf. 82n.

νᾶες ἄρισται ‖ πόντον ἐπιπλώοντι: Cf. *Od.* 7.327–28 (Alcinous to Odysseus), εἰδήεις δὲ καὶ αὐτὸς ἐνὶ φρεσὶν ὅσσον ἄρισται ‖ νῆες ἐμαὶ καὶ κοῦροι ἀναρρίπτειν ἅλα πηδῶι. Naval power is one more respect in which the Phaeacian royal couple foreshadow Philadelphus and Arsinoe (cf. further *Od.* 7.108–9, 8.555–63; Vox 1989, 90; above 38–39n.). πόντον ἐπιπλώσας begins a hexameter at *Il.* 3.47, and cf. *Arg.* 1.548–49 (the gods admire the Argonauts), οἳ τότ' ἄριστοι ‖ πόντον ἐπιπλώεσκον.

Rossi (1989) retains the transmitted ἄριστοι as an example of a superlative treated as a two-termination form (cf. *Hymn. Hom. Dem.* 157, with Richardson's note; *Od.* 4.442; Hes. *Theog.* 408; Pind. fr. 152 M; Aratus *Phain.* 625, 628 [ἔσχατος]; Kastner 1967, 21–39). Wilamowitz also kept ἄριστοι, but on the grounds that T. here treated ναῦς as masculine; neither defense is convincing (cf. Latte 1968, 528), especially in a place where no metrical necessity demands or would protect the rarity.

ἐπιπλώοντι: For the Doric form cf. above, p. 56.

91–92 Philadelphus's universal rule has many models: Zeus (*Il.* 12.241–42; Aratus *Phain.* 2–4, etc.), Apollo (*Hymn. Hom. Ap.* 22–24, 29), and particularly Alexander, who came to rule ἡ οἰκουμένη ἅπᾶσα, as indeed the oracle at Siwa had foretold (Quint. Curt. 4.7.26). How readily such claims ease the transition from human to divine at this period is clear from Euhemeros's narrative in which the sanctuary of Zeus Triphylios was established by Zeus himself "while he was still among men and ruled the whole world

⟨τῆς οἰκουμένης ἀπάσης⟩" (Diod. Sic. 6.1.6); cf. further Bosworth 1999. Such claims to universal "world" rule are in fact commonplace in both pharaonic and Ptolemaic texts (cf. Hornung 1957, 123–25; Huss 1994, 104 n.162) and more generally in Hellenistic panegyric (cf. Doblhofer 1966, 49–50); T.'s "remarkable hyperbole" (Gow) is in fact perfectly at home within an oriental rhetoric of kingship. The Callimachean version of these verses is the unborn Apollo's prophecy of Philadelphus's empire, ἀμφοτέρη μεσόγεια καὶ αἳ πελάγεσσι κάθηνται, | μέχρις ὅπου περάτη τε καὶ ὁπ‑πόθεν ὠκέες ἵπποι |'Ηέλιον φορέουσιν (*H.* 4.168–70); it is noteworthy that these verses of Callimachus contain one of the few now commonly accepted "Egyptianizing" references in the *Hymns*: ἀμ‑φοτέρη μεσόγεια as Upper and Lower Egypt (cf. Mineur 1984 ad loc.; above, p. 49). Callimachus's association of Philadelphus and the sun also seems to draw on traditional expressions of the extent of kingly control (cf., for example, Lichtheim 1976, 40–41 [Amenhotep II]: "He bound the heads of the Nine Bows, he holds the Two Lands in his hand . . . [Amun] himself made him rule what his eye encircles, what the disk of Re illuminates; he has taken all of Egypt, south and north are in his care. The Red Land brings him its dues, all countries have his protection; his borders reach the rim of heaven, the lands are in his hand in a single knot. . . . His portion is that on which Re shines, to him belongs what Ocean encircles . . .").

For the division of the world into land, sea, and rivers cf. Hes. *Theog.* 108–9; Eur. *HF* 1296–97, with Wilamowitz and Bond ad loc.; *Arg.* 3.164–66; Dion. Perieg. 1–2, etc.

αἶα: A choice epic word, only here in T. (where γαῖα would be metrically impossible).

ποταμοὶ κελάδοντες: Another high-style phrase (cf. *Il.* 18.576).

93–94 At vv. 75–78 the transition between verse-paragraphs was effected by a triple anaphora of πολύς leading to the repeated μυρίαι/ μυρία and the theme of plenty; here another anaphora of πολύς and the image of gleaming bronze lead toward ὄλβος.

At one level the verses depict Ptolemy, like Hieron amidst his forces at 16.78–81, as an epic hero on the model of an Agamemnon or an Achilles; note esp. *Il.* 2.476–83, Agamemnon like Zeus, Ares, and Poseidon (a combination that Ptolemy's universal rule recreates) and "foremost and outstanding amidst the many heroes"; and 2.576–80, Agamemnon as both ἄριστος and as leading "by far the most (πολὺ πλεῖστοι) troops." For the combination of cavalry and ἀσπιδιῶται cf. *Il.* 2.553–54, 16.167. On the other hand, the present tense need not refer to preparations for an imminent battle; rather, the image is timeless and visual, and we may think of the monumental temple images of pharaohs encircled by their armies (good examples at Frankfort 1948, figs. 9–10; cf. 102n.). Jerome records a figure of 200,000 foot soldiers and 20,000 cavalry for Philadelphus (*PL* 25.559 Migne = *FGrHist* 260 F42); App. *Praef.* 10 puts the cavalry at 40,000. At the end of the "Grand Procession" came "the cavalry and infantry forces, all of them marvelously armed (καθωπλισμέναι θαυμασίως); there were 57,600 foot soldiers and 23,200 cavalry" (Ath.5.202f–3a); for a consideration of these figures cf. Winnicki 1989a. For an Egyptian version of Philadelphus's vast armies cf. the honorific text cited by Sauneron 1960, 87: "Ses soldats sont plus nombreux que le sable du rivage."

ἱππῆες: For the Ptolemaic cavalry cf. Mooren 1975, 146–68; Rice 1983, 123–25. The royal "war horses" are noted by Praxinoa at 15.51–52.

πολλοὶ δέ μιν ἀσπιδιῶται: The word order mimics the sense of Ptolemy "surrounded" by his forces; the primary reference is to the Graeco-Macedonian phalanx and Ptolemy's mercenary forces (cf. 14.66–67). There seems no reason to think of Ptolemy's "bodyguards."

χαλκῶι μαρμαίροντι: The flavor is again epic (cf. *Il.*13.801, 16.663–64; Alcaeus fr. 140 V [a catalogue of weapons ready for war]). μαρμαίροντι . . . ἀμφαγέρονται approaches very close to the rhyming pattern of v. 29 (where see note).

σεσαγμένοι: The ordinary sense "laden down with" perhaps "lends a touch of humour to the line" (Rossi), but cf. ἀχθόμενοι at 16.79 and βαρυνόμενοι at 22.143; Herodotus also uses this passive with the sense "equipped," and without obvious humorous intent (7.62.2, 70.2, etc.).

95–97 We now move back from Ptolemaic wealth and power as displayed in military might and foreign conquest to the peaceful plenty of Egypt (cf. vv. 79–81), which is itself the result of secure boundaries. Thus the "Pithom Stele" declares that in 273 Philadelphus and Arsinoe visited Pithom "to protect Egypt from foreigners" (Roeder 1959, 122; cf. p. 117). In Hecataeus of Abdera's account it was the idealized Sesoosis whose conquests secured for the Egyptians "eternal security and plentiful ease" (Diod. Sic. 1.56.1–3), though he seems also to have laid great stress on the geographical "fortifications" of Egypt in every direction (Diod. Sic. 1.30–31). For peace as a theme in Hellenistic panegyric more generally cf. Doblhofer 1966, 76–77.

ὄλβωι: Wealth, and the display of wealth, had always been central to the self-presentation of Greek elites (cf., for example, Pind. *Ol.* 1.10, 2.11, 22, 53–56; fr. 119), and Hellenistic kings were no exceptions (cf. Préaux 1978, 208–12); nowhere perhaps was this more the case than in Ptolemaic Alexandria, where, as the Adonis festival of *Idyll* 15 makes clear, ostentatious τρυφή was an important element of royal presentation (cf. Hunter 1996, 117; Weber 1993. 226–28). The wealth of North Africa in grain, minerals (cf. Diod. Sic. 1.49.2), and ivory (cf. 124n.) meant that there was genuine substance behind the presentation, as is clear from the extremely rich extant coinage of Philadelphus (cf. von Reden 2001). πλοῦτος is the first "virtue" of Egypt at Herodas 1.28, and under the influence of the "Grand Procession," Athenaeus extols the Ptolemaic kingdom as the richest there has ever been and singles out Philadelphus as remarkable in this regard, even by Ptolemaic standards (Ath.5.203b–c; cf. App. *Praef.* 10); a late third-century epitaph refers to the παλαίπλουτοι βασιλῆες | Aἰγύπτου (*GV* 1508.9–10 Peek). For the negative presentation of Philadelphus's paraded wealth cf. Plut. *Arat.* 15 (Antigonus about Aratus): "Formerly he used to overlook us, fixing his hopes elsewhere, and he admired the wealth of Egypt, hearing tales of its elephants, and fleets, and palaces; but now that he has been behind the scenes and seen that everything in Egypt is empty posturing and painted sets (τραγωιδίαν καὶ σκηνογραφίαν), he has come over entirely to us"; a similar tradition will lie behind Plut. *Mor.* 341a, in which Philadelphus appears in a list of kings who, in contrast to Alexander, "spent their lives making merry in processions and theaters."

Jerome gives a figure of 14,800 talents of silver and 1,500,000 artabae of grain as the annual income from Egypt (*PL* 25.560 Migne). (For an attempt to quantify Ptolemaic income cf. Préaux 1978, 1: 363–66; 1939.) Vv. 96–97 make plain the reciprocity that is claimed for this situation: Ptolemy's wealth, which derives in good measure from the agricultural work of the people, is in turn used to secure the frontiers and deter invasion, and thus to guarantee that the people will be allowed to live and work in peace (cf.

Bresciani 1978, 34–35), and for such ideas in kingship theory cf. already Isoc. *Nic.* 21, ἅπαντα γὰρ τὰ τῶν οἰκούντων τὴν πόλιν οἰκεῖα τῶν καλῶς βασιλευόντων ἐστί. Peace, such as results from the rule of a "good king" (cf.16.90–97; Men. Rhet. 377.13–24 Sp. [= p. 92 R-W]; Schubart 1937, 14) or a just people (Hes. *WD* 228–29) is regularly extolled in the priestly decrees in honor of later Ptolemies (cf. *OGIS* 56.12 [Euergetes I], 90.10–15 [= Austin 1981, no. 227, Epiphanes]); for a pharaonic example that strongly suggests vv. 97–101 cf. Lichtheim 1976, 77 = Davies 1997, 185 (Merneptah): "One walks free-striding on the road, for there's no fear in people's hearts; fortresses are left to themselves, wells are open for the messengers' use. Bastioned ramparts are becalmed, sunlight only wakes the watchman; Medjai are stretched out asleep, Nau and Tekten are in the fields they love. The cattle of the field are left to roam, no herdsmen cross the river's flood, etc." (cf. further Peden 1994, 21, 219 [Ramses III]).

The reference to "all [other] kings" and the optative καταβρίθοι, "would outweigh [sc. if a competition were arranged]," suggest the competitive displays of wealth and *euergesia* in which Hellenistic kings indulged (cf. Weber 1993, 72–73, 334–35), and there is likely to be a connection between this passage and the similar treatment of the theme at Callim. *H.* 1.84–86 (Zeus and kings): ἐν δὲ ῥυηφενίην ἔβαλές σφισιν, ἐν δ᾽ ἅλις ὄλβον· | πᾶσι μέν, οὐ μάλα δ᾽ ἶσον. ἔοικε δὲ τεκμήρασθαι | ἡμετέρωι μεδέοντι· περιπρὸ γὰρ εὐρὺ βέβηκεν.

καταβρίθοι: "Would press down," in other words, "outweigh"; the image picks up the heavy bronze of the previous verse. Taken literally the image is, as Gow notes, "illogical, for in the scales Ptolemy's wealth would cause the opposing scale to rise, not sink." He compares καθέλκει at Callim. fr. 1.9, where see Massimilla's note.

ἐπ' ἆμαρ ἕκαστον: A further suggestion of the Ptolemaic insistence upon bookkeeping and census records.

οἶκον: As Σ see, the resonance is specifically "treasury, stronghold," not just "palace" (cf. LSJ s.v. I.3).

ἔργα περιστέλλουσιν: "Look after their fields" (cf. LSJ s.v. ἔργον I.3a); "attend to their works/crafts" (cf. v. 81) is not impossible, but the following context strongly suggests agricultural labor. K's περιστέλλονται may well be right (cf. Eur. *HF* 1129, τὰ σὰ περιστέλλου κακά).

ἔκηλοι: "undisturbed" (cf. Campbell on *Arg.* 3.219). The language of this verse is similar to *Hymn. Hom.* 20.5–7 (Hephaestus's gifts have civilized mankind): νῦν δὲ δι' Ἥφαιστον κλυτοτέχνην ἔργα δαέντες | ῥηιδίως αἰῶνα τελεσφόρον εἰς ἐνιαυτὸν | εὔκηλοι διάγουσιν ἐνὶ σφετέροισι δόμοισιν. Hazzard (2000, 108) interestingly associates these verses with surviving ordinances of Philadelphus against robbers (λῃσταί) and evildoers (κακοῦργοι) (cf. *PHibeh* II.198.92–100 [probably later than *EP*]), and we may also be reminded of Praxinoa's exclamation about the safety of Alexandrian streets at 15.46–50; the primary reference of the verse seems, however, to be to security from foreign attack.

98–101 No one attacks Egypt across the desert from east or west; hence πεζός is opposed to attack from the north by ship (vv. 100–101) (cf. *Od.* 11.58; *Il.* 24.438, ἐν νηὶ θοῆι ἢ πεζός). The alternatives, "military attack" and "raids on farms," form a traditional pair (cf. Bacchyl. 18.5–10). The verses may, however, have a specific reference: in his account of the "First Syrian War" Pausanias (1.7) reports how projected attacks on Egypt from the west by Magas of Cyrene and from the north and east by Antiochus were aborted. Such specificity is not, of course, necessary (cf. Men.

Rhet. 377.13–19 [p. 92 R-W]: "[Because of the emperor] the earth is tilled in peace, the sea sailed without danger, piety towards God is increased, honours are given to all in due fashion. 'We fear neither barbarians nor enemies. The emperor's arms are a safer fortress for us than our cities' walls. We acquire prisoners as slaves, not by going to war ourselves, but by receiving them from the emperor's victorious hands'" [trans. Russell-Wilson]).

πολυκήτεα: The epic-style compound (cf. *Od.* 3.158, μεγακήτεα πόντον) is more likely to be a reference to (especially) crocodiles and hippopotamuses than just to the large fish of the river, but it is typical of Alexandrian poetry that these exotic creatures are not explicitly named and are "naturalized" by a Homeric-style adjective. The Nile itself fights for Ptolemy's kingdom, as allegedly in 321 when hundreds of Perdiccas's invading army were eaten by crocodiles (Diod. Sic. 18.35.6). The motif is traditional (cf. Isoc. *Bus.* 12–13: "[Egypt] is protected by the immortal wall of the Nile [ἀθανάτωι δὲ τείχει τῶι Νείλωι τετειχισμένην], which is designed by nature to provide not only protection but also sufficient sustenance for the country, since it is impregnable and difficult for attackers, but good for commerce and serving many purposes for those who live within its bounds"; Bonneau 1964, 74–78). The Nile's "monsters" are themselves a sign of the river's special fertility, as Strabo, commenting on the fact that the river has τὰ κήτη μείζω καὶ πλείω, remarks (15.1.23). At Aesch. *Pers.* 33–34, ὁ μέγας καὶ πολυθρέμμων | Νεῖλος, editors are divided between "much-nurturing" and "full of monsters" (cf. Broadhead ad loc.). Barchiesi (1996, 14–15) suggests that T.'s πολυκήτεα Νεῖλον is imitated at Hor. *Carm.* 4.14.47–48, *beluosus . . . Oceanus*.

ἐστάσατο: Aorist of repeated action, like ἐξήλατο (v. 100) (cf. K-G I 162).

κώμαις: Chosen to suggest the small agricultural and administrative units of Egypt (cf. Bevan 1927, 143, etc.).

100–101 suggest the cattle raids of which Nestor tells, or a pirate raid, such as are commonly described in the *Odyssey* (cf. 14.257–86 [a raid on Egyptian fields]). The verses are indeed full of epic language, θοᾶς ... ναός, θωρηχθείς, ἀνάρσιος. For the central importance of cattle in the Egyptian economy cf. Schnebel 1925, 320–23; Kees 1961, 86–91.

Αἰγυπτίῃσιν: Scanned as four syllables, with the central iota treated consonantally; this is a standard Homeric prosody (cf. West on *Od.* 4.83).

102 πλατέεσσιν ... πεδίοισι: If pressed, this is more obviously appropriate to the Delta and the Fayum than to the Nile Valley.

ἐνίδρυται: Apparently "is settled," though the use is far more natural of a whole people, as at *Epigr.* 18.5, τοὶ Συρακούσσαις ἐνίδρυνται (where see Gow's note), than of one ruler. As the verb is standardly used of temples and statues (cf. v. 125; LSJ s.v.), it may evoke the gigantic images of the ruler displayed on Egyptian temples throughout the countryside, like the Theban images of Ramses II ("Osymandyas") described by Hecataeus of Abdera (Diod. Sic. 1.48): it is these images that deter potential aggressors (cf. 93–94n.). We may also think of great enthroned statues, such as those of Amenhotep III at Thebes (the "Colossi of Memnon"). Be that as it may, though military prowess is an inevitable part of any ideology of kingship (cf., for example, Isoc. *Euag.* 31–32, μόνος πρὸς πολλοὺς καὶ μετ' ὀλίγων πρὸς ἅπαντας τοὺς ἐχθρούς; Préaux 1978, 195–99), the idea that the national security depends on just one "invincible" warrior-king finds many echoes in pharaonic texts (cf., for example, Lichtheim 1973, 198–99 [Sesostris III]; 1976, 41 [Amenhotep II], 62–63 [Ramses II]; Frankfort 1948, 8–9; Hornung 1957, 126–28; Spalinger 1982, 120–221). On the so-called Satrap Stele, Soter is "a person of youthful vigour, strong in his two arms, wise in spirit, leader of the soldiers . . . not turning his back, striking his adversaries in the face in the midst of the battle . . . in the midst of the battle none could stand against him, because of the might of his arm there was no parrying his hand" (Bevan 1927, 30; cf. Roeder 1959, 101). On the "Pithom Stele" also, Philadelphus is described in very conventional language as "der starke König, der Jüngling, der Große der Fremdländer, hoch an Arm am Tage des Zusammenstoßes und des Kampfes; der die Feinde bändigt, der die Gegner vertreibt, der den Widersache niederwirft durch viele starke Taten, der die Herzen aus den Leichen der menschen herausreißt . . ." (Roeder 1959, 117).

103 ξανθοκόμας: The standard hair color of epic heroes, such as Achilles (*Il.* 1.197) and Menelaos (18.1). Cf. [Arist.] *Physiog.* 812a16: "Those with sandy hair are brave; the model is the lion." *Epica Adesp.* 9, col.III 9 Powell may describe Arsinoe's hair as ξανθός, as the *coma Berenices* was *flaua* (Cat. 66.62). Gow notes that "Ptolemy would hardly be called ξανθοκόμης if he were really not so," but this may be optimistic.

ἐπιστάμενος δόρυ πάλλειν: Skill with the spear was a central element of Macedonian warrior culture, but here the αἰχμητής (v. 56) Philadelphus emulates both Achilles (cf. 55n.) and Alexander, who was very commonly portrayed in sculpture with a spear (Stewart 1993), 161–71), symbolizing his territorial conquests of "spear-won land"; this too was how the Ptolemies held Egypt

(Diod. Sic. 18.43). A fragmentary hexameter from a (contemporary?) poem gives Soter's father, Lagos, the epic epithet δορικλειτός (*SH* 922.9), and at *SH* 979.6–7 Philopator is celebrated as τὸν ἄριστον | ἐν δορὶ καὶ Μούσαις κοίρανον, which would fit Philadelphus as well. A hieroglyphic text tells of Philadelphus's enemies "effondrés devant son épée" (Sauneron 1960, 87).

104–5 Philadelphus not only preserves but also adds to what he received from Soter (cf. Nicander fr. 104.1 [on Attalus], ὦ κλῆρον ἀεὶ πατρώιον ἴσχων; Lichtheim 1973, 119 [Sesostris III], "I have made my boundary farther south than my fathers, I have added to what was bequeathed me," but both territory and revenues are at issue here). Philadelphus thus shows that Soter's confidence in him (vv. 41–42) was well placed; *Od.* 2.225–27 (41–42n. above) seems to be echoed again here.

μέλει: Cf. 46n.; royal ἐπιμέλεια is a standard theme of honorific inscriptions (cf. Schubart 1937, 8).

πατρώια πάντα: A Homeric formula (cf. *Od.* 17.80, 20.336; Bulloch on Callim. *H.* 5.133).

οἷ' ἀγαθῶι βασιλῆι: Cf. 14.64 (Philadelphus is generous), οἷα χρὴ βασιλῆ'. The "good king" conjures up for us later theoretical discussions, such as Philodemos's *On the Good King According to Homer*, and a didactic and gnomic flavor was always an important part of encomium, as Pindar, Isocrates, and others amply demonstrate. Nevertheless, the principal intertext here is *Il.* 3.178–79 (the *teikhoskopia*): οὗτός γ' Ἀτρεΐδης εὐρὺ κρείων Ἀγαμέμνων, | ἀμφότερον βασιλεύς τ' ἀγαθὸς κρατερός τ' αἰχμητής; according to Plut. *Mor.* 331c, v. 179 was judged by Alexander to be the greatest of all Homeric verses, and it is this standard against which Philadelphus is to be measured (and not found wanting). Cf. further Xen. *Mem.* 3.2.

The whole Agamemnon-section of the *teikhoskopia* is relevant here, particularly vv. 167–70 on his stature, βασιλῆι γὰρ ἀνδρὶ ἔοικε, and for Agamemnon as a model of outstanding kingly virtues cf. already Isoc. *Panath.* 72–83.

106–14 As though to block off a possible unfavorable interpretation of the previous verse (i.e., Philadelphus is concerned only with acquisition and possession), T. now moves to the theme of royal *euergesia* and *philanthropia* (cf. Doblhofer 1966, 55–57); Philadelphus, far from being a mere hoarder of wealth on the model of the Herodotean Croesus, is as openhanded as T. encourages patrons to be at 16.22 ff. The proper use of wealth is, of course, a traditional theme of patronage poetry (cf. Pind. *Pyth.* 1.90–91, εἴπερ τι φιλεῖς ἀκοὰν ἀδεῖαν αἰ- | εἰ κλύειν, μὴ κάμνε λίαν δα‾ πάναις; *Ol.* 2.92–95, . . . τεκεῖν μή τιν᾿ ἑκατόν γε ἐτέων πόλιν | φίλοις ἄνδρα μᾶλλον | εὐεργέταν πραπίσιν ἀφθονέστερόν τε χέρα | Θήρωνος; *Nem.* 1.31–32, οὐκ ἔραμαι πολὺν ἐν | μεγάρωι πλοῦτον κατακρύψαις ἔχειν, | ἀλλ᾿ ἐόντων εὖ τε παθεῖν καὶ ἀκοῦ- | σαι φίλοις ἐξαρκέων; *Isthm.* 1.67–68; Hunter 1996, 104–9). So, too, pharaonic inscriptions are full of lists of royal gifts and expenditures, and the "Rosetta Stone" praises Epiphanes for the "large expenditures" he has made for the well-being of Egypt (*OGIS* 90.11–13 = Simpson 1996, 261). Hecataeus of Abdera described a group of "mortal kings" who had achieved immortality because of their benefactions, and *euergesia* lies at the heart of Hecataeus's notion of proper kingship and the divinization of kings (Diod. Sic. 1.13, 20.5, 90.3; Murray 1970, 159–60); here too, then, T. may be indebted not merely to traditional ideas of Greek praise poetry.

106 ἐνὶ: Cf. 3–4n.

107 The acquisitive and apparently tireless activities of ants may be regarded negatively as miserly hoarding, as here and at Crates, *SH* 359.6–7, or positively as sensible forethought, as at Hes. *WD* 778, Hor. *Sat.*1.1.32–40, and Virg.*Georg.* 1.186. For ancient ant-lore cf. Davies and Kathirithamby 1986, 37–46; *Der neue Pauly* s.v. Ameise, and for the rejection of hoarding cf. Lichtheim 1980, 15 (a high royal official): "The people reckoned me as openhanded, for I despised the piling up of riches." There seems no reason to see here a reference to the famous gold-digging ants of India (Hdt. 3.102; Kerkhecker 1999, 239–40).

ἀεὶ . . . μογεόντων: For the hyperbaton cf. 2.137, ἔτι δέμνια θερ-μά (with Gow's note). μογεῖν is mildly pejorative in this context: Ptolemy, by contrast, achieves everything easily, like a god.

108–9 From a Greek perspective, donations to temples and priests are a crucial part of elite or royal εὐσεβεία and display (cf. Pind. fr. 119 [Theron's ancestors], πλεῖστα μὲν δῶρ᾿ ἀθανάτοις ἀνέ-χοντες, | ἕσπετο δ᾿ αἰενάου πλούτου νέφος; Xen. *Ages.* 1.34); such gifts were a very important factor in the competition between Hellenistic kings for power and prestige in the Greek world (cf. *OGIS* 214, Seleukos I's donations to the temple of Apollo at Didyma; Bringmann, von Steuben, and Schmidt-Donaus 1995–2000). On the Egyptian side, no theme is more prominent in pharaonic texts than the benefits conferred by the king upon existing temples and the creation of new shrines; the pattern here is Horus's piety toward Osiris: "The king was the son of the gods, and he had to care for them, as an earthly son cares for his parents" (Roeder 1960b, 277). For Philadelphus cf. "Pithom Stele"; Roeder 1959, 122–24, 127, 178–79 ("who enriches the temples . . . all temples are awash with his donations"); Huss 1994, esp. 28–29, for

Philadelphus's foundations; Otto 1905, 1: 384–91; Thompson 1988, 106–54; Goyon 1988; for further Ptolemaic examples cf. *OGIS* 56.10 (Euergetes), 90.14–19 (Epiphanes).

ἐρικυδέες: In Homer "of gods and their descendants . . . [and] their gifts" (LSJ s.v.); particularly relevant perhaps is *Il.* 3.65 (= 20.265), θεῶν ἐρικυδέα δῶρα.

αἰεί with correption of the final syllable may be retained (cf. *Od.* 13.255; *Hymn. Hom. Aphr.* 201).

ἀπαρχομένοιο: Sc. Πτολεμαίου. The meaning is that Ptolemy offers "firstfruits" (of harvests, the spoils from conquest, etc.) to the temples but also makes other donations on other occasions. It was standard for great men to offer a part of new gains, or (e.g.) commemorative statues in their place, to the temples as part of self-advertisement. Ptolemy is again behaving in traditional ways; cf. Herodotus's account of Croesus's dedications at Delphi, which included "firstfruits of his paternal inheritance" and wealth confiscated from an enemy (1.92).

110–11 Further anaphora of πολύς (cf. vv. 75–78, 93) continues a central theme of the poem. The distinction between "kings" and "republics" suggests the universality of Philadelphus's generosity: he is the benefactor of the whole civilized world.

ἰφθίμοισι . . . βασιλεῦσι: Strongly Homeric in flavor. These "kings" may include "subject kings," such as the Ptolemaic agent Philocles, king of Sidon (cf. *SIG* 390–91), and (depending on the chronology) Magas of Cyrene (cf. *OGIS* 22 for honors to Philadelphus in Cyrene), but the sense—which should in any case not be pressed too hard—includes gifts to all other *basileis*, as (pace Gow) the principal subject is Philadelphus's wealth, here used in "relations with other potentates," not merely the "administration of his own empire." The Spartan *basileus*, Areus, who is honored by Philadelphus in a surviving inscription (*SIG* 433) may be a special case, given Spartan "kingship" traditions, but we may also think of such men as the "king of the Bithynians" who claimed friendly relations with Philadelphus in mid-century (Welles, *RC* no. 25). That Philadelphus is able to make large gifts to "powerful kings" is, of course, a measure of his own wealth and power (cf. Weber 1993, 334 n. 5) and places him within a tradition of idealized rulers (cf. Hecataeus of Abdera on Sesoosis; Diod. Sic. 1.58). On the use of the term βασιλεύς by the *diadochoi* cf. Mooren 1983, 212–15; Hammond and Walbank 1988, 172–75.

πτολίεσσι: T. uses the epic form in πτολ- only here and at 22.157 (πτολίεθρα). Benefactions to cities were a crucial, perhaps *the* crucial, weapon in the foreign policy of Hellenistic kings (cf. Bringmann 1993; Buraselis 1993; Ma 1999, 180–242). For the Ptolemies, donations of grain were particularly easy benefits to bestow (cf. Préaux 1978, 202–3). For examples of Philadelphus's donations cf. Habicht 1970, 116–20 (Byzantium and the Black Sea coast); Welles, *RC* no. 14 (Miletos) = Burstein 1985, no. 95; Shear 1978 (Athens); Hazzard 2000, 109.

ἀγαθοῖσιν ἑταίροις: Ptolemy's "brave companions" are the descendants of the *hetairoi* of Macedonian kings, particularly of course Alexander (cf. Hammond 1989, 53–58). The standard term for the king's courtiers and advisors is φίλοι, but it is probable that ἑταῖροι survived in use long after it disappears from official records (cf., for example, Ath. 6.251c [= Timon fr. 6 Di Marco], a *hetairos* of Antigonos; Polyb. 14.11.1, a *hetairos* of Philopator), and in any case ἑταῖροι is here used, rather than φίλοι, for its Homeric and Macedonian resonance. On the king's "friends" cf. Mooren 1975; Herman 1980–81; Walbank 1984, 68–71; Weber 1993,

139–40; Kerkhecker 1997. Generosity to one's "friends" was a normal ideal of Greek elite cultures (cf. Xen. *Ages.* 1.17–19; Men. *Sam.* 15–16, etc.), as of Macedonian kingship traditions. Hellenistic kings practiced such generosity with enthusiasm (cf. Welles, *RC* nos. 10–12, a large gift of land by Antiochus I to a φίλος); as all of Egypt "belonged" to Ptolemy, he was in a position to make very large gifts indeed (cf. Koenen 1993, 30). Like gifts to kings and cities, such gifts were, of course, quintessentially political: Alexander is said to have defined "the best king" as ὁ τοὺς φίλους δωρεαῖς συνέχων, τοὺς δὲ ἐχθροὺς διὰ τῶν εὐεργεσιῶν φιλοποιούμενος (*Gnom. Vat.* 82, *WS* 10 [1888] 6; cf. Isocr. *Euag.* 45).

112–14 In his lavish patronage of the arts, Philadelphus is praised for actually doing what poets often advise (real or potential) patrons to do (cf. 16.42 ff.). Drama flourished at Alexandria, but the verses suggest (for example) rhapsodic and kitharoidic contests, rather than those for full-fledged drama; cf. 15.98, the singer ἅτις καὶ πέρυσιν τὸν ἰάλεμον ἀρίστευσε.

Although Διωνύσου probably belongs primarily with ἀγῶνας, the word order groups Διωνύσου τις ἀνήρ, which unmistakably evokes the "Artists of Dionysus." In the "Grand Procession" marched "the poet Philikos, who was the priest of Dionysus, and all the Artists of Dionysus" (Ath. 5.198b), and Philadelphus freed the members of the Guild, together with schoolteachers, gymnastic trainers, and those who were victorious at the principal Alexandrian contests, from the salt tax (*PHal* 1.260–65; Fraser 1972, 2: 870–71; Rice 1983, 54); later in the century one group of Artists at Ptolemais-Hermiou styles itself οἱ περὶ τὸν Διόνυσον καὶ Θεοὺς Ἀδελφούς (*OGIS* 50–51). Such generosity to the Artists is again a form of royal philanthropy by no means limited to the Ptolemies (cf. Price 1984,

30–32). For the Artists at Alexandria and elsewhere cf. Sifakis 1967; Rice 1983, 52–58; Stefanis 1988: Lightfoot 2002.

ἱερούς . . . ἀγῶνας: The most notable were the "isolympic" Ptolemaia in honor of Soter (cf. *SIG* 390 [= Austin 1981, no. 218]; "Kallias" decree 55–64 [= Shear 1978]; Callim. fr. 384), but there were many other Alexandrian festivals also at which poets could display their wares (cf. Koenen 1977; Weber 1993, 165–82; Fraser 1972, 1: 231–33; Perpillou-Thomas 1993, 151–75). *EP* itself has often been associated with the Ptolemaia (perhaps of 271/0)—a thesis that would certainly suit the prominence of Soter in the poem—but that is at least not a *necessary* hypothesis. What is, however, clear is that T. would include himself and this song in the praise of 113; he is a poet who, like Odysseus (*Od.* 11.367–68), is ἐπιστάμενος. To judge by a surviving scholium on the lost ending of *Idyll* 24, that poem was composed as, or at least in the manner of, a "competition piece."

κατ᾽ . . . ἵκετ᾽: κατά is regularly used with verbs of motion to indicate purpose (cf. Ar. *Clouds* 239, ἦλθες δὲ κατὰ τί; LSJ s.v. κατά B III.1), but the current example seems influenced by καταβαίνειν "enter a contest" (cf. LSJ s.v. I.3).

λιγυρὰν . . . ἀοιδάν: Cf. 15.135; *Od.* 12.183 (the Sirens); Hes. *WD* 659 (Hesiod victorious in a poetry competition), etc. The light dactyls of v. 113, set off by the initial spondees of v. 114, perhaps suggest the tunefulness of song. Despite τέχνας in the following verse, however, the temptation to see here a "programmatic" link with the λιγὺς ἦχος of the Callimachean cicada (fr. 1.29) should probably be resisted.

δωτίναν: An epic word confers dignity upon an otherwise "sordid" subject; for the poetic treatment of monetary pay for poetry cf. Hunter 1996, 97–109; Barchiesi 1996. Cash prizes had long been the norm at poetic festivals: one extant list for a festival of Artemis at Eretria c. 340 offers 120 dr., 30 dr., and 20 dr. for first, second, and third place, respectively, in the contest for rhapsodes, and 200 dr., 150 dr., and 100 dr. for kitharodes (*IG* XII.9.189). Prizes and/or what would today be called "appearance fees" could be very substantial, and Ptolemy was no doubt at the top of the league in this matter; a textually difficult sentence appended to the account of the "Grand Procession" (Ath. 5.203a) seems to suggest golden crowns as prizes "in the contest." Cf. in general Sifakis 1967, index s.v. "prizes."

τέχνας: Both "craft" in a professional sense and "poetic skill," as most famously at Callim. fr. 1.17.

115–16 Philadelphus's generous patronage of poetry and *mousike* generally leads to further singing in his honor. ἀντ᾽ εὐεργεσίης picks up ἀντάξιον to suggest the reciprocal relation between poet and patron.

Μουσάων δ᾽ ὑποφῆται: Cf. 16.29 (with Gow's note), 22.116 (with Sens's note); poets are inspired media who transmit the Muses' words to men. The phrase is here particularly appropriate, as it evokes the Hesiodic connection between kings and Muses—Μουσάων . . . Πτολεμαῖον frames v. 115—from the *Theogony* passage that has been so central to the whole poem (*Theog.* 80–93). Whether the phrase specifically evokes the Alexandrian Museum (Weber 1993, 322) seems doubtful.

ἀντ᾽ εὐεργεσίης: Cf. Antipater of Thessalonica, *AP* 9.92.3–4 (= *GP* 83–84), the poet thanks his patron (a suggestive analogy for *EP*): ὡς καὶ ἀοιδὸς ἀνὴρ ξενίων χάριν ἀνταποδοῦναι | ὕμνους εὐ- έρκταις οἶδε παθὼν ὀλίγα.

ἀνδρί: Gods may have higher rewards (cf. Griffiths 1979, 81), but ὀλβίωι reminds Philadelphus of his specially privileged position (cf. 95–97n.).

117 The Homeric model is *Od.* 1.95 (Athena's plans for Telemachus), ἠδ᾽ ἵνα μιν κλέος ἐσθλὸν ἐν ἀνθρώποισι ἔχηισιν; both Telemachus and Philadelphus will do their fathers justice (cf. 13n.). Such close borrowing from Homer embodies the point of the verse: Homer's famous poetry is known to all and has the power to confer fame, but Homer is not the only poet. Very close to Homer and T. is Pliny *Epist.* 3.21.6 (on Martial's praise of Pliny): *quid homini potest dari maius, quam gloria et laus et aeternitas?*

118–20 For these themes, cf. 16.59 (money is no good to you when dead, so spend it on poetry while you are alive) and 16.30–57 (poetry confers immortal fame), a passage that has many points of detailed contact with these verses and is itself indebted to Simonides' use of the theme of Homeric fame at fr. 11.10–18 West, Hor. *Carm.* 4.9.25–28 (note *longa nocte* ~ ἀέρι παι κέκρυπται); Kurke 1991, 225–39; Barchiesi 1996, 25–29. The theme is recurrent in Pindar's epinicians (cf., for example, *Nem.* 6.29–30, παροιχομένων γὰρ ἀνέρων | ἀοιδαὶ καὶ λόγοι τὰ καλά σφιν ἔργ᾽ ἐκόμισαν) and occurs of course also in prose encomium (cf. Isoc. *Euag.* 3–4: *logos* will make the *arete* of Evagoras "ever remembered by all men"). Here the Atreidai are remembered, but all their plunder forgotten (because, presumably, not commemorated in epic song); for this contrast between the transient blessings of ὄλβος and the true blessing of *kleos* cf. Pind. *Nem.* 7.58–63; *Isthm.* 1.47–52 ("pay," *misthos*, is what a "manual worker" receives, whereas the victor in the games or in war "receives the highest profit," a good report among men). This focus on wealth is here obviously determined by the Ptolemaic context, but the (almost Cynic) idea is in essence not much different from 16.40–47, where the riches of Simonides' patrons would have done them no good in death— for even the rich die—had they not used some of it while alive to hire a poet. For the great riches of Troy that the Greeks secured cf. Aesch. *Ag.* 820; Eur. *Tro.* 18–19; Virg. *Aen.* 2.4; Philostr. *Her.* 25.12, etc.

καὶ: More naturally "for the Atreidai as well [as Ptolemy]," rather than (Gow) "even for the Atreidai." The clear warning to the patron is continued in the echo in κτεάτισσαν of κτεατίζεται (v. 105).

μυρία τῆνα: Cf. 16.38, 42: τὰ πολλὰ καὶ ὄλβια τῆνα. The central section of the poem, devoted to Egypt and the virtues of Ptolemy, is framed by the notion of vast number (v. 77 ~ v. 118).

ἀέρι: "Dark mist," associated in early poetry with the Underworld and with "hiding" and making things invisible (Hes. *Theog.* 729–30; *Od.* 11.15; *LfgrE* s.v. ἀήρ). Odysseus, a hero made famous by Homer, was twice surrounded by such a mist (*Od.* 7, 13) but did in the end achieve a *nostos*. We ought perhaps here think of the Phaeacian treasure that Odysseus hid on Ithaca in a σπέος ἠεροειδές (*Od.* 13.366). The text has often been doubted, and Gallavotti accepts Pflugk's Ἄιδι πάντα (cf. Campbell on *Arg.* 3.61 for the resulting prosody), but the assumed corruption is at best implausible.

ὅθεν πάλιν οὐκέτι νόστος: For the language cf. *Od.* 3.241; *Arg.* 4.1235; Cat. 3.11–12, *qui nunc it per iter tenebricosum | illud unde negant redire quemquam.*

121–22 Lit. "This man, alone of men of the past and of those of whose still warm footprints the dust, trodden down on its surface, bears the imprint." The basic dichotomy is probably not "the dead

v. the living," but rather the Homeric distinction between "heroes of the past" and οἱ νῦν; T.'s second category will therefore include not just the living, but also men of the recent past who were "like us." The origins of T.'s elaborate periphrasis are obscure; despite 18.20 (Helen), οἷα Ἀχαιιάδων γαῖαν πατεῖ οὐδεμί' ἄλλα, it is tempting to think that there may be a pharaonic tradition in play here (cf. *ANET* 231 [Hatshepsut expelling the Hyksos]: "I have made distant those whom the gods abominate, and earth has carried off their foot[prints]"). Castiglione (1967) studies representations of (probably) gods' footprints in Egyptian temples, and cf. Stephens (2003) 167.

μοῦνος: The claim to uniqueness, a mode of "amplification" (αὔξησις), is standard in the language of both Greek (cf. Isoc. *Euag.* 16 [Peleus, the only man to have the gods sing the wedding hymn at his wedding], *Helen* 16 [Helen was Zeus's only mortal daughter], *Panath.* 76 [Agamemnon, the only leader of all Greece]; Arist. *Rh.* 1.1368a11; Hunter on 4.33) and pharaonic praise (cf. Roeder 1959, 125–26, on Philadelphus's establishment of Ptolemais Theron and the transport of elephants ["no king has ever done the like"]; Hornung 1957, 125–26; Huss 1994, 103). The truth claims of such rhetoric are not to be pushed too hard; some have wished to see a hit at Antiochos, who had instituted divine honors for his father Seleukos, but apparently not for his mother (so Prott 1898, 467; Meincke 1965, 137).

προτέρων: In other words, men of the heroic age, a sense prepared by the preceding verses: here is an aspect in which Ptolemy surpasses the Atreidai. For this sense of πρότεροι cf. *Arg.* 3.919; Nikitinski 1996, 195–99.

θερμά: "Warm, fresh," of footprints (cf. Xen. *Cyn.* 5.5; Ovid *Met.* 7.775; [probably] Erinna, *SH* 401.19–20).

123–25 The verses most probably refer to the cult of the Theoi Soteres (cf. note on ἀρωγούς below), established by Philadelphus early in his reign (after the death of Berenice), rather than to individual deifications, but the matter is unclear and the verses too nonspecific for firm chronolgical conclusions to be drawn (cf. further 50n.; Weber 1993, 216–17); the texts relating to the establishment of the Ptolemaia (112–14n.) do not mention divine honors at that time for Berenice (cf. Fraser 1972, 1: 224; Rice 1983, 122). Σ quotes Lycus of Rhegium, *FGrHist* 570 F16, for a "very large shrine" built by Philadelphus to his parents, but we simply cannot say how strictly the plural ναούς is to be interpreted. For a pharaonic example of the theme of these verses cf. Roeder 1959, 58 (Ramses II honoring his father): "You have fashioned him from gold and precious stones . . . you have made a statue of him in electron"; and one of Isis's standard claims is that she instituted that "parents should be cherished (φιλοστοργεῖσθαι) by a child" (1.19 Totti). More broadly, in building shrines for his parents, Philadelphus is doing what Egyptian rulers constantly boast of having done for their divine "parents"—namely, the gods (cf., for example, Davies 1994, 41: "Lord of the Two Lands, Nebkheperure, who makes monuments and they come into existence immediately for his fathers, all the gods. He has built their temples anew and he has fashioned [their] images in electrum").

θυώδεας picks up a theme of vv. 29–39 (the sweet smells of Olympus); as Griffiths (1979, 73) notes, "The resplendent fixtures of the shrines which Ptolemy builds . . . rather conspicuously resemble those of the halls of Zeus."

χρυσῶι . . . ἐλέφαντι: Cf. *Od.* 23.200 (Odysseus making the signature bed), δαιδάλλων χρυσῶι τε καὶ ἀργύρωι ἠδ' ἐλέφαντι. Chryselephantine thrones, including "the throne of Soter" (17n.), a vast wealth of gold, and 600 tusks of Ethiopian ivory (Ath. 5.201a) were carried in the "Grand Procession"; this display, like T.'s claim here, symbolizes Philadelphus's control of the gold mines and elephant-hunting grounds to the south and southeast of Egypt (cf. 87n.; Fraser 1972, 1: 178–79; Casson 1993; Burstein 1993, 43–46; 1996). As Philadelphus seems to have been the first systematically to exploit these sources of wealth (cf. Agatharcides, p. 42 Burstein; *OGIS* 54.10–13), they are not something he inherited from his father, and as such there is a particular encomiastic point here. For the significance of gold in pharaonic representations cf. Daumas 1956, and for chryselephantine statues in general cf. Lapatin 2001.

ἀρωγούς: σωτήρ and βοηθός are standard terms of praise for Hellenistic kings (Schubart 1937, 13–15; Habicht 1970, 156 n. 76; Nock 1972, 720–35), but the former, whose power derives from its resonance of Zeus Soter (cf. Isoc. *Euag.* 57), became a "title" for the first Ptolemy; it is tempting to see in ἀρωγός an allusion to that title. Unfortunately, it is not certain that this title was regularly used for Ptolemy I as early as the probable date of *EP.* Diod. Sic. 20.100.3–4 records that in 304 the Rhodians asked the oracle of Zeus-Ammon at Siwa whether they should honor the son of Lagos as a god, and with oracular approval they set up a *temenos* to him; modern scholarship has combined this narrative with a report in Paus.1.8.6 that it was the Rhodians who gave Ptolemy the title Σωτήρ (cf. Habicht 1970, 233–34; Préaux 1978, 248–49; Weber 1993, 58 n. 3). This composite construction has, however, been doubted; Hazzard (2000, 1–24) argues that "Soter" was a name regularly used for Ptolemy I only after 262 (cf. also Hazzard 1992). "Soter" may occur as a title, alongside the Egyptian "protector," in a demotic document of 304, which also names

Berenice with her husband (Bresciani 1983), but Clarysse (1987, 30 n. 78) describes the reading as "rather uncertain from a palaeographical point of view."

In its original application, Σωτήρ means "deliverer" from foreign foes and aggression, but the association with Zeus Soter and the growth of dynastic cult lent wider applicability to gods with the power to intervene and "help." For such ideas within Egyptian tradition cf. Koenen 1983, 154–57.

126 Cf. *Od.* 3.273–74 (Aigisthos), πολλὰ δὲ μηρία κῆε θεῶν ἱεροῖς ἐπὶ βωμοῖς, | πολλὰ δ᾽ ἀγάλματ᾽ ἀνῆψεν κτλ.

πιανθέντα: Transferred from βοῶν to μηρία (cf. K-G I 263), but the transference makes the point that Philadelphus's offerings (the thighs) are indeed πίων, rich with fat (πῖαρ), in the approved (by gods) manner.

127 Cf. *Il.* 2.550–51 (Erechtheus and Athens), ἔνθα δέ μιν ταύροισι καὶ ἀρνειοῖς ἱλάονται | κοῦροι Ἀθηναίων περιτελλομένων ἐνιαυτῶν. The choice of a Homeric passage referring to cult for a divinized king is obviously pointed; Σ'b produces reasons why μιν in the Homeric verse cannot refer to Athena herself, and DuQuesnay (1981, 144 n. 93) suggests that T. is making a philological, as well as a literary, point about the Homeric verse. Be that as it may, T.'s verse most naturally refers to sacrifices on a particular day each month (perhaps the day of Soter's birthday or founding of the cult), such as are later attested on the Canopus decree for Euergetes (*OGIS* 56.33) and are known for other Hellenistic kings (cf. Schmidt 1908, 12–16; Clausen on Virg. *Ecl.* 1.43). Annual sacrificial offerings to deceased family members (ἐναγίσματα), such as those established by Epicurus in his will (D.L. 10.18), are familiar from earlier Greek traditions.

128 ἰφθίμα τ' ἄλοχος: A Homeric phrase (*Il.* 5.415; *Od.* 12.452, etc); Arsinoe is no less heroized than her husband.

129 νυμφίον: νυμφίος is twice used in Homer (*Il.* 23.223; *Od.* 7.65) of a "young man," in one case a man who has already had a daughter. It is clear from the scholiastic explanations of these two passages that grammarians believed the word could be much more widely used than just "bridegroom" (cf. *LfgrE* s.v.), and it is certainly true that νύμφα is correspondingly so used (cf. Pind. fr. 52v, νύμφαν ἀριστόποσιν, of Hera; *Il.* 3.130; *Od.* 4.743; Callim. *H.* 4.215, etc.). There is, however, likely to be special point here: Arsinoe's love for Philadelphus continues as strongly as the love and desire a new wife feels for her "new husband," both on the wedding night and in the first period of marriage; cf. the later description of Protesilaos and Laodamia at Philostr. *Her.* 11.1: ἐρᾶι [sc. ὁ Πρωτεσίλεως]. . . . καὶ ἐρᾶται, καὶ διακείνται πρὸς ἀλλήλους ὥσπερ οἱ θερμοὶ τῶν νυμφίων. For such poetic intimacy with the royal couple, cf. Callimachus's teasing of Berenice in the *Coma*, and for the Egyptian background to these ideas cf. 38–39n. above. Like Zeus-Hera, Heracles-Hebe, and Soter-Berenice, the paradigmatic marriage of Philadelphus and Arsinoe is an endlessly repeated series of "weddings"; the wife "enfolding her husband in her arms" may evoke both the language of wedding hymns (cf. Eubulus fr. 102 K-A [= 104 Hunter]; Cat. 61.97–106, 64.330–32) and *Il.* 14.346, ἀγκὰς ἔμαρπτε Κρόνου παῖς ἣν παράκοιτιν, in a lovemaking that explicitly replays the first union of Zeus and Hera (cf. vv. 294–96). For the use of νύμφα in Ptolemaic court poetry cf. Gelzer 1982, 24.

ἀγοστῶι: A disputed Homeric gloss, appropriate to the epic flavor of the union of Philadelphus and Arsinoe. The sense here must be "forearms" (cf. *Σ Il.* 14.452; Livrea on *Arg.* 4.1734; Rengakos 1994, 31–32).

130 ἐκ θυμοῦ στέργοισα: And thus a complete contrast to the ἄστοργος γυνή of v. 43. Arsinoe is standardly described in Egyptian texts, after the fashion of a pharaoh's wife, as "Mistress of Loveliness, sweet in love . . . who loves her brother" (e.g., Roeder 1959, 121; Koenen 1983, 159–60) and may perhaps have been given the appellation Φιλάδελφος before her death and before the establishment of the cult of the Theoi Adelphoi in 272/1 (cf. Fraser 1972, 1: 217, 2: 367; and (against) Burstein 1982, 201–2); Φιλάδελφος was not used of Ptolemy himself until a later period.

κασίγνητόν τε πόσιν τε: Cf. *Il.* 16.432, Ἥρην δὲ προσέειπε κασιγνήτην ἄλοχον τε (cf. 18.356); the echo prepares for the explicit comparison in the following verses.

131–32 If the Egyptian paradigm of brother-sister marriage was Isis and Osiris (cf. Koenen 1983, 158–59), Zeus and Hera were the obvious Greek couple; in fact, however, it is unclear how commonly the analogy between Olympian and Ptolemaic marriages was drawn (cf. Weber 1993, 274; Hazzard 2000, 89–93). An anecdote about the wedding of Philadelphus and Arsinoe at Plut. *Mor.* 736f suggests that the analogy was easily evoked, but in any case it here comes naturally enough in a poem that has been concerned throughout with analogies between Zeus and Ptolemy. While Soter is living the Olympian life on Olympus (vv. 16–33), his son is doing the same on earth: Olympus and the Ptolemaic court are reciprocal spheres (note βασιλῆας 'Ολύμπου).

It is likely enough that Callim. fr. 75.4–7 alludes to a poem in which Sotades humorously drew the analogy between Zeus and Philadelphus in the matter of incest and may have suffered for so doing (cf. Pretagostini 1984, 144–47; Cameron 1995, 18–22). Sotades presumably overstepped the mark by inappropriately explicit jesting (fr. 1 Powell) in an obviously mocking meter (cf. Hunter 1996, 78–79), but there is a considerable difference between that and the graceful and coy rhetoric of these verses. It is a great pity that we do not know more of *SH* 961, a fragmentary poem that seems to involve Hera, Arsinoe, and the language of weddings. Other than Sotades, it is only in later texts that strong disapproval of the incestuous union is expressed (cf. Plut. *Mor.* 736 f.), and— despite the repeated assertions of modern scholars—it is far from clear what the contemporary Greek reaction in Alexandria and elsewhere actually was. It is noteworthy that Pausanias 1.7.1 makes Ptolemy's marriage the result of *eros* (which so often explains shameful behavior; cf. Candaules' delusions at Hdt. 1.7.8), but also in keeping with Egyptian practice (an assertion that is at best a partial truth).

ἐξετελέσθη: Probably an aorist of repeated action (cf. 129n.).

οὓς τέκετο 'Ρέα: Cf. *Il.* 15.187 (Poseidon speaks), τρεῖς γάρ τ' ἐκ Κρόνου εἰμὲν ἀδελφεοί, οὓς τέκετο 'Ρέα, the only example of 'Ρέα (scanned as a monosyllable) in Homer (cf. Janko on *Il.* 14.203–4). Stephens (2003, 163) suggests that the echo is a very pointed one: Callimachus had evoked and rejected this Homeric passage in telling of the coming-to-power of Zeus/Philadelphus (*H.* 1.58– 67), so the parallel between heavenly and earthly "Zeus" is here very strong.

133–34 Iris acts as a kind of personal attendant who prepares the bed for the royal couple (cf. *Od.* 7.335–38, etc.); the idea is a very unusual one. In the *Iliad* Iris is a messenger at the beck and call of Zeus, but in literature after Homer she becomes more and more closely associated with Hera, culminating in her amusingly unpleasant role in Callimachus's *Hymn to Delos;* it is possible that the current verses are intended to reverse Callimachus's unflattering presentation. Simon (1953, 58–65) argued that the many scenes on vases (*LIMC* s.v. Iris I, figs. 42–60) of (probably) Iris pouring (Styx water?) for Zeus and Hera represented oaths of fidelity sworn by the gods at the *hieros gamos* (cf. Aesch. *Eum.* 214, Ἥρας τελείας καὶ Διὸς πιστώματα). If this is correct, it would give Iris a much closer connection with the divine marriage than any literary text can provide. Be that as it may, Iris is elsewhere found leading marriage processions (*LIMC* s.v. Iris I, figs. 84, 101, 124–26), and *LIMC* s.v. Iris I, fig.75, is (probably) a Roman painting of the *hieros gamos* with Iris conducting the bride (cf. Gazaille 1980). It seems likely, then, that T. was drawing on a more widespread iconographic tradition than we can now recover; nevertheless, two other influences are probable. As the Olympian marriage is like an (endlessly repeated) wedding, so the bed of Zeus and Hera is specially prepared every night, like the special decoration that a marriage bed received; for this idea cf. Eur. *Med.* 1026–27; Callim. fr. 75.16, δεύτερον ἐστόρ-νυντο τὰ κλισμία; *Arg.* 4.1141–46 (the "wedding" in the cave, which Vatin [1970, 78–81] regarded as modeled on Ptolemaic court weddings); Moschus *Europa* 164; Xen. *Eph.* 1.8; Oakley and Sinos 1993, 35. Secondly, it is also tempting to think that there was a specific analogy in Ptolemaic court practice and/or religion for Iris's Olympian role, but what that might have been we can only speculate. Unfortunately we know nothing of Aeschylus's Θαλαμόποιοι.

ἐν δὲ λέχος: A version of the familiar μία χλαῖνα to denote the pleasures of sexual relations (Asclepiades, *AP* 5.169.3–4 [= *HE* 814–15], etc.).

ἰαύειν: "For the sleeping," an infinitive of purpose.

χεῖρας φοιβήσασα μύροις: Perhaps a reference to a courtly or religious ritual, but the point of this, as of the following, phrase remains obscure. Both bride and groom used perfumes on the day of the wedding, and it may be that this custom is here transferred to the attendant who prepared the bed. Wilamowitz (1924, 2: 135) suggested that the point was that this task was so holy that even a virgin still had to cleanse herself before carrying it out.

ἔτι παρθένος: In some traditions Iris eventually married Zephyrus (cf. Alcaeus fr. 327 Voigt; Lightfoot on Parthenius fr. 2), but it is not obvious what the point of such an allusion here would be. If it was normal for a virgin to prepare the marriage bed, then the point might be that Iris is "to this day a virgin," and thus able to continue to perform this task for Zeus and Hera. It may also be relevant that virgins normally used only simple oil, not scented perfumes (μύρα) (cf. Callim. *H.* 5.15–16; fr. 110.77–78), but Iris is allowed to break such human boundaries. White (1999, 52) interprets στόρνυσιν (v. 133) as a "historical present," which makes clear the allusion to her later marriage to Zephyrus.

135–37 A three-verse closure that seems closely related to the six-verse closure of Callim. *H.* 1 (cf. on ἀρετήν below); T.'s verses are wholly dactylic, and this rhythm also predominates in the Callimachean passage (broken only by the successive spondees in the indignant outburst of v. 93). The poet bids farewell to Ptolemy, as though finishing a "Hymn to Ptolemy" (cf. 8n.), and then produces a version of the most common hymnic close: "I shall remember . . ." (cf. *Hymn. Hom. Dem.* 495, with Richardson's note; *Hymn. Hom. Ap.* 545–46; *Hymn. Hom. Herm.* 579–80, etc.; for a bucolic reworking cf. 1.144–45).

χαῖρε ἄναξ: Cf. the last verse of *Hymn. Hom.* 15 to Heracles, χαῖρε ἄναξ Διὸς υἱέ· δίδου δ' ἀρετήν τε καὶ ὄλβον; in view of the regularity of the χαῖρε ἄναξ formula (cf. *Hom. Hymn* 19.48, 21.5, 31.17, 32.17), it would be hazardous to posit direct allusion here, though one son of a Soter has replaced another, and Philadelphus is proved by this poem as another true descendant of Heracles. All of Callimachus's *Hymns* close with a version of the traditional χαῖρε formula, and χαῖρε ἄναξ are the first words of the last verse of the *Hymn to Apollo.*

σέθεν: Cf. above, p. 56.

ἡμιθέων: Despite Gow's reservations, it seems clear that T. here treats Ptolemy, just addressed in the hymnic χαῖρε ἄναξ mode, as a ἡμίθεος (cf. 5n. for the meaning of this term); the series of analogies and likenesses that have run playfully throughout the poem have raised him from the "best of men" with which he began to this position. The poem thus proves its own contention that it is poetry that confers status. *Hymn. Hom.* 31 (Helios) and 32 (Selene) move at their close from the χαῖρε ἄναξ/ἄνασσα formula to promise song about the great deeds of ἀνδρῶν (or φωτῶν) ἡμιθέων.

δοκέω: Parenthetic (cf. LSJ s.v. I.2).

οὐκ ἀπόβλητον: Cf. *Il.* 2.360–61 (Nestor to Agamemnon), ἀλλά, ἄναξ, αὐτός τ' εὖ μήδεο πείθεό τ' ἄλλωι· | οὔ τοι ἀπόβλητον ἔπος ἔσσεται, ὅττι κεν εἴπω. As Agamemnon is a principal paradigm for Ptolemy, so Nestor is the Homeric "wise advisor" par excellence and a figure who is adopted as such in Hellenistic discussions of kingship. T. thus takes the position of a Pindar or a Simonides advising princes; φθέγξομαι suggests the "prophetic" voice of archaic lyric (cf. Pind. *Ol.* 2.92, αὐδάσομαι ἐνόρκιον λόγον ἀλαθεῖ νόωι).

As Gow notes, this is the only place in the certainly genuine poems where a vowel remains short before βλ or γλ, which was always a very rare license in classical poetry (West 1982, 16–17); for other instances in Hellenistic poetry cf. Gow and Page on *HE* 2301.

ἀρετήν: A version of a traditional formula found at the close of *Hymn. Hom.* 15 (Heracles) and 20 (Hephaestus) and *CEG* 334 to Apollo (sixth cent.): δίδου δ᾿ ἀρετήν τε καὶ ὄλβον. Callimachus expanded upon this formula at the close of his *Hymn to Zeus*, and it is unlikely that the two passages are unconnected (cf., for example, Perrotta 1978, 180–86; Griffiths 1977–78, 100): χαῖρε, πάτερ, χαῖρ᾿ αὖθι· δίδου δ᾿ ἀρετήν τ᾿ ἄφενός τε. | οὔτ᾿ ἀρετῆς ἄτερ ὄλβος ἐπίσταται ἄνδρας ἀέξειν | οὔτ᾿ ἀρετὴ ἀφένοιο· δίδου δ᾿ ἀρετήν τε καὶ ὄλβον. Socrates' famous prayer to Pan at the end of the *Phaedrus* (279b8–c3) may be viewed as a "philosophic" version of this traditional hymnic request: "Dear Pan and all you gods of this place, grant me that I may become beautiful within; and that what is in my possession outside me may be in friendly accord with what is inside. And may I count the wise man as rich; and may my pile of gold be of a size which only a man of moderate desires could bear or carry" (trans. C. Rowe).

After vv. 135–37a one expects δίδου δ᾿ ἀρετήν τε καὶ ὄλβον addressed to Ptolemy, but Ptolemy cannot give ἀρετή (in any sense; cf. below)—only Zeus and the gods can do that in traditional Greek thought—though he certainly could bestow ὄλβος upon the poet; the subtext will not be lost on any patron or audience, especially after vv. 112–14. Rather, however, than make a direct appeal, T. closes the poem with a witty gesture of resignation that places a prayer in the mouth of Ptolemy rather than the poet and returns the initiative to Zeus: it is not so much that Ptolemy does not need to ask for ὄλβος because he has that in abundance already, as that the ὄλβος has been "conferred" and celebrated by the poet in the poem we have just heard, and he promises to do more in the future. There must, however, be a role left for Zeus—ἐκ δὲ Διὸς βασιλῆες—and that will be in the field of ἀρετή, the traditional subject around which encomium is organized (cf. Isoc. *Euag.* 8; Arist. *Rh.* 1.9). The clausula of the poem is thus to be seen as a typical game with the poetic tradition; T.'s "piety" is no less amusing than Callimachus's fussy explanation of why one should ask for *both* "wealth" and "virtue."

A statue of Ἀρετή was paraded beside Soter in the "Grand Procession" (Ath. 5.201d; cf. Rice 1983, 109–10). Although on honorific inscriptions ἀρετή may refer to martial prowess, this is by no means always exclusively the case with Hellenistic kings, for whom *arete* can be a general state of wisdom and beneficent power, befitting an ἀγαθὸς βασιλεύς and manifested in (for example) the preservation of peace and the distribution of wealth: "Als Inbegriff aller Sittlichkeit bedeutet ἀρετὴ weniger ein Tun als ein Sinn, ein Verhalten, aus dem alle sittlichen Handlungen folgen; sie richtet sich auf das so viel gerühmte καλῶς ἔχον. Häufig umfassen ἀρετὴ und εὔνοια alles, was am König gefeiert, was von ihm erwartet werden kann" (Schubart 1937, 5); this view is well exemplified in the honors paid by the Island League to Philadelphus ἀρετῆς ἕνεκεν καὶ εὐνοίας τῆς εἰς τοὺς Νησιώτας (*SIG* 390.45–46) or in the declaration of the priests at Canopus that Euergetes and his wife have left behind ἀθάνατον εὐεργεσίαν καὶ τῆς αὐτῶν ἀρετῆς μέγιστον ὑπόμνημα (*OGIS* 56.18). The *arete* of a king may be very specifically directed, or more generally be a marker of a beneficent reign, representing something like a combination of the four Platonic virtues of ἀνδρεία, σωφροσύνη, δικαιοσύνη, and φρόνησις/σοφία (*Rep.* 4.427e–28a) (cf., for example, Dio Chrys. 3.9–10 for this combination in a king). *Arete* is something for which one is always searching; it is the object of a pursuit, not—like riches—something that one either has or does not. That others may praise one's *arete* does not mean that the pursuit is at an end; Aristotle's poem for Hermeias (*PMG* 842; cf. Rutherford 2001, 92–97), which associates the pursuit of *arete* with Heracles, the Dioscuri, Achilles, and Ajax, all of whom, with the partial exception of Ajax, are good models for Ptolemy, makes that very clear. Thus it is no disrespect to Ptolemy's current status to urge him to "ask for *arete*." The common interpretation of *arete* here as "successful martial deeds" for which Ptolemy will have to ask Zeus because he has not yet achieved anything in this field (so, for example, Wilamowitz 1906, 54–55, though with important observations; Gow; Meincke 1965, 142) is not only false to the whole strategy of the poem (esp. vv. 86–94) but also operates with much too narrow a conception of *arete*. It is not, however, necessary to see here a specific riposte to contemporary ethical ideas (e.g., Chrysippos, *SVF* III fr. 215) that made *arete* achievable only through individual (intellectual) effort and not as a divine gift (so Pohlenz 1965, 26).

REFERENCES

Assmann, J. 1975. *Ägyptische Hymnen und Gebete.* Zurich.

Austin, M. M. 1970. *Greece and Egypt in the archaic age.* PCPS Supplement 2. Cambridge.

———. 1981. *The Hellenistic world from Alexander to the Roman conquest.* Cambridge.

Bagnall, R. 1976. *The administration of Ptolemaic possessions.* Leiden.

Barbantani, S. 1998. Un epigramma encomiastico «Alessandrino» per Augusto (*SH* 982). *Aevum Antiquum* 11: 255–344.

———. 2001. *ΦΑΤΙΣ ΝΙΚΗΦΟΡΟΣ: Frammenti di elegia encomiastica nell' età delle guerre galatiche.* Milan.

Barchiesi, A. 1996. Poetry, praise, and patronage: Simonides in book 4 of Horace's *Odes. ClAnt* 15: 5–47.

Barthelmess, P. 1992. *Der Übergang ins Jenseits in den thebanischen Beamtengräbern der Ramessidenzeit.* Heidelberg.

Bassett, S. E. 1919. Versus tetracolos. *CP* 14: 216–33.

Bastianini, G., and C. Gallazzi, eds. 2001. *Posidippo di Pella, Epigrammi (P.Mil. Vogl. VIII 309).* Milan.

Bernsdorff, H. 1996. Parataktische Gleichnisse bei Theokrit. In *The-*

ocritus, edited by M. A. Harder, R. F. Regtuit, and G. C. Wakker, 71–88. Groningen.

Bevan, E. 1927. *A history of Egypt under the Ptolemaic dynasty*. London.

Bianchi, R. S. 1988. The pharaonic art of Ptolemaic Egypt. In *Cleopatra's Egypt: Age of the Ptolemies*, 55–80. Brooklyn.

Bing, P. 1988. *The well-read Muse: Present and past in Callimachus and the Hellenistic poets*. Göttingen.

Bonneau, D. 1964. *La crue du Nil*. Paris.

Bosworth, A. B. 1996. *Alexander and the East*. Oxford.

———. 1999. Augustus, the *Res Gestae* and Hellenistic theories of apotheosis. *JRS* 89: 1–18.

Bousquet, J. 1988. La stèle des Kyténiens au Létôon de Xanthos. *REG* 101: 12–53.

Bouvier, H. 1985. Hommes de lettres dans les inscriptions delphiques. *ZPE* 58: 119–35.

Bowman, A. K., and E. Rogan, eds. 1999. *Agriculture in Egypt*. Oxford.

Brandenburg, H. 1966. *Studien zur Mitra*. Münster.

Bresciani, E. 1978. La spedizione di Tolomeo II in Siria in un ostrakon demotico inedito da Karnak. In *Das ptolemäische Ägypten*, edited by H. Maehler and V. M. Strocka, 31–37. Mainz.

———. 1983. Un nouveau texte démotique daté du 28 Nov. 304 a. J.-C. à Deir el Bahari. *MDAI(K)* 39: 103–5.

Bringmann, K. 1993. The king as benefactor: Some remarks on ideal kingship in the age of Hellenism. In *Images and ideologies: Self-definition in the Hellenistic world*, edited by A. W. Bulloch et al., 7–24. Berkeley.

Bringmann, K., H. von Steuben, and B. Schmidt-Donaus, eds. 1995–2000. *Schenkungen hellenistischer Herrscher an griechische Städte und Heiligtümer*. 3 vols. Berlin.

Brioso Sánchez, M. 1976, 1977. Aportaciones al estudio del hexametro de Teocrito. *Habis* 7: 21–56, 8: 57–75.

Brunner, H. 1964. *Die Geburt des Götterkönigs: Studien zur Überlieferung eines altägyptischen Mythos*. Wiesbaden.

Bubeník, V. 1989. *Hellenistic and Roman Greece as a sociolinguistic area.* Amsterdam.

Buchheit, V. 1960. *Untersuchungen zur Theorie des Genos Epideiktikon von Gorgias bis Aristoteles.* Munich.

Buecheler, F. 1875. De bucolicorum Graecorum aliquot carminibus. *RhM* 30: 33–61.

Bundy, E. L. 1972. The "quarrel between Kallimachos and Apollonios." Part I: The epilogue of Kallimachos's *Hymn to Apollo. CSCP* 5: 39–94.

Buraselis, K. 1993. Ambivalent roles of centre and periphery: Remarks on the relation of the cities of Greece with the Ptolemies. In *Centre and periphery in the Hellenistic world*, edited by P. Bilde et al., 251–70. Aarhus.

Burkert, W. 1979. Kynaithos, Polycrates, and the Homeric Hymn to Apollo. In *Arktouros: Hellenic studies presented to Bernard M. W. Knox*, 53–62. Berlin.

Burstein, S. M. 1982. Arsinoe II Philadelphus: A revisionist view. In *Philip II, Alexander the Great and the Macedonian heritage*, edited by W. L. Adams and E. N. Borza, 197–212. Washington, D.C.

———. 1985. *The Hellenistic age from the battle of Ipsos to the death of Kleopatra VII.* Cambridge.

———. 1989. *Agatharchides of Cnidus, On the Erythraean Sea.* London.

———. 1991. Pharaoh Alexander: A scholarly myth. *AncSoc* 22: 139–45.

———. 1993. The hellenised fringe: The case of Meroe. In *Hellenistic history and culture*, edited by P. Green, 38–54. Berkeley.

———. 1996. Ivory and Ptolemaic exploration of the Red Sea: The missing factor. *Topoi* 6/2: 799–807.

Burton, J. 1992. The function of the symposium theme in Theocritus' *Idyll* 14. *GRBS* 33: 227–45.

———. 1995. *Theocritus's urban mimes: Mobility, gender, patronage.* Berkeley.

Cadell, H. 1998. À quelle date Arsinoé II Philadelphe est-elle décédée? In *Le culte du souverain dans l'Égypte ptolémaique au IIIe siècle avant notre ère*, edited by H. Melaerts, 1–3. Louvain.

Cairns, F. 1972. *Generic composition in Greek and Roman poetry.* Edinburgh.

———. 1976. The distaff of Theugenis—Theocritus *Idyll* 28. *PLLS* 1: 293–305.

Cameron, A. 1995. *Callimachus and his critics.* Princeton.

Casson, L. 1993. Ptolemy II and the hunting of African elephants. *TAPA* 123: 247–60.

Castiglione, L. 1967. Tables votives à empreintes de pied dans les temples d'Égypte. *AOrientHung* 20: 239–52.

Cavarzere, A. 1996. *Sul limitare: Il «motto» e la poesia di Orazio.* Bologna.

Chamoux, F. 1956. Le roi Magas. *RH* 216: 18–34.

Chantraine, P. 1973. *Grammaire homérique.* 2 vols. Paris.

Clarysse, W. 1987. Greek loan-words in demotic. In *Aspects of demotic lexicography,* edited by S. P. Vleeming, 9–33. Louvain.

———. 1998. Ethnic diversity and dialect among the Greeks of Hellenistic Egypt. In *The two faces of Graeco-Roman Egypt,* edited by A. M. F. W. Verhoogt and S. P. Vleeming, 1–13. Leiden.

———. 2000. Ptolémées et temples. In *Le décret de Memphis,* 41–65. Actes du Colloque de la Fondation Singer-Polignac. Paris.

Clausing, A. 1913. Kritik und Exegese der homerischen Gleichnisse im Altertum. Diss., Freiburg.

Clauss, J. J. 1986. Lies and allusions: The addressee and date of Callimachus' *Hymn to Zeus. ClAnt* 5: 155–70.

Coarelli, F. 1990. La *pompé* di Tolomeo Filadelfo e il mosaico nilotico di Palestrina. *Ktema* 15: 225–51.

Cohen, G. M. 1995. *The Hellenistic settlements in Europe, the Islands, and Asia Minor.* Berkeley.

Coleman, K. M. 1988. *Statius, Silvae IV.* Oxford.

Cribiore, R. 1995. A hymn to the Nile. *ZPE* 106: 97–106.

Cunningham, I. C. 1965. Herodas 1.26ff. *CR* 15: 7–9.

D'Alessio, G. B. 1997. *Callimaco.* 2d ed. 2 vols. Milan.

Darms, G. 1981. Die Ionismen des Papyrus Antinoae in der Pharmakeutria des Theokrit. *Glotta* 59: 165–208.

Daumas, F. 1956. La valeur de l'or dans la pensée égyptienne. *RHR* 149: 1–17.

———. 1958. *Les mammisis des temples égyptiens*. Paris.

Davies, B. G. 1994. *Egyptian historical records of the later Eighteenth Dynasty*. Vol. 6. Warminster.

———. 1997. *Egyptian historical inscriptions of the Nineteenth Dynasty*. Jonsered.

Davies, M., and J. Kathirithamby. 1986. *Greek insects*. London.

Deubner, L. 1941. *Ololyge und Verwandtes*. Abhandlungen der Preussischen Akademie der Wissenschaften. Berlin.

Di Benedetto, V. 1956. Omerismi e struttura metrica negli idilli dorici di Teocrito. *ASNP* 25: 48–60.

———. 1994. Callimaco di fronte al modello omerico: il fr. 228 Pf. *RFIC* 122: 273–78.

Dietze, G. 1994. Philae und die Dodekascoinos in ptolemäischer Zeit. *AncSoc* 25: 63–110.

Doblhofer, E. 1966. *Die Augustuspanegyrik des Horaz in formalhistorischer Sicht*. Heidelberg.

Dover, K. J. 1971. *Theocritus, Select Poems*. London.

Dunand, F. 1981. Fête et propagande à Alexandrie sous les Lagides. In *La fête, pratique et discours*, 13–40. Paris.

DuQuesnay, I. M. LeM. 1981. Vergil's first *Eclogue*. *PLLS* 3: 29–182.

Durrbach, F. 1921. *Choix d'inscriptions de Délos*. Paris.

Effe, B. 1995. Alexandrinisches Herrscherlob: Ambivalenzen literarischer Panegyrik. In *Affirmation und Kritik: Zur politischen Funktion von Kunst und Literatur im Altertum*, edited by G. Binder and B. Effe, 107–23. Trier.

Empereur, J.-Y. 1998. *Alexandria rediscovered*. London.

Färber, H. 1936. *Die Lyrik in der Kunsttheorie der Antike*. Munich.

Fantuzzi, M. 1980. Ἐκ Διὸς ἀρχώμεσθα: Arat. *Phaen*. 1 e Theocr. XVII 1. *MD* 5: 163–72.

———. 1988. *Ricerche su Apollonio Rodio*. Rome.

————. 1993. Teocrito e la poesia bucolica. In *Lo spazio letterario della Grecia antica,* edited by G. Cambiano, L. Canfora, and D. Lanza, I.2: 145–95. Rome.

————. 1995. Variazioni sull'esametro in Teocrito. In *Struttura e storia dell'esametro greco,* edited by M. Fantuzzi and R. Pretagostini, 221–64. Rome.

————. 2000. Theocritus and the "demythologizing" of poetry. In *Matrices of genre,* edited by M. Depew and D. Obbink, 135–51. Cambridge, Mass.

————. 2001. Heroes, descendants of *hemitheoi:* The prooemium of Theocritus 17 and Simonides fr. 11 W. In *The new Simonides: Contexts of praise and desire,* edited by D. Boedeker and D. Sider, 232–41. New York.

Fantuzzi, M., and R. Hunter. 2002. *Muse e modelli: La poesia ellenistica da Alessandro Magno ad Augusto.* Rome.

Farnell, L. R. 1921. *Greek hero cults and ideas of immortality.* Oxford.

Foertmeyer, V. 1988. The dating of the pompe of Ptolemy II Philadelphus. *Historia* 37: 90–104.

Frankfort, H. 1948. *Kingship and the gods.* Chicago.

Fraser, P. M. 1972. *Ptolemaic Alexandria.* 3 vols. Oxford.

Fraustadt, G. 1909. Encomiorum in litteris Graecis usque ad Romanam aetatem historia. Diss., Leipzig.

Gaertringen, F. Hiller von. 1906. *Inschriften von Priene.* Berlin.

Gazaille, M. 1980. Deux représentations d'Iris inspirées l'une d'Hésiode et l'autre de Théocrite. In *Mélanges d'études anciennes offerts à Maurice Lebel,* edited by J.-B. Caron, M. Fortin, and G. Maloney, 103–11. Quebec.

Gelzer, T. 1982. Kallimachos und das Zeremoniell des ptolemäischen Königshauses. In *Aspekte der Kultursoziologie,* edited by J. Stagl, 13–30. Berlin.

Gerber, D. E. 1981. Theocritus, *Idyll* 17.53–7. *Corolla Londiniensis* 1: 21–24.

Giangrande, G. 1970. Der stilistische Gebrauch der Dorismen im Epos.

Hermes 98: 257–77 (= *Scripta Minora Alexandrina* [Amsterdam 1980] 1: 65–85).

———. 1971. Review of *Studies in Greek encomiastic poetry of the early Byzantine period*, by T. Viljamaa. *GGA* 223: 211–16.

Gold, B. K., ed. 1982. *Literary and artistic patronage in ancient Rome*. Austin.

Goldhill, S. 1991. *The poet's voice*. Cambridge.

Goodenough, E. R. 1928. The political philosophy of Hellenistic kingship. *YCS* 1: 55–102.

Gow, A. S. F. 1965. *Machon*. Cambridge.

Goyon, J.-C. 1988. Ptolemaic Egypt: Priests and the traditional religion. In *Cleopatra's Egypt: Age of the Ptolemies*, 29–39. Brooklyn.

Griffin, J. 1984. Augustus and the poets: "Caesar qui cogere posset." In *Caesar Augustus: Seven aspects*, edited by F. Millar and E. Segal, 189–218. Oxford.

Griffiths, F. T. 1977–78. The date of Callimachus' *Hymn to Delos*. *Maia* 29/30: 95–100.

———. 1979. *Theocritus at court*. Leiden.

Grzybek, E. 1990. *Du calendrier macédonien au calendrier ptolémaique: Problèmes de chronologie hellénistique*. Basel.

Guarducci, M. 1926. Poeti vaganti e conferenzieri dell'età ellenistica. *RAL* 6.2: 629–65.

Gutzwiller, K. J. 1992a. Callimachus' *Lock of Berenice*: Fantasy, romance, and propaganda. *AJP* 113: 359–85.

———. 1992b. The nautilus, the halcyon, and Selenaia: Callimachus's *Epigram* 5 Pf. = 14 G-P. *ClAnt* 11: 194–209.

———. 1996. The evidence for Theocritean poetry books. In *Theocritus*, edited by M. A. Harder, R. F. Regtuit, and G. C. Wakker, 119–48. Groningen.

Habicht, C. 1970. *Gottmenschentum und griechische Städte*. 2d ed. Munich.

Hammond, N. G. L. 1989. *The Macedonian state*. Oxford.

Hammond, N. G. L., and F. W. Walbank. 1988. *A history of Macedonia*. Vol. 3. Oxford.

Harder, M. A., R. F. Regtuit, and G. C. Wakker, eds. 1996. *Theocritus.* Groningen.

———. 1998. *Genre in Hellenistic poetry.* Groningen.

Hardie, A. 1983. *Statius and the Silvae.* Liverpool.

Harvey, A. E. 1955. The classification of Greek lyric poetry. *CQ* 5: 157–75.

Hatzikosta, S. 1981. The dual in Theocritus. *MPhL* 4: 73–87.

Hauben, H. 1970. *Callicrates of Samos.* Louvain.

Hazzard, R. A. 1992. Did Ptolemy I get his surname from the Rhodians in 304? *ZPE* 93: 52–56.

———. 2000. *Imagination of a monarchy: Studies in Ptolemaic propaganda.* Toronto.

Hazzard, R. A., and M. P. Fitzgerald. 1991. The regulation of the Ptolemaieia: A hypothesis explored. *Journal of the Royal Astronomical Society of Canada* 85: 6–23.

Head, B. V. 1911. *Historia Numorum.* 2d ed. Oxford.

Hendriks I. H. M., P. J. Parsons, and K. A. Worp. 1981. Papyri from the Groningen Collection I: Encomium Alexandreae. *ZPE* 41: 71–83.

Henrichs, A. 1989. Zur Perhorreszierung des Wassers der Styx bei Aischylos und Vergil. *ZPE* 78: 1–29.

Herman, G. 1980–81. The "friends" of the early Hellenistic rulers: Servants or officials? *Talanta* 12/13: 103–49.

Herz, P. 1992. Die frühen Ptolemaier bis 180 v. Chr. In *Legitimation und Funktion des Herrschers,* edited by R. Gundlach and H. Weber, 51–97. Stuttgart.

Hinds, S. 1998. *Allusion and intertext.* Cambridge.

Hölbl, G. 2001. *A history of the Ptolemaic empire.* London.

Hollis, A. S. 1990. *Callimachus, Hecale.* Oxford.

Hopkinson, N. 1984. *Callimachus, Hymn to Demeter.* Cambridge.

Hornung, E. 1957. Zur geschichtlichen Rolle des Königs in der 18. Dynastie. *MDAI(K)* 15: 120–33.

———. 1967. Der Mensch als "Bild Gottes" in Ägypten. In *Die Gottebenbildlichkeit des Menschen,* edited by O. Loretz, 123–56. Munich.

Horrocks, G. 1997. *Greek: A history of the language and its speakers.* London.

Hunt, A. S., and J. Johnson. 1930. *Two Theocritus papyri.* London.

Hunter, R. L. 1983. *Eubulus, The fragments.* Cambridge.

————. 1993. *The Argonautica of Apollonius: Literary studies.* Cambridge.

————. 1996. *Theocritus and the archaeology of Greek poetry.* Cambridge.

————. 1999. *Theocritus: A selection.* Cambridge.

————. 2001. Virgil and Theocritus: A note on the reception of the *Encomium to Ptolemy Philadelphus. SemRom* 4: 159–63.

Huss, W. 1994. *Der makedonische König und die ägyptischen Priester.* Stuttgart.

Huttner, U. 1997. *Die politische Rolle der Heraklesgestalt im griechischen Herrschertum.* Stuttgart.

Jamot, P. 1895. Fouilles de Thespies. *BCH* 19: 321–85.

Jones, C. P., and C. Habicht. 1989. A Hellenistic inscription from Arsinoe in Cilicia. *Phoenix* 43: 317–46.

Käppel, L. 1992. *Paian: Studien zur Geschichte einer Gattung.* Berlin.

Kastner, W. 1967. *Die griechischen Adjektive zweier Endungen auf -ΟΣ.* Heidelberg.

Kees, H. 1956. *Totenglauben und Jenseitsvorstellungen der alten Ägypter.* 2d ed. Berlin.

————. 1961. *Ancient Egypt: A cultural topography.* London.

Kennedy, G. A. 1991. *Aristotle, On Rhetoric.* New York.

Kerkhecker, A. 1997. Μουσέων ἐν ταλάρωι—Dichter und Dichtung am Ptolemäerhof. *A&A* 43: 124–44.

————. 1999. *Callimachus' book of Iambi.* Oxford.

Kidd, D. A. 1997. *Aratus, Phaenomena.* Cambridge.

Kirsten, E., and I. Opelt. 1989. Eine Urkunde der Gründung von Arsinoe in Kilikien. *ZPE* 77: 55–66.

Koch, W. 1924. Die ersten Ptolemäerinnen nach ihren Münzen. *Zeitschrift für Numismatik* 34: 67–106.

Koenen, L. 1977. *Eine agonistische Inschrift aus Ägypten und frühptolemäische Königsfeste.* Meisenheim.

————. 1983. Die Adaptation ägyptischer Königsideologie am Ptolemäerhof. In *Egypt and the Hellenistic world*, edited by E. van't Dack, P. van Dessel, and W. van Gucht, 143–90. Louvain.

————. 1993. The Ptolemaic king as a religious figure. In *Images and ideologies: Self-definition in the Hellenistic world*, edited by A. W. Bulloch et al., 25–115. Berkeley.

Koenen, L., and D. B. Thompson. 1984. Gallus as Triptolemos on the Tazza Farnese. *BASP* 21: 111–56.

Koster, S. 1970. *Antike Epostheorien*. Wiesbaden.

Kunst, C. 1887. *De Theocriti versu heroico*. Leipzig.

Kurke, L. 1991. *The traffic in praise: Pindar and the poetics of social economy*. Ithaca.

Kurtz, D. C. 1975. *Athenian white lekythoi*. Oxford.

Kyrieleis, H. 1975. *Bildnisse der Ptolemäer*. Berlin.

Lada-Richards, I. 1999. *Initiating Dionysus: Ritual and theatre in Aristophanes' Frogs*. Oxford.

Lapatin, K. D. S. 2001. *Chryselephantine statuary in the ancient Mediterranean world*. Oxford.

Latte, K. 1968. *Kleine Schriften zu Religion, Recht, Literatur und Sprache der Griechen und Römer*. Munich.

Lattimore, R. 1962. *Themes in Greek and Latin epitaphs*. Urbana.

Legrand, P. E. 1898. *Étude sur Théocrite*. Paris.

Leutner, W. G. 1907. The article in Theocritus. Ph.D. diss., Johns Hopkins University.

Levi, M. A. 1975. L'idillio XVII di Teocrito e il governo dei primi Tolomei. *RIL* 109: 202–9.

Lichtheim, M. 1973. *Ancient Egyptian literature: A book of readings*. Vol. 1, *The Old and Middle Kingdoms*. Berkeley.

————. 1976. *Ancient Egyptian literature: A book of readings*. Vol. 2, *The New Kingdom*. Berkeley.

————. 1980. *Ancient Egyptian literature: A book of readings*. Vol. 3, *The Late Period*. Berkeley.

Lightfoot, J. 2002. Nothing to do with the *technitai* of Dionysus? In

Greek and Roman actors, edited by P. Easterling and E. Hall, 209–24. Cambridge.

Lincoln, B. 1980. The ferryman of the dead. *JIE* 8: 41–59.

Lissarrague, F. 1990. *The aesthetics of the Greek banquet*. Princeton.

Lloyd, A. B. 1975. *Herodotus, Book II: Introduction*. Leiden.

Loprieno, A. 1988. *Topos und Mimesis: Zum Ausländer in der ägyptischen Literatur*. Wiesbaden.

Loraux, N. 1986. *The invention of Athens: The funeral oration in the classical city*. Cambridge, Mass.

Lorton, D. 1971. The supposed expedition of Ptolemy II to Persia. *JEA* 57: 160–64.

Ma, J. 1999. *Antiochos III and the cities of western Asia Minor*. Oxford.

Maehler, H., and V. M. Strocka, eds. 1978. *Das ptolemäische Ägypten*. Mainz.

Martin, J. 1956. *Histoire du texte des Phénomènes d' Aratos*. Paris.

Mastrocinque, A., ed. 1979. *La Caria e la Ionia meridionale in epoca ellenistica*. Rome.

Meincke, W. 1965. Untersuchungen zu den enkomiastischen Gedichten Theokrits. Diss., Kiel.

Melaerts, H., ed. 1998. *Le culte du souverain dans l'Égypte ptolémaique au IIIe siècle avant notre ère*. Louvain.

Merkelbach, R. 1981. Das Königtum der Ptolemäer und die hellenistischen Dichter. In *Alexandrien*, edited by N. Hinske, 27–35. Mainz.

Minas, M. 1994. Die Pithom-Stele: Chronologische Bemerkungen zur frühen Ptolemäerzeit. In *Aspekte spätägyptischer Kultur*, edited by M. Minas and J. Zeidler, 203–11. Mainz.

Mineur, W. H. 1984. *Callimachus, Hymn to Delos*. Leiden.

Modena, A. 1992. The behaviour of prepositives in Theocritus' hexameter. *Glotta* 70: 55–60.

Molinos Tejada, T. 1990. *Los dorismos del Corpus Bucolicorum*. Amsterdam.

Mooren, L. 1975. *The Aulic titulature in Ptolemaic Egypt: Introduction and prosopography*. Brussels.

———. 1983. The nature of the Hellenistic monarchy. In *Egypt and the*

Hellenistic world, edited by E. van't Dack, P. van Dessel, and W. van Gucht, 205–40. Louvain.

Mørkholm, O. 1991. *Early Hellenistic coinage*. Cambridge.

Murray, O. 1970. Hecataeus of Abdera and pharaonic kingship. *JEA* 56: 141–71.

———. 1996. Hellenistic royal symposia. In *Aspects of Hellenistic kingship*, edited by P. Bilde et al., 15–27. Aarhus.

Naville, E. 1885. *The store-city of Pithom and the route of the exodus*. London.

———. 1902–3. La stèle de Pithom. *ZÄS* 40: 66–75.

Nightingale, A. W. 1995. *Genres in dialogue*. Cambridge.

Nikitinski, O. 1996. *Kallimachos-Studien*. Frankfurt.

Nock, A. D. 1930. Σύνναος Θεός. *HSCP* 41: 1–62.

———. 1972. *Essays on religion and the ancient world*. Oxford.

North, H. F. 1966. Canons and hierarchies of the cardinal virtues in Greek and Latin literature. In *The classical tradition*, edited by L. Wallach, 165–83. Ithaca.

Nöthiger, M. 1971. *Die Sprache des Stesichorus und des Ibycus*. Zurich.

Oakley, J. H., and R. H. Sinos. 1993. *The wedding in ancient Athens*. Madison.

Obbink, D. 2001. The genre of *Plataea*: Generic unity in the new Simonides. In *The new Simonides: Contexts of praise and desire*, edited by D. Boedeker and D. Sider, 65–85. New York.

O'Neil, E. G. 1942. The localization of metrical word-types in the Greek hexameter. *YCS* 8: 105–78.

Onians, R. B. 1954. *The origins of European thought*. 2d ed. Cambridge.

Otto, E. 1971. Der Mensch als Geschöpf und Bild Gottes in Ägypten. In *Probleme biblischer Theologie*, edited by H. W. Wolff, 335–48. Munich.

Otto, W. 1905. *Priester und Tempel im hellenistischen Ägypten*. 2 vols. Leipzig.

Page, D. L. 1955. *Sappho and Alcaeus*. Oxford.

Parsons, P. J. 1983. 3551: Theocritus, *Idyll* xvii 94–105, xxviii 1–19. In *The Oxyrhynchus Papyri*, L: 127–29. London.

————. 1992. Simonides, Elegies. In *The Oxyrhynchus Papyri*, LIX: 4–50. London.

Pease, A. 1926. Things without honor. *CP* 21: 27–42.

Peden, A. J. 1994. *Egyptian historical inscriptions of the Twentieth Dynasty*. Jonsered.

Pendergraft, M. 1986. Aratean echoes in Theocritus. *QUCC* 24: 47–54.

Pernot, L. 1993. *La rhétorique de l'éloge dans le monde gréco-romain*. 2 vols. Paris.

Perpillou-Thomas, F. 1993. *Fêtes d' Égypte ptolémaique et romaine d' après la documentation papyrologique grecque*. Louvain.

Perrotta, G. 1978. *Poesia ellenistica: Scritti minori*. Vol. 2. Rome.

Pfeiffer, R. 1922. *Kallimachosstudien*. Munich.

————. 1968. *History of classical scholarship from the beginnings to the end of the Hellenistic age*. Oxford.

Pichon, R. 1902. *Index verborum amatoriorum*. Paris.

Pohlenz, M. 1965. *Kleine Schriften*. Vol. 2. Hildesheim.

Posener, G. 1960. *De la divinité du Pharaon*. Paris.

Préaux, C. 1939. *L'économie royale des Lagides*. Brussels.

————. 1952. Sur les communications de l'Éthiopie avec l'Égypte hellénistique. *CE* 53: 257–81.

————. 1978. *Le monde hellénistique*. Paris.

Pretagostini, R. 1984. *Ricerche sulla poesia alessandria*. Rome.

————. 2000. La nascita di Tolomeo II Filadelfo in Teocrito, *Idillio* XVII e la nascita di Apollo in Callimaco, *Inno a Delo*. In *Letteratura e riflessione sulla letteratura nella cultura classica*, edited by G. Arrighetti, 157–70. Pisa.

Price, S. R. F. 1984. *Rituals and power*. Cambridge.

Prott, H. v. 1898. Das ἐγκώμιον εἰς Πτολεμαῖον und die Zeitgeschichte. *RhM* 53: 460–76.

Pulleyn, S. 1997. *Prayer in Greek religion*. Oxford.

Quaegebeur, J. 1971a. Ptolémée II en adoration devant Arsinoé II divinisée. *BIFAO* 69: 191–217.

———. 1971b. Documents concerning a cult of Arsinoe Philadelphos at Memphis. *JNES* 30: 242–43.

———. 1998. Documents égyptiens anciens et nouveaux relatifs à Arsinoé Philadelphe. In *Le culte du souverain dans l'Égypte ptolémaique au IIIe siècle avant notre ère*, edited by H. Melaerts, 73–108. Louvain.

Race, W. 1982. *The classical priamel from Homer to Boethius.* Leiden.

———. 1987. Pindaric encomium and Isokrates' *Evagoras. TAPA* 117: 131–55.

Reed, J. D. 2000. Arsinoe's Adonis and the poetics of Ptolemaic imperialism. *TAPA* 130: 219–51.

Reeve, M. D. 1989. Conceptions. *PCPS* 35: 81–112.

Reger, G. 1994. *Regionalism and change in the economy of independent Delos.* Berkeley.

Reinsch-Werner, H. 1976. *Callimachus Hesiodicus.* Berlin.

Rengakos, A. 1993. *Der Homertext und die hellenistischen Dichter.* Stuttgart.

———. 1994. *Apollonios Rhodios und die antike Homererklärung.* Munich.

Rice E. E. 1983. *The Grand Procession of Ptolemy Philadelphus.* Oxford.

Ritter, H.-W. 1965. *Diadem und Königsherrschaft.* Munich.

Robert, J., and L. Robert. 1983. *Fouilles d'Amyzon en Carie.* Vol. 1. Paris.

Robert, L. 1938. *Études épigraphiques et philologiques.* Paris.

———. 1963. *Noms indigènes dans l'Asie-Mineure gréco-romaine.* Paris.

———. 1966. Sur un décret d' Ilion et sur un papyrus concernant des cultes royaux. In *Essays in honor of C. Bradford Welles*, 175–211. New Haven.

Roeder, G. 1959. *Die ägyptische Götterwelt.* Zurich.

———. 1960a. *Kulte, Orakel und Naturverehrung im alten Ägypten.* Zurich.

———. 1960b. *Mythen und Legenden um ägyptische Gottheiten und Pharaonen.* Zurich.

Rohde, E. 1898. *Psyche.* 2 vols. Tübingen.

Rossi, M. A. 1989. *Theocritus' Idyll XVII: A stylistic commentary.* Amsterdam.

Rostropowicz, J. 1982. Remarks to *Id.* XVII, lines 43 and 44 of Theocritus. *Eos* 70: 233–35.

Rowlandson, J., ed. 1998. *Women and society in Greek and Roman Egypt.* Cambridge.

Ruijgh, C. J. 1971. *Autour de "te" épique: Études sur la syntaxe grecque.* Amsterdam.

Russell, D. A., and N. G. Wilson. 1981. *Menander Rhetor.* Oxford.

Rutherford, I. 2001. *Pindar's paeans.* Oxford.

Saller, R. P. 1982. *Personal patronage under the early empire.* Cambridge.

Sauneron, S. 1960. Un document Égyptien relatif à la divinisation de la reine Arsinoé II. *BIAO* 60: 83–109.

Schechter, S. 1965. Theocritus 17.2 once again. *RhM* 108: 184–85.

Scheidel, W. 1996. Finances, figures and fictions. *CQ* 46: 222–38.

Schiappa, E. 1999. *The beginnings of rhetorical theory in classical Greece.* New Haven.

Schlatter, G. 1941. Theokrit und Kallimachos. Diss., Zurich.

Schlott, A. 1969. *Die Ausmasse Ägyptens nach altägyptischen Texten.* Tübingen.

Schmidt, W. 1908. *Geburtstag im Altertum.* Giessen.

Schmitt, H. H. 1991. Zur Inszenierung des Privatlebens des hellenistischen Herrschers. In *Hellenistische Studien,* edited by J. Seibert, 75–86. Munich.

Schnebel, M. 1925. *Die Landwirtschaft im hellenistischen Ägypten.* Munich.

Schubart, W. 1937. Das hellenistische Königsideal nach Inschriften und Papyri. *APF* 12: 1–26.

Schwinge, E.-R. 1986. *Künstlichkeit von Kunst: Zur Geschichtlichkeit der alexandrinischen Poesie.* Munich.

Selden, D. 1998. Alibis. *ClAnt* 17: 289–412.

Sens, A. 1994. Hellenistic reference in the proem of Theocritus, *Idyll* 22. *CQ* 44: 66–74.

———. 1997. *Theocritus, Dioscuri (Idyll 22).* Göttingen.

Shear, T. L. Jr. 1978. *Kallias of Sphettos and the revolt of Athens in 286 B.C.* Princeton.

Sherwin-White, S. 1978. *Ancient Cos.* Göttingen.

Sifakis, G. 1967. *Studies in the history of Hellenistic drama.* London.

Simon, E. 1953. *Opfernde Götter.* Berlin.

Simon, F.-J. 1991. *Τὰ κύλλ' ἀείδειν: Interpretationen zu den Mimiamben des Herodas.* Frankfurt.

Simpson, R. S. 1996. *Demotic grammar in the Ptolemaic sacerdotal decrees.* Oxford.

Slater, W. J. 1969. *Lexicon to Pindar.* Berlin.

Slings, S. R. 1993. Hermesianax and the tattoo elegy. *ZPE* 98: 29–37.

Smith, R. R. R. 1988. *Hellenistic royal portraits.* Oxford.

Sourvinou-Inwood, C. 1995. *"Reading" Greek death to the end of the classical period.* Oxford.

Spalinger, A. J. 1982. *Aspects of the military documents of the ancient Egyptians.* New Haven.

Stefanis, I. E. 1988. *ΔΙΟΝΥΣΙΑΚΟΙ ΤΕΧΝΙΤΑΙ.* Heraklion.

Steinmeyer-Schareika, A. 1978. *Das Nilmosaik von Palestrina und eine ptolemäische Expedition nach Äthiopien.* Bonn.

Stephens, S. A. 2003. *Seeing double: Intercultural Poetics in Ptolemaic Alexandria.* Berkeley.

Stewart, A. 1993. *Faces of power.* Berkeley.

Tarn, W. W. 1910. The dedicated ship of Antigonus Gonatas. *JHS* 30: 209–22.

———. 1926. The First Syrian War. *JHS* 46: 155–62.

———. 1928. Ptolemy II. *JEA* 14: 246–60.

———. 1929. Ptolemy II and Arabia. *JEA* 15: 9–25.

Thompson, D. J. 1988. *Memphis under the Ptolemies.* Princeton.

———. 1998. Demeter in Graeco-Roman Egypt. In *Egyptian religion: The last thousand years*, edited by W. Clarysse, A. Schoors, and H. Willems, 699–707. Louvain.

———. 2000. Philadelphus' procession: Dynastic power in a Mediterranean context. In *Politics, administration and society in the Hellenistic and Roman world*, edited by L. Mooren, 365–88. Studia Hellenistica 36. Louvain.

Tondriau, J. L. 1948a. Princesses ptolémaiques comparées ou identifiées à des déesses. *BSAA* 37: 12–33.

————. 1948b. Rois Lagides comparés ou identifiés à des divinités. *CE* 23: 127–46.

Too, Y. L. 1998. *The idea of ancient literary criticism.* Oxford.

Troxler, H. 1964. *Sprache und Wortschatz Hesiods.* Zurich.

Turner, E. G. 1984. Ptolemaic Egypt. In *Cambridge Ancient History*, VII.1: 118–74. 2d ed. Cambridge.

Vahlen, J. 1907. *Opuscula academica.* 2 vols. Leipzig.

Valbelle, D. 1990. *Les neufs arcs.* Paris.

Van't Dack, E., and H. Hauben. 1978. L'apport égyptien à l'armée navale lagide. In *Das ptolemäische Ägypten*, edited by H. Maehler and V. M. Strocka, 59–94. Mainz.

Vatin, C. 1970. *Recherches sur le mariage et la condition de la femme mariée à l'époque hellénistique.* Paris.

Verdier, C. 1972. *Les éolismes non-épiques de la langue de Pindare.* Innsbruck.

Visser, E. 1938. *Götter und Kulte im ptolemaischen Alexandrien.* Amsterdam.

Von Reden, S. 2001. The politics of monetization in third-century BC Egypt. In *Money and its uses in the ancient Greek world*, edited by A. Meadows and K. Shipton, 65–76. Oxford.

Vox, O. 1989. Particolari teocritei dall' "Encomio di Tolomeo." *Corolla Londiniensis* 5: 87–90.

Walbank, F. W. 1984. Monarchies and monarchic ideas. In *Cambridge Ancient History*, VII.1: 62–100. 2d ed. Cambridge.

————. 1996. Two Hellenistic processions: A matter of self-definition. *SCI* 15: 119–30.

Wallace-Hadrill, A. 1981. The emperor and his virtues. *Historia* 30: 298–323.

————. 1982. Civilis princeps: Between citizen and king. *JRS* 72: 32–48.

Weber, G. 1993. *Dichtung und höfische Gesellschaft.* Stuttgart.

West, M. L. 1982. *Greek metre.* Oxford.

————. 1997. *The east face of Helicon.* Oxford.

————. 1998–2000. *Homeri Ilias.* 2 vols. Stuttgart.

White, H. 1981. Theocritus, Ptolemy Philadelphus and Colonus. *Corolla Londiniensis* 1: 149–58.

———. 1982. On a line of Theocritus. *Corolla Londiniensis* 2: 165–67.

———. 1999. Notes on Theocritus. *Myrtia* 14: 39–56.

White, P. 1993. *Promised verse: Poets in the society of Augustan Rome*. Cambridge, Mass.

Wilamowitz-Moellendorff, U. von. 1886. *Isyllos von Epidauros*. Berlin.

———. 1906. *Die Textgeschichte der griechischen Bukoliker*. Berlin.

———. 1924. *Hellenistische Dichtung*. 2 vols. Berlin.

———. 1962. *Kleine Schriften*. Vol. 4. Berlin.

Williams, F. 1981. *ΔΙΕΡΟΣ*: Further ramifications. *MPhL* 5: 84–93.

Winnicki, J. K. 1989a. Das ptolemäische und das hellenistische Heerwesen. In *Egitto e storia antica dall'ellenismo all'età araba*, edited by L. Criscuolo and G. Geraci, 213–30. Bologna.

———. 1989b, 1991. Militäroperationen von Ptolemaios I. und Seleukos I. in Syrien in den Jahren 312–311 v.Chr. *AncSoc* 20: 55–92, 22: 147–201.

———. 1994. Carrying off and bringing home the statues of the gods. *JJurPap* 24: 149–90.

Wörrle, M. 1977, 1978. Epigraphische Forschungen zur Geschichte Lykiens. *Chiron* 7: 43–66, 8: 201–46.

Zabkar, L. 1988. *Hymns to Isis in her temple at Philae*. Hanover.

Zanker, G. 1989. Current trends in the study of Hellenic myth in early third-century Alexandrian poetry: The case of Theocritus. *A&A* 35: 83–103.

Zibelius-Chen, K. 1988. *Die ägyptische Expansion nach Nubien: Eine Darlegung der Grundfaktoren*. Wiesbaden.

Zinato, A. 1974. Nota su διερός. *BIFGPadova* 1: 173–79.

GENERAL INDEX

Italic numbers refer to pages of the Introduction, roman numbers to notes by line number in the Commentary.

INDEX OF GREEK WORDS

Italic numbers refer to pages of the Introduction, roman numbers to notes by line number in the Commentary.

INDEX LOCORUM

Italic numbers refer to pages of the Introduction, roman numbers to notes by line number in the Commentary.

HELLENISTIC CULTURE AND SOCIETY

General Editors: Anthony W. Bulloch, Erich S. Gruen,
A. A. Long, and Andrew F. Stewart

Compositor:	Integrated Composition Systems
Text:	General, 10/15 Janson;
	Greek, Porson
Display:	Janson
Printer and binder:	Maple-Vail Manufacturing Group